PENGUIN BOOKS

A *Treasury of*
Foolishly Forgotten Americans

Michael Farquhar is the author of *A Treasury of Royal Scandals,*
A Treasury of Great American Scandals, and *A Treasury of Deception.*
A former writer and editor at *The Washington Post* specializing
in history, he is coauthor of *The Century: History as It Happened
on the Front Page of the Capital's Newspaper.* His work has been
featured in a number of publications, and he has appeared as a
commentator on such programs as the History Channel's *Russia:
Land of the Tsars* and *The French Revolution.*

A Treasury of

Foolishly
Forgotten
Americans

★

Pirates, Skinflints, Patriots,
and Other Colorful Characters
Stuck in the Footnotes of History

★

Michael Farquhar

PENGUIN BOOKS

PENGUIN BOOKS

Published by the Penguin Group
Penguin Group (USA) Inc., 375 Hudson Street, New York,
New York 10014, U.S.A.
Penguin Group (Canada), 90 Eglinton Avenue East, Suite 700,
Toronto, Ontario, Canada M4P 2Y3
(a division of Pearson Penguin Canada Inc.)
Penguin Books Ltd, 80 Strand, London WC2R 0RL, England
Penguin Ireland, 25 St Stephen's Green, Dublin 2,
Ireland (a division of Penguin Books Ltd)
Penguin Group (Australia), 250 Camberwell Road, Camberwell,
Victoria 3124, Australia (a division of Pearson Australia Group Pty Ltd)
Penguin Books India Pvt Ltd, 11 Community Centre,
Panchsheel Park, New Delhi – 110 017, India
Penguin Group (NZ), 67 Apollo Drive, Rosedale, North Shore 0632,
New Zealand (a division of Pearson New Zealand Ltd)
Penguin Books (South Africa) (Pty) Ltd, 24 Sturdee Avenue,
Rosebank, Johannesburg 2196, South Africa

Penguin Books Ltd, Registered Offices:
80 Strand, London WC2R 0RL, England

First published in Penguin Books 2008

10 9 8 7 6 5 4 3

Frontispiece by Patterson Clark

LIBRARY OF CONGRESS CATALOGING IN PUBLICATION DATA
Farquhar, Michael.
A treasury of foolishly forgotten Americans : pirates, skinflints, patriots, and other colorful
characters stuck in the footnotes of history / Michael Farquhar.
p. cm.
Includes bibliographical references.
ISBN 978-0-14-311305-8
1. United States—History—Anecdotes.   2. United States—Biography—Anecdotes.
I. Title.
E179.F29   2008
978—dc22   2007026997

Printed in the United States of America
Set in Bembo
Designed by Elke Sigal

In memory of my father,

Gerald William Farquhar

1929–2007

Glory is fleeting, but obscurity is forever.

—Napoléon Bonaparte

Contents

Introduction

"History is the essence of innumerable biographies," Thomas Carlyle once wrote. However, only a relative handful ever get read, which is unfortunate because so many fascinating American lives are overlooked in favor of the nation's more familiar icons.

Almost a century before Martin Luther King Jr. had his dream, Tunis Campbell acted on a nearly identical one. For fifty years the FBI was associated entirely with J. Edgar Hoover, but there were five directors before him. And one of them, William J. Burns, was such an esteemed detective that Sir Arthur Conan Doyle dubbed him "America's Sherlock Holmes." Sitting Bull and Geronimo are universally identified as great Native American chiefs, but what about Sarah Winnemucca, a powerful Indian leader in her own right?

The murderous Pilgrim, the Quaker martyr, the socialite explorer, and all the other men and women chronicled here may not necessarily have shaped the American experience, but they undoubtedly added to its unique texture. And though the course of history would probably have continued to run unimpeded had Anna Jarvis not created Mother's Day, before she went crazy, or had Alexander "Boss" Shepherd left the nation's capital a muddy morass, somehow it would have been a little less American.

A Treasury of

Foolishly Forgotten Americans

1

John Billington:
Mayflower Murderer

Not every passenger aboard the *Mayflower* was a God-fearing Pilgrim; one was a murderer in the making. His name was John Billington, an ornery fellow with a foul mouth, who, along with his badly behaved children, made the miserable journey across the Atlantic even more unbearable. He would go on to do far worse.

The Billington family—John, his wife Eleanor, and their two sons—were among the majority of *Mayflower* passengers known as "Strangers," who, unlike the Separatists, or "Saints," were not necessarily seeking religious freedom in the New World. It is unclear how they came to board the ship, but once they did they were nothing but trouble. Pilgrim leader William Bradford, who became governor of the Plymouth Colony, called them "an ill-conditioned lot . . . unfit for the company," and "one of the pro-fanest families among [the Pilgrims]." John Billington was by some accounts the ringleader of an aborted mutiny aboard the *Mayflower,* while his son Francis almost blew up the ship when he fired a musket near several kegs of powder—"a rash act," writes scholar Albert Borowitz, "that threatened to send them to colonize the ocean floor." Things didn't get much better when the Pilgrims reached Plymouth.

Billington was one of the signers of the Mayflower Compact, which was produced partly as a result of the shipboard rebellion. He and the other signers promised to work for "the general good of the Colony; unto which we promise all due submission and obedience." It became quickly apparent that he had no intention of keeping his part of the pact. As if disease and starvation weren't difficult enough during that first harsh winter of 1620–21, the Pilgrims had to contend with Billington's big mouth and bad temper. He bullied his neighbors and refused to honor a summons for the military service that was required of every able-bodied colonist. That was bad enough, but when he bad-mouthed the colony's military chief, Myles Standish, making "opprobrious speeches against him," as Governor Bradford wrote, it was clear that the time had come for some serious attitude adjustment—Pilgrim-style. He was sentenced to be bound by his neck and heels, an excruciating ordeal that made every muscle feel like it was on fire. Suddenly, all his bluster seemed to disappear. As the ropes were applied, he humbled himself and begged for mercy, after which the sympathetic magistrates released him. Billington, however, had not learned his lesson.

In 1624 he was implicated in a scandal involving two settlers named John Oldham and John Lyford, who were expelled from the Plymouth Colony for writing seditious letters critical of its governance. Billington weaseled his way out of that mess, but his obnoxious behavior continued. He was still nasty to his neighbors, and a feud with one of them—a recent colony arrival aptly named John Newcomen—would lead to murder.

The cause of the quarrel with Newcomen remains uncertain, but on a summer day in 1630 it culminated in a nearby wood when Billington ambushed his adversary and shot him. Though grievously wounded, Newcomen lived long enough to identify his attacker, who, after spending several days in the forest, was promptly arrested. What resulted was New England's first murder trial. Billington, wrote Governor Bradford, "was found guilty of willful murder by plain and notorious evidence," and condemned to hang. The sentence was stayed, however, because the colony's leaders were uncertain whether they had the legal authority to execute him. They consulted with John Winthrop, governor of the Massachusetts Bay Colony, who replied that Billington "ought to die and the land be purged from blood." And so that September, the *Mayflower* murderer met his fate.[1]

"This, as it was the first execution among [the Pilgrims] . . . was a matter of great sadness unto them," Bradford wrote. Yet for the sake of peace and quiet, Billington's demise may well have been cause for a second Thanksgiving.

---

1. It is often erroneously stated that Billington's was the first execution in the American colonies. That distinction actually belongs to Captain George Kendall, who, in 1608, was put to death in Virginia after being charged with spying for Spain.

2

Mary Dyer:
Quaker Martyr

It was a cruel lesson in conformity—or a cruel joke, had the theocratic Puritans of Massachusetts been feeling the least bit frisky. Mary Dyer and two of her fellow Quakers were led to the elm tree on Boston Common, from which they had been condemned to hang. Each was fitted with a noose, and, as Mary watched, Marmaduke Stephenson and William Robinson were dropped to their deaths. Then it was her turn. She ascended the ladder, and the rope around her neck was looped over the tree branch. Just then, however, came word of a reprieve. The Puritans had planned it all along.

★

The Religious Society of Friends, or Quakers, as they were commonly called, faced a hostile reception from their fellow Christians when they first came to Massachusetts in 1656. Whipping and mutilation; fines, prison, banishment, and even death by hanging were the instruments of persecution used against the pacifist sect that—along with so-called witches—the ruling Puritans found so threatening to their established order. Quakers were denounced as "open and capitall blasphemers, open seducers from the glorious

Trinity, . . . and from the Holy Scriptures as the rule of life, open ennemyes of government itself as established in the hands of any but men of theire owne principles, . . . and malignant and assiduous promoters of doctrines directly tending to subvert both our churches and state." All this because the Quakers dared to believe that it was the Holy Spirit who would lead them to righteousness, not the clerical authority that formed the basis of the Puritan power structure. Mary Dyer was determined to bear witness against this state of extreme intolerance, even if she had to lay down her life.

Though her impact was profound, only the barest sketch of her life survives. She was described by the Quaker chronicler George Bishop as "a Comely Grave Woman, and of Goodly Personage, and one of good Report, having a Husband of an Estate, fearing the Lord, and a Mother of Children." Mary and her husband, William, had come to the Massachusetts Bay Colony from England in 1635 seeking religious tolerance. Little did they know that such freedom of belief was reserved only for the Puritans who ran the place.

Even before she joined the Society of Friends, Mary offended the Massachusetts authorities because of her close association with Anne Hutchinson—"the instrument of Satan," as Governor John Winthrop called her—who was banished from Massachusetts for having dared challenge Puritan orthodoxy and who went on to cofound the colony of Rhode Island. Hutchinson stressed the individual's intuition as a means for reaching God rather than the observance of institutionalized beliefs and the precepts of ministers.[1] Her approach appealed to Mary and closely resembled the Quaker tenets she would later adopt. As a result, the two women formed an enduring bond.

---

1. "As I do understand it, laws, commands, rules and edicts are for those who have not the light which makes plain the pathway," Hutchinson wrote. "He who has God's grace in his heart cannot go astray."

During the course of their friendship, Hutchinson, a midwife, helped deliver Mary's stillborn baby—a girl with severe defects—then secretly buried the child to avoid the superstition and controversy that would have been aroused at a time when even the slightest abnormality might be considered the mark of the devil. Mary, in turn, stood by Anne's side during her heresy trials, and eventually followed her to exile in Rhode Island.

The relationship between the two women prompted Governor Winthrop, once an admirer of Mary's, to condemn her as a woman "notoriously infected with Mrs. Hutchinson's errors, and very censorious and troublesome (she being of a very proud spirit, and much addicted to revelations)." That, he was convinced, was what caused Mary to deliver the "monster" he never actually saw but vividly described in his journal:

> It was so Monstrous and Mis-shapen as the like that scarce been heard of. It had no Head but a Face, which stood so low upon the Breast, as the Ears, which were like an Ape's, grew upon the Shoulders.
>
> The Eyes stood far out, so did the Mouth. The Nose was hooking upward. The Breast and back was full of sharp prickles, like a Thornback [an ocean dweller with thorny spines]. The Navel and all the Belly with the distinction of the Sex were where the lower part of the Back and Hips should have been, and those back parts were on the side the Face stood.
>
> The Arms and Hands, with the Thighs and Legs, were as other Children's, but instead of Toes it had upon each Foot Three Claws, with Talons like a young Fowl.
>
> Upon the Back above the Belly it had two great Holes, like Mouths, and in each of them stuck out a piece of Flesh.
>
> It had no Forehead, but in the place thereof, above the Eyes, Four Horns, whereof two were above an Inch long, hard and sharp, the other two were somewhat shorter.

The Dyers were counted among Rhode Island's leading citizens after following Anne Hutchinson and her family into exile there in 1638. William held a number of high offices and was, in fact, one of the signers of the Portsmouth Compact that established the new colony. In 1652 Mary accompanied him on business to England, where she converted to the Quaker doctrines recently established by George Fox. Five years later, when she returned to Boston en route to her home in Rhode Island, she was promptly arrested. The first Quakers had arrived in Massachusetts the year before, and since that time the Puritans, under Governor John Endecott, had enacted harsh measures against them. Mary was only released from prison when her husband, who had not converted, promised on pain of great penalty to usher her out of the colony and not allow anyone to speak to her along the way.

She was not home for long before she ventured back to Massachusetts in 1659 to visit Marmaduke Stephenson and William Robinson, two fellow Rhode Island Quakers who had been imprisoned for having entered the colony to bear witness against the persecuting spirit that existed there. Mary was arrested as well. That September she and the others were brought before the Court of Assistants and banished from Massachusetts. Failure to leave carried an automatic death sentence. Mary did return to Rhode Island, briefly, but Stephenson and Robinson remained in Massachusetts "to try the bloody laws unto death." Mary soon rejoined them, resulting in the farce that was played out on Boston Common. It was merely a dress rehearsal for what was to come.

If the Puritans believed they had frightened Mary Dyer into submission with the mock execution, they underestimated her religious zeal, which rivaled their own. She was every bit as willing to die for her faith as they were to kill for theirs. "My life is not accepted," she wrote to the authorities after her reprieve, "neither availeth me, in comparison with the lives and liberty of the Truth and Servants of the living God, for which in the Bowels of Love and Meekness I sought you; yet nevertheless with wicked Hands have you put two of them to Death, which makes me to feel that the Mercies of the Wicked is cruelty; I rather chuse to Dye than to live, as from you, as Guilty of their Innocent Blood."

The Massachusetts authorities sent her back to Rhode Island, making much of their mercy in the face of popular indignation over the executions of Stephenson and Robinson. But six months later Mary defiantly returned to Boston and was arrested yet again. She was brought before the magistrates on May 31, 1660.

"Are you the same Mary Dyer that was here before?" inquired Governor Endecott.

"I am the same Mary Dyer that was here the last General Court," she replied.

"You will own yourself a Quaker, will you not?" the governor continued.

"I own myself to be reproachfully so called," Mary answered.

"Sentence was passed upon you the last General Court; and now likewise," Endecott pronounced. "You must return to the prison, and there remain till tomorrow at nine o'clock; then thence you must go to the gallows, and there be hanged till you are dead."

"This is no more than what thou saidst before," she rejoined.

"But now," said the governor, "it is to be executed. Therefore prepare yourself tomorrow at nine o'clock."

"I came in obedience to the will of God the last General Court, desiring you to repeal your unrighteous laws of banishment on pain of death," she declared. "And that same is my work now, and earnest request, although I told you that if you refused to repeal them, the Lord would send others of his servants to witness against them."

Endecott then sneeringly asked if she was a "prophetess," to which she replied that she spoke the words the Lord spoke in her, and now the thing was come to pass. As she continued to speak of her calling, the exasperated governor abruptly interrupted. "Away with her!" he screeched. "Away with her!"

The next day Mary Dyer once again stood at the base of the great elm tree on Boston Common. As she ascended the ladder, she rebuffed all pleas to repent and save herself. It was then that Captain John Webb, commander of the military guard, told her she was guilty of spilling her own blood. "Nay," she answered. "I came to keep blood-guiltiness from you, desiring you to repeal the unrighteous and unjust law of banishment upon pain of death, made against the innocent servants of the Lord, therefore my blood will be required at your hands who willfully do it; but for those that do it in the simplicity of their hearts, I do desire the Lord to forgive them. I came to do the will of my Father, and in obedience to his will I stand even to the death." And so she did.

3

Anne Bonny:
Pirate of the Caribbean

Anne Bonny was all sympathy when she came to see her condemned lover, Caribbean pirate "Calico Jack" Rackham, on the day of his execution. "If you'd fought like a man," she snarled, "you wouldn't be hanged like a dog!" It was a touching farewell worthy of a fellow pirate, which is exactly what Anne was. Though women were typically strictly forbidden aboard pirate ships, Calico Jack recognized that certain savage something in his girlfriend and made an exception. Together, the swashbuckling couple and the rest of their cutthroat crew prowled the waters of the West Indies, plundering merchant ships and terrorizing innocents during that romanticized period of history known as the Golden Age of Piracy.

As the privileged daughter of William Cormac, a wealthy plantation owner in what would become South Carolina, Anne might have made a respectable match and settled into genteel anonymity. But there was something feral about her, even at an early age. Some unsubstantiated accounts say that as a teenager she stabbed a servant girl to death with a carving knife, and later beat an unwelcome suitor bloody. Whatever the case, Anne Cormac was clearly not destined for proper Charleston society.

In 1718, at age twenty, she eloped with a drifter named James Bonny and settled with him in the Bahamas. It was a fateful move, for there she met Calico Jack. Historian Clinton Black notes that Rackham took Anne like he did any ship he plundered: with "no time wasted, straight up alongside . . . every gun brought to play, and the prize boarded." There is no evidence of any resistance on Anne's part, and soon enough the adulterous couple was out to sea.

Bonny quickly established herself as one of the most ferocious pirates in Rackham's crew. Yet oddly enough, she wasn't the only woman. Mary Read had spent most of her life at sea disguised as a man. And so she was when Rackham captured the Dutch merchant vessel she was working on and invited her to join his band of pirates. According to one story, Anne developed a crush on Mary, thinking she was a man. This apparently drove Calico Jack wild with jealousy, and he threatened to slit Read's throat. It was then that Mary opened her shirt to reveal her breasts and said, "As you can see, sir, I am no threat to you." After that Anne Bonny and Mary Read became inseparable friends—and one terrifying team.

Victims of their raids reported the two women screaming like banshees as they boarded a captured ship, wielding their weapons as seasoned marauders. In one instance, a woman named Dorothy Thomas was attacked while alone in a canoe on the north side of Jamaica and forced aboard Rackham's sloop for an ordeal that can only be imagined. A report on the deposition she gave later stated that Bonny and Read "wore Mens Jackets, and long Trouzers, and Handkerchiefs tied about their Heads; and that each of them had a Machet and Pistol in their Hands, and cursed and swore at the Men, to murther the Deponent; and that they should kill her, to prevent her coming against them; and the Deponent further said, That the Reason of knowing and believing them to be Women then was, by the largeness of their Breasts."

Throughout the summer and early fall of 1720, Rackham and his crew conducted raid after raid, with Bonny and Read often leading the charge. But on the night of October 22, their reign of terror on the seas came to an end. A British navy vessel captained by pirate hunter Jonathan Barnett overpowered their anchored sloop and disabled it. After firing only one shot, Rackham realized there was no hope and called for quarter, which Barnett granted. Bonny and Read wanted no part of it, however. They put up a fierce fight with their pistols and cutlasses while the rest of the crew cowered in the ship's hold. At one point Anne reportedly screamed down at them, "If there's a man among ye, ye'll come up and fight like the men ye are to be!" When that failed to motivate them, she fired into the hold and killed one of the crew. It was an act of defiant rage that would have done Blackbeard proud.

In spite of their frenzied resistance, Bonny and Read were overpowered and taken prisoner with the rest of the crew. Calico Jack and the other men were tried, convicted, and sentenced to death that November. After his kiss-off from Anne and subsequent execution, Rackham's corpse was subjected to a rather ghastly ordeal: It was placed upright in a metal cage known as a gibbet and left to rot on the Jamaica coast, as a warning to other pirates. A week later the women were tried. One witness who had been taken prisoner described them as "very profligate, cursing and swearing much, and very ready and willing to do most any Thing on Board." Another testified that "when they saw any Vessel, gave chase, or Attacked, they wore Men's Cloathes; and at other Times, they wore Women's Cloaths; That they did not seem to be Kept, or detain'd by Force, but of their own Free-Will and Consent."

Neither woman offered a defense, and each was duly condemned to hang. Right after the sentence was read, however, both informed the court that they were pregnant. An examination proved this to be true, and the sentences were suspended. Mary Read died in prison soon after, perhaps during childbirth, but Anne Bonny's fate remains a mystery. Some historians speculate that her wealthy father used his influence with the British authorities to get her released, but no direct evidence of this has ever been produced. Only one thing is certain: She fought like a man, and, unlike Calico Jack, she wasn't hanged like a dog.

4

Tom Quick:
"The Indian Slayer"

Back in the days when Native Americans were still seen as "savages," the town of Milford, Pennsylvania, dedicated a monument in 1889 to Tom Quick, the lionized "Indian Slayer" who once roamed the wilds of the region picking off members of the Delaware Nation. "Maddened by the death of his Father at the hands of Savages," an inscription on the memorial read, "Tom Quick never abated his hostility to them until the day of his death, a period of over forty years." By some accounts, the body count reached ninety-nine Delaware, though local historians limit it to four or five. The true number, like so much of Tom Quick's life, is obscured by legend. The only certainty is that Milford had seen fit to memorialize a serial killer.

One of Quick's few documented victims was his boyhood friend Mushwink, the son of a Delaware chieftain. The two had grown up together after the Quick family became the first white settlers of the northeastern Pennsylvania area around Milford in 1733. The local Delaware—by then a defeated tribe paying tribute to the six-nation Iroquois Confederacy—treated the Quicks kindly, and Tom and Mushwink became constant companions.

Together they explored the great forests of the region, where Tom learned to hunt and trap with great skill and daring. The boys were like brothers, each practically adopted into the other's family. It was an idyll not destined to last.

William Penn had established good relations with the Delaware when he led a group of English Quakers to the new colony of Pennsylvania in 1682. His successors, however, were not so benevolent. Fraudulent land grabs, like the infamous Walking Purchase of 1737,[1] and an ever-expanding European immigrant population pushed the Delaware farther and farther west, away from their homeland along the river for which they were named. It was only around the Quick homestead, their traditional burial grounds, that the Delaware remained in any significant numbers.

The increasing bitterness of the displaced tribe came to full fruition during the French and Indian War, when the British and the French, along with their Native American allies, clashed over territory, particularly around the Ohio River Valley. The Delaware, allied with the French, launched fierce raids into their former lands in eastern Pennsylvania, burning homes, pillaging livestock, and scalping men, women, and children alike. "Just now arrived in town an express from our frontiers with the bad news that eight families of Pennsylvania were cut off last week," Benjamin Franklin, then postmaster of the colony, wrote to London in 1755. "Thirteen men and women were found scalped and dead and twelve children missing." It was during this time that Tom Quick turned homicidal.

---

1. The Walking Purchase was a land swindle in which the Pennsylvania authorities tricked the Delaware into ceding a large tract of their territory by producing a bogus treaty from 1686 that they said had been lost. Under its terms, the Indians had supposedly agreed to hand over land that extended from the fork of the Delaware and Lehigh rivers to as far as a man could walk in a day and a half. The Delaware agreed to honor the "lost" treaty, anticipating the distance walked through the wilderness wouldn't be too great. But the colonists selected to complete the task ran along a path that had been carefully cleared, and covered more than twice the distance the Indians expected.

The Quick family and their white neighbors had taken refuge from the marauding tribe in a fortified stone house across the Delaware River in New Jersey. They had only carried with them a month's worth of supplies, however, and as hunger and illness threatened to deplete them in the winter of 1756, Tom, his father, and a brother-in-law ventured back across the frozen river to a mill owned by Tom's father. There they worked all night grinding corn. The following morning, heavily laden with sacks of cornmeal, the men started back. Nearly midway across the river, amid Delaware war cries, shots rang out from the Pennsylvania shore. Tom's father fell. Rushing to his aid, Quick found the old man stricken. "I'm a dead man," he gasped. "I can go no further. Leave me. Run for your lives."

With the Delaware war party rapidly approaching, Tom had little choice but to flee to the other side of the river with his brother-in-law as the Indians fell upon his father. Safe on the shore, he watched helplessly as they stripped the elder Quick of his silver buttons and shoe buckles, then scalped him. Tom could just make out the features of the Delaware leader leaning over his father and desecrating his corpse. It was his boyhood friend, Mushwink. Overwhelmed with rage, Tom swore revenge. His oath is recorded in the Quick family papers: "The blood of the whole Indian race is not sufficient to atone for the blood of my father."

Tales of the murderous rampage that followed were legion, often told in the same reverential tone reserved for other American folk heroes such as Davy Crockett and Daniel Boone. An introductory poem to a book of Quick's exploits, published in 1851, read:

> Hero of many a wondrous tale,
> Full of his dev'lish cunning!
> Tom never flunked or turned pale,
> Shooting as he was running.

In one perhaps apocryphal story, Quick ambushed a Delaware family and killed them all. Asked later why he hadn't spared the life of the innocent baby, he reportedly snorted, "because nits make lice." Another oft-repeated tale had Tom splitting rails one day when he was suddenly surrounded by seven Delaware warriors. They demanded that he come with them. Quick pretended to agree, but asked the warriors for their help splitting one last log. The Indians apparently saw no reason to deny this simple request. They dropped their guns and plunged their hands into a split in the log that Tom had opened with a wedge. With his enemies thus positioned, Quick suddenly knocked out the wedge, trapping the warriors' fingers in the wood. At his leisure, he then killed them one by one.

Such stories, which grew richer with each retelling, are difficult to substantiate. But late in 1764 there was an encounter that is well documented. Tom was at a tavern near present-day Reading, Pennsylvania, when an intoxicated Delaware approached and offered to drink with him. Quick refused, but the Indian persisted. "You hate Delawares," he said. "I hate you." When Tom continued to ignore him, the Indian taunted, "You kill Delawares. I kill your father." Perhaps Quick didn't recognize Mushwink. After all, it had been almost ten years since his father's murder. "Prove it," Tom demanded. With that, Mushwink produced the silver buttons cut from the elder Quick's coat and gleefully mimicked the old man's death agonies. Enraged, Quick jumped up, grabbed a musket mounted on the tavern wall, aimed it at Mushwink, and forced him outside. "Indian dog," he roared, "you'll kill no more white men." He then shot his former friend in the back and returned to the tavern.

With the French and Indian War over and trade with the Delaware resumed, Mushwink's murder was seen as a dangerous breach of the peace. Quick was arrested, but the local townspeople arranged his escape. He was free to resume his murderous career, which, some say, lasted another thirty years. Smallpox finally finished him off in 1796.

As the years passed, the famed "Indian Slayer" gradually faded into obscurity. But his memory was revived in 1997, when a vandal defaced his memorial in Milford. The nine-foot-tall zinc obelisk was removed and repaired, but there was sharp resistance to returning it to its former place of prominence. Behavior that was once seen as heroic was now condemned as barbaric. "Lynchings in the South were part of history, too, so are we going to start putting up monuments to the grand wizards of the KKK?" Chuck Gentle Moon Demund, interim chief of the Delaware Nation, said in 2004.

Given the controversy, Tom Quick's monument remains hidden away from public view. When asked for the exact location, Lori Strelecki, curator of the Pike County Historical Society's The Columns Museum, was rather Quick with her response: "If I told you, I'd have to kill you."

5

Mary Jemison:
"The White Woman
of the Genesee"

It was a spring day in 1758, with the French and Indian War in full fury, when the terror every frontier family dreaded most was visited upon the Jemisons. A raiding party of six Shawnee warriors and four Frenchmen burst into their home near what is now Gettysburg, Pennsylvania, and took them and another family captive. The three adults and seven children were marched through the forest until they reached the spot where most of them would be slain. Only young Mary Jemison, who was about fifteen, and a little boy from the other family were spared. The two children were driven farther into the woods while the rest were killed. Both then had to watch as the bloody scalps of their loved ones were meticulously scraped, dried, and stretched over hoops by the Indians who treated them as trophies.

"Those scalps I knew at the time must have been taken from our family, by the color of the hair," Mary Jemison recalled many years later. "My mother's hair was red, and I could easily distinguish my father's and the children's from each other. That sight was most appalling; yet I was obliged to endure it without complaining."

What happened to Mary Jemison was hardly unique at a time when European settlers were routinely abducted by Native Americans. But her story, first published in 1824, was among the most widely read of the Indian captivity narratives that once abounded—perhaps because it offered something different. Not only was Mary snatched away by Indians, a familiar enough horror to many readers, but she also lived among them for the rest of her life. Thus her account provided a tantalizing glimpse into an alien society that both frightened and fascinated so many people.

The narrative is marred somewhat by the unfortunate intrusions of James E. Seaver, the writer to whom Mary told her story at the end of her life. He infused commonly held prejudices against Native Americans into the tale, not to mention an abundance of his own overwrought language (like this bathos-laden passage: "But alas! how transitory are all human affairs! how fleeting are riches! how brittle the invisible thread on which all earthly comforts are suspended!"). Still, Mary Jemison does manage to be heard, and her portrait of the native people is far more balanced and sympathetic than most. She had, after all, become one of them.

After the murder and mutilation of her family, Mary was taken to Fort Duquesne (now Pittsburgh) and given to two Seneca sisters who adopted her as a replacement for their dead brother. This was a common practice among some tribes, who believed the spirit of their loved ones resided in those they adopted, including white prisoners. She was ceremoniously dressed as a Seneca maiden and initiated into the tribe at their village on the Ohio River. "In the course of that ceremony, from mourning [the dead warrior] they became serene," Mary recalled. "Joy sparkled in their countenances, and they seemed to rejoice over me as over a long-lost child. I was made welcome among them as a sister to the two squaws before mentioned, and was called

Deh-he-wä-mis; which, being interpreted, signifies a pretty girl, a handsome girl, or a pleasant, good thing. That is the name by which I have ever since been called by the Indians."

Although she missed her family terribly and struggled to retain her native identity, Mary adapted well to the life of a Seneca woman. She tended crops, dressed game, and after several years was married to a Delaware chief by the name of Sheninjee. "The idea of spending my days with him at first seemed perfectly irreconcilable to my feelings," she told Seaver; "but his good nature, generosity, tenderness, and friendship toward me soon gained my affection; and strange as it may seem, I loved him."

Mary's contentment was made plain when she actively resisted being returned to the white world. The British offered a bounty on all those who had been taken captive during the French and Indian War, but when a Dutchman named John van Sice tried to redeem her, she ran away and hid for three days. Similarly, when a Seneca chief ordered her returned to the British, she disappeared with her child, a boy named Thomas, until it was safe to return to her tribe—the people she now considered her family. "With them was my home," she said.

A period of peace followed the French and Indian War, during which time (Sheninjee having died) Mary married her second husband, a Seneca warrior named Hiokatoo. The couple had six children, all named with a nod to their mother's past and the relatives from whom she had been parted. Two boys named John and Jesse joined their half brother, Thomas, along with four daughters called Jane, Nancy, Betsey, and Polly. Mary described the Seneca people during the lull in hostilities (with what appear to be some of James Seaver's linguistic flourishes tossed into the text):

No people can live more happy than the Indians did in times of peace, before the introduction of spiritous liquors among

> *them. Their lives were a continual round of pleasures. Their*
> *wants were few, and easily satisfied, and their cares were*
> *only for today—the bounds of calculation for future comfort*
> *not extending to the incalculable uncertainties of tomorrow. If*
> *peace ever dwelt with men, it was in former times, in the*
> *recess from war, among what are now termed barbarians. The*
> *moral character of the Indians was (if I may be allowed the*
> *expression) uncontaminated. Their fidelity was perfect, and*
> *became proverbial. They were strictly honest; they despised*
> *deception and falsehood; and chastity was held in high ven-*
> *eration, and a violation of it was considered sacrilege. They*
> *were temperate in their desires, moderate in their passions,*
> *and candid and honorable in the expression of their senti-*
> *ments, on every subject of importance.*

The peaceful interlude lasted until the American Revolution, when the Seneca (among other tribes) were enticed by the British to help subdue the rebellious colonists. Mary Jemison had a unique perspective on the conflict and witnessed horrors committed by both sides. She described the ghastly execution by the Indians of an American officer named Thomas Boyd, who was stripped naked, tied to a tree, and menaced by tomahawks and scalping knives. An incision was then made in his abdomen, and his intestines were slowly drawn out. Finally the prisoner was beheaded, his head stuck on a pole, and the rest of his body was left to rot unburied. It was a brutal killing, but Mary also recalled the destruction of her village in western New York by American forces under Major General John Sullivan. "A part of our corn they burnt," she said, "and threw the remainder into the river. They burnt our houses, killed what few cattle and horses they could find, destroyed our fruit trees, and left nothing but the bare soil and timber." A number of Indians starved or froze to death as a result. Mary survived by working for two escaped slaves who hired her to help them husk corn on their farm.

"I have laughed a thousand times to myself," she told Seaver, "when I have thought of the good old negro who hired me, who, fearing that I should get taken or injured by the Indians, stood by me constantly when I was husking, with a loaded gun in his hand, in order to keep off the enemy; and thereby lost as much labor of his own as he received from me, by paying good wages."

After the Revolutionary War, Mary was given another opportunity to return to the white world—only this time without her oldest son, Thomas, who the Seneca leaders believed would one day make a great warrior. "The chiefs refusing to let him go was one reason for my resolving to stay," she recalled; "but another, more powerful if possible, was that I had got a large family of Indian children that I must take with me; and that, if I should be so fortunate as to find my relatives, they would despise them, if not myself, and treat us as enemies, or, at least, with a degree of cold indifference, which I thought I could not endure."

Mary was rewarded for her decision to stay with an enormous tract of land around New York's Genesee River. It was a munificent bequest, but she would find little peace there in her later years, thanks to murderous infighting among her sons. A lingering quarrel between Thomas and his half brother John came to a bloody conclusion in 1811, when John beat Thomas to death at their mother's home while she was away. "I returned soon after, and found my son lifeless at the door, on the spot where he was killed," she remembered. "No one can judge my feelings on seeing this mournful spectacle; and what greatly added to my distress was the fact that he had fallen by the murderous hand of his brother." It was a terrible tragedy for any mother, but Mary had to endure it again when John killed his other brother,

Jesse, in another drunken rampage. John himself was later killed by some companions. Mary blamed the booze, and reflected upon its destructive effects on her family and her community:

> To the introduction and use of that baneful article which has made such devastation in our tribes, and threatens the extinction of our people . . . I can with greatest propriety impute the whole of my misfortune in losing my three sons. But as I have before observed, not even the love of life will restrain an Indian from sipping the poison that he knows will destroy him. The voice of nature, the rebukes of reason, the advice of parents, the expostulations of friends, and the numerous instances of sudden death, all are insufficient to restrain an Indian who has once experienced the exhilarating and inebriating effects of spirits from seeking his grave in the bottom of a bottle.

After a lifetime of adventure and heartbreak, Mary told her story to James Seaver in 1823. By then she was an old woman of about eighty, careworn but still lively and engaging. "When she looks up, and is engaged in conversation, her countenance is very expressive," wrote Seaver. "But from her long residence with the Indians, she has acquired the habit of peeping from under the eyebrows, as they do, with the head inclined downward." The book that followed was a best seller with numerous editions, and "the White Woman of the Genesee," as Mary was called, became familiar to generations of readers. But there was more to Mary Jemison than Seaver was able to capture with his purple prose. As she later told a visitor before her death in 1833, "I did not tell them who wrote it down half of what it was."

6

William Dawes:
The *Other* Midnight Rider

William Dawes had the misfortune of being at the right place, but with the wrong rhyme. While his fellow patriot and midnight rider, Paul Revere, was immortalized in verse by Henry Longfellow, Dawes is all but forgotten. It's a grave injustice to a man whose efforts on that fateful April night in 1775 were every bit as valiant as Revere's. So listen, children, and you shall hear of the midnight ride of William Dawes.

Tension between Britain and the American colonists in Massachusetts had reached a breaking point in the spring of 1775. Independent-minded rebels had repeatedly defied British authority with numerous acts of subversion like the Boston Tea Party, and now the mother country was determined to enforce some strict discipline. Colonial ringleaders John Hancock and Samuel Adams were to be arrested, and a large cache of arms and ammunition stored in the town of Concord destroyed. "Keep the measure secret until the moment of execution, it can hardly fail of success," the Earl of Dartmouth assured the royal governor of Massachusetts, General Thomas Gage. "Any efforts of the people unprepared to encounter with a regular force, cannot be very formidable."

Secrets were hard to keep in Boston, however. Word of British preparations buzzed around town throughout the day on April 18, and a network of informers within the tight-knit community kept leading citizens Paul Revere and Dr. Joseph Warren apprised of their every movement. A highly placed source among the British—some historians believe it was General Gage's American wife—confirmed to Dr. Warren that plans were indeed underway to arrest Samuel Adams and John Hancock, who were known to be in the town of Lexington, and then to destroy the weapons and ammunition stored at Concord. Armed with this information, Dr. Warren sent Revere *and* William Dawes, both established and reliable couriers, on an urgent mission to warn Hancock and Adams.

Each man took a different route to Lexington to ensure that if one was intercepted by British regulars patrolling the region, the other could still relay the vital message. Dawes left town through the gate at Boston Neck, a narrow isthmus that provided the only land access to and from the mainland. He was "mounted on a slow-jogging horse," according to his biographer Henry W. Holland, "with saddle-bags behind him, and a large flapped hat upon his head to resemble a countryman on a journey." Accounts vary as to how Dawes actually got through the closely guarded gate. Some say he joined a group of farmers returning to the mainland from Boston; others that he knew the British sentries on duty because of his frequent travels as a tanner by trade. Whatever the case, it is said that no sooner had he passed through the gate than orders arrived to stop all movement out of town.

Dawes made his way on his slow horse south across Boston Neck to Roxbury, and then west and north through Brookline, Brighton, Cambridge, and Menotomy (now Arlington) to Lexington—a nearly seventeen-mile journey that took about three hours. While his ride had none of the dazzle and flash of

steeple lights that Revere's did (at least none that's known because, unlike his fellow messenger, Dawes didn't leave a record),
it was every bit as heroic. The countryside was crawling with red-
coats determined to stop any alarms from reaching Lexington,
and Dawes deftly avoided them to deliver his message. Although
no record exists of his alerting people along the way, he almost
certainly did. "I can't imagine him riding mute," says Bill Fowler,
professor of history at Northeastern University and former director of the Massachusetts Historical Society. Still, Revere gets
all the credit and, says Fowler, "poor Dawes sort of limps along."
Historian David Hackett Fischer and others say that's because
Revere was much better connected with the leaders of the towns
along his route and thus better equipped to rally them. But the
fact remains that both Revere and Dawes accomplished their
mission, against great odds, by reaching Lexington and warning
Hancock and Adams.

After a brief rest in Lexington, Dawes and Revere set out
together to warn the town of Concord about the British approach. They were joined by a third man, unheralded like Dawes,
named Dr. Samuel Prescott. About halfway through their journey, during which they alerted a number of homesteads along
the way, the riders were intercepted by four well-armed British
Regulars. "God damn you! Stop!" one shouted. "If you go one
inch further you are a dead man!" The three tried to push through
the officers, but were overpowered. They were ordered off the
road and directed at gunpoint to an enclosed pasture. The officers "swore if we did not turn into that pasture they would blow
our brains out," Revere later recalled. Prescott saw an opportunity for escape, however. "Put on!" he whispered to Revere, and
both men spurred their horses to a gallop. Prescott turned left,
jumped a low stone wall, and disappeared into the woods. He
was the only rider to reach Concord that night. Revere was
quickly surrounded and captured.

Dawes escaped during the confusion and raced to a nearby farm with two officers in pursuit. Upon reaching the abandoned farmhouse, his horse was spooked and stopped abruptly. Dawes was pitched to the ground, and the horse ran off. Helpless now, he devised a clever feint. "Halloo, my boys," he shouted into the empty house. "I've got two of them." Unsure how many armed people might be inside, the British officers who had given chase rode off. Dawes then limped back to Lexington.

With the revolutionary spark ignited, Dawes joined the army in the siege of Boston, fought at Bunker Hill, and won a commission as commissary to the Continental Army. Dawes family lore also has it that he later returned to the empty house where he had fooled the British soldiers and recovered the watch he lost in his fall. He died on February 25, 1799, at age fifty-three, and is buried at King's Chapel in Boston. There he lies all but forgotten, a fate that might have been shared by Revere had it not been for Longfellow. The injustice of it all was captured in another, less-celebrated poem written by Helen F. Moore and published in *Century Magazine* in 1896:

> *I am a wandering, bitter shade,*
> *Never of me was a hero made;*
> *Poets have never sung my praise,*
> *Nobody crowned my brow with bays;*
> *And if you ask me the fatal cause,*
> *I answer only, "My name was Dawes"*

> *'TIS all very well for the children to hear*
> *Of the midnight ride of Paul Revere;*
> *But why should my name be quite forgot,*
> *Who rode as boldly and well, God wot?*
> *Why should I ask? The reason is clear—*
> *My name was Dawes and his Revere.*

WHEN the lights from the old North Church flashed out,
Paul Revere was waiting about,
But I was already on my way.
The shadows of night fell cold and gray
As I rode, with never a break or a pause;
But what was the use, when my name was Dawes!

HISTORY rings with his silvery name;
Closed to me are the portals of fame.
Had he been Dawes and I Revere,
No one had heard of him, I fear.
No one has heard of me because
He was Revere and I was Dawes.

7

James T. Callender:
Muckraker for the
First Amendment

The United States had barely emerged as a new nation before it was rent by what George Washington called "the baneful effects of the spirit of party." Ideological factions clashed fiercely, often using newspapers and pamphlets as the vehicles to promote their agendas. Writers for these blatantly partisan publications savaged politicians with whom they disagreed, and few of the founding fathers—not even Washington—were spared their venomous quills. A scandalmonger by the name of James T. Callender was among the most vicious of these literary character assassins who roamed the early Republic. During his brief but colorful career, Callender relentlessly hounded the nation's first leaders and published a number of salacious stories about them that endure to this day. In the process, he ran afoul of one of the most odious laws ever enacted by the U.S. government.

A fugitive Scot from British sedition laws, Callender arrived in America in 1792 and soon established himself as a rabid anti-Federalist whose screeds against the party in power attracted the attention of the Republican opposition. Thomas Jefferson secretly funded and encouraged him, while others fed him the dirt that fueled his vituperative rants. Alexander Hamilton was an early target: Callender learned that in 1792 this leading Federalist had been investigated by James Monroe and others for alleged financial improprieties involving a scoundrel named James Reynolds while serving as the nation's first secretary of the treasury. Hamilton had denied any pecuniary misdeeds, explaining to the investigators that he was actually guilty of adultery with Reynolds's wife, Maria, and that the couple had blackmailed him.[1] The money he had given Reynolds was not for any illegal speculation with public funds, as had been charged, but from his own pocket as hush money for his sexual sins. Monroe took Hamilton at his word, with reservations, and the matter was concluded.

Five years later, however, documents from the investigation were leaked to Callender, probably by John Beckley, a former clerk of the House of Representatives who had been assigned by Monroe to copy them.[2] Callender gleefully published the papers, neglecting to include Hamilton's humiliating explanation of his dealings with Reynolds and Monroe's note of the same. With all the hyperbole typical of his trade, Callender grossly exaggerated Hamilton's supposed corruption and excoriated him for his abuse of the public trust: "The funding of certificates to the extent of perhaps thirty-five millions of dollars, at eight times the price which the holders had paid for them, presents, in itself, one of the most egregious, the most impudent, the most oppressive, and the most provoking bubbles that ever burlesqued the legislative proceedings of any nation."

Faced with Callender's damning charges, Hamilton did something few politicians would ever dare: He publicly confessed his

---

1. The otherwise brilliant Hamilton apparently continued his affair with Maria even after he had been blackmailed.

2. Hamilton believed Monroe had been involved in leaking the documents, and the two nearly came to a duel. Ironically, it was Aaron Burr, who later killed Hamilton in their famous duel, who diffused the situation.

affair with Maria Reynolds to save his reputation. "The charge against me is a connection with one James Reynolds for purposes of improper pecuniary speculation," he wrote in a ninety-seven-page pamphlet. "My real crime is an amorous connection with his wife Maria, for a considerable time with his privity and connivance, if not originally brought on by a combination between the husband and wife with the design to extort money from me. This confession is not made without a blush."

Hamilton's revealing pamphlet titillated the nation and absolutely thrilled Callender, who continued his assault on the founder and dismissed his tortured admission as a flimsy cover for his real crimes. "If you have not seen it, no anticipation can equal the infamy of this piece," he wrote to Jefferson. "It is worth all that fifty of the best pens in America could have said against him."

Having demolished Hamilton's reputation, or so he believed, Callender set his sights on the Federalist president John Adams—a friend of British tyranny, Republicans claimed, with kingly pretensions of his own and an enduring enmity for freedom-loving France. Why, Callender demanded to know in an editorial for the Republican organ the *Aurora,* was Adams withholding information about a failed U.S. diplomatic mission to France? Could it be that the president, so favorable to Britain in its war with France, had deliberately undermined it? What Callender didn't know was that the American envoys had been insulted by French officials—identified in coded dispatches as X, Y, and Z—who had demanded significant cash bribes before they would deign to meet with the U.S. delegation. Fearing the XYZ Affair, as it came to be called, would provoke a war that the United States could ill afford to fight, Adams wanted to keep secret the dispatches that detailed the French outrages. His hand was forced, however, by a Republican-led demand from Congress that the dispatches be released. Predictably, anger over France's affront to American pride was sharply aroused, and the cries for war were resounding. It was in this belligerent atmosphere that Callender and his Republican cohorts found themselves threatened not only by angry mobs, but by the law.

During what became known as the Quasi-War with France, President Adams, enjoying widespread support from an inflamed public, signed into law the Alien and Sedition Acts. They were "rightly judged by history as the most reprehensible acts of his presidency," writes David McCullough, Adams's biographer. The Alien Act gave the president the legal right to expel any foreigner he considered "dangerous." And while Callender's Republican supporters helped him avoid the consequences of this law by arranging for his citizenship,[3] the Sedition Act was another matter. Clearly unconstitutional and aimed at people like Callender, it made any "false, scandalous, and malicious" writing against the government, Congress, or the president, or any attempt "to excite against them . . . the hatred of the good people of the United States, or to stir up sedition," crimes punishable by fines and imprisonment.

Callender was determined to take a stand against the Sedition Act, and, if necessary, become a martyr to it. He left his young sons in Philadelphia, which in the midst of war hysteria had become dangerously hostile to him, and moved to Jefferson's home state of Virginia. There he penned *The Prospect Before Us,* a scorching blast against the president—that "repulsive pedant" and "gross hypocrite" who was to face Jefferson in the upcoming election of 1800. "The reign of Mr. Adams has hitherto been one continued tempest of malignant passions," Callender wrote. "The grand object of his administration has been to calumniate and destroy every man who differs from his opinion." He called the president "a hoary-headed incendiary" determined to make war on France, and "in his private life, one of the most egregious

---

3. They needn't have bothered, since the Alien Act was never invoked.

fools upon the continent." There were a number of other seditious epithets guaranteed to provoke the president. Callender described him as "that strange compound of ignorance and ferocity,
of deceit and wickedness," a "hideous hermaphroditical character which has neither the force and firmness of a man, nor the
gentleness and sensibility of a woman," and "a wretch whose soul
came blasted from the hand of nature . . . a wretch that has neither the science of a magistrate, the politeness of a courtier, nor
the courage of a man."

Jefferson was pleased by Callender's toxic tract. "Such papers
cannot fail to produce the best results," he assured the author.
Adams was decidedly less enthusiastic, and Callender was promptly
arrested for sedition. His subsequent trial was a sham presided over
by U.S. Supreme Court Justice Samuel Chase, who was later im-
peached (and acquitted) for his conduct during the proceedings.

"James Thomson Callender, by his writings attached hereto,
has maliciously defamed the President of the United States, John
Adams," declared prosecutor Thomas Nelson. "The accused is
a person of wicked, depraved, and turbulent mind and is disposed toward evil. He has written and caused to be published
these words with the bad intent of bringing him into contempt,
and to excite the hatred of the people against him and their government."

All efforts by the defense to argue on their client's behalf
were thwarted by Chase, a Federalist who was determined to see
Callender convicted. In one typical exchange, Nelson referenced
a sentence from *The Prospect Before Us:* "So great is the violence
of the President's passions, that under his second administration,
America would be in constant danger of a second quarrel."

"This is the same as saying, 'Do not re-elect the present
President, for he will involve you in a war,' " Nelson declared.
"It predicts the future. How can that be true? Therefore, it must
be false, scandalous, and uttered with malicious intent."

"It is an opinion," countered defense attorney George Hay. "A political opinion does not purport to be a fact. It can neither be true nor false."

"Your objection is irrelevant," Chase snapped.

"Your Honor," Hay responded, "are you ruling that it is against the law to have an opinion, to speak your mind during the Presidency of John Adams?"

"Your argument is disrespectful, irritating, and highly incorrect," Chase said sharply. "I will have no more of that, young man."

The outcome of the case was almost preordained, and Callender was convicted. "If your calumny, defamation, and falsehood were to be tolerated," Chase lectured after the verdict was announced, "it would reduce virtue to the level of vice. There could be no encouragement to integrity, and no man, however upright in his conduct, could be secure from slander." Concluding his speech, the justice gave the convicted man an opportunity to speak. "Do you have any contrition to express that might bring about a diminution of your sentence?" he asked. Callender remained defiant. "I may be insolent," he said. "I have written some words that may be abusive. But the insolence and abusiveness of liberty, sir, are far preferable to the groveling decorum of the Court and the funereal silence of despotism."

Sentenced to nine months in prison and a $200 fine, Callender became a martyr for the First Amendment and the Republican cause, as perhaps he had intended all along. Adams was defeated in the election that followed (one of the most bitter in American history, and the only time a president and vice president ever ran against each other). It was in the wake of this victory, however, that the nation's preeminent muckraker did something astonishing: He turned on the man who had silently supported him and who was now president.

Callender expected to be rewarded for all the services he had rendered Jefferson and the Republicans—not the least of which had been his defiance of the Sedition Act, which contributed to the public's disenchantment with Adams—and the $50 the new president gave him as "charity" simply wouldn't suffice. At the very least, he wanted to be reimbursed for the $200 fine that had been levied against him as part of his sentence, and he wanted to be Richmond's postmaster as well. Callender simmered with resentment when his requests were ignored. "I now begin to know what Ingratitude is," he wrote to Secretary of State James Madison in 1801. Driven now by this festering sense of betrayal, Callender intimated to Jefferson's secretary, Meriwether Lewis, and others that he had compromising information about the president and was prepared to publish it. The $50 he had received was not charity, he said, but his due—hush money, in fact, for all he knew about Jefferson's secret machinations against the Federalists.

The president was furious when he received the reports of Callender's threats. "Such a misconstruction of my charities puts an end to them forever," he announced, a bit disingenuously, having actively (albeit secretly) supported and funded Callender's crusades against Adams and others. "He knows nothing of me which I am not willing to declare to the world myself," Jefferson continued. "I knew him first as the author of *The Political Progress of Britain,* a work I had read with great satisfaction, and as a fugitive from persecution [in Britain] for this very work. I gave him from time to time such aides as I could afford, merely as a man of genius suffering under persecution, and not as a writer in our politics. It is long since I wished he would cease writing on them, as doing more harm than good." Callender gave lie to the president's pretensions when he published the letters Jefferson had written him encouraging his attacks. It was merely an opening salvo, to be followed by an explosive story that shocked the nation and remains part of the third president's legacy.

"It is well known that the man, whom it delighteth the people to honor, keeps and for many years has kept, as his concubine, one of his slaves," Callender wrote in the September 1, 1802, edition of the Richmond *Recorder*. "Her name is Sally. The name of her eldest son his Tom. His features are said to bear a striking though sable resemblance to those of the President himself. . . . By this wench Sally, our President has had several children. There is not an individual in the neighborhood of Charlottesville who does not believe the story, and not a few who know it."

By exposing the president to contempt and ridicule with the Sally Hemings story, Callender effectively banished himself for good from the party he had once so stoutly supported. He was vilified in the Republican press, and even bludgeoned nearly to death by the same lawyer who had defended him in his sedition trial. Drinking heavily now, but unbowed, Callender continued his assault on Jefferson and Hemings, whom he referred to as "Dusky Sally," with all the signature vitriol he had used against the Federalists. And he dredged up other scandals from the president's past as well, including his attempted seduction of his best friend's wife.

It was only a drunken misadventure that finally silenced James Callender forever. On July 17, 1803, his bloated corpse was found floating in three inches of murky water on the James River. His many enemies may have delighted in the irony of his drowning in the muck. But it is a tribute to this unlikely hero of the First Amendment that, in the face of egregious laws, physical intimidation, and prison, it was the only thing that could keep him quiet.

8

John Ledyard:
The Explorer Who Dreamed
of Walking the World

The weary traveler arrived in Russia battered and bloody, his clothes in shreds and his only companion, a dog, dead. For two months he had trudged on foot across the frozen expanses of northern Sweden and Finland with only a wool cloak to protect him from the sub-Arctic winter and an iron will to propel him forward. He still had far to go.

★

Long before Lewis and Clark set out on their historic journey across North America, John Ledyard tried to walk around the world. It was an audacious undertaking by a man "of fearless courage and enterprise," as Thomas Jefferson described him; a restless wanderer propelled by the romance of discovery. Already he had circumnavigated the globe as part of Captain James Cook's famed third voyage, and in the process became the first American to see Hawaii, Alaska, and the Pacific Northwest. "Behold me the greatest traveler in history," he wrote, a bit immodestly. "An eccentric, irregular, unafraid, unaccountable, curious & without vanity, majestic as a comet."

In the end Ledyard fell short of his quest, intercepted in Siberia by order of Catherine the Great and escorted out of Russia. Still, he managed to traverse a third of the earth's land mass (though not all on foot)—a feat that inspired the Lewis and Clark expedition two decades later. And ultimately, his failure didn't matter. It was Ledyard's bold adventures and ambitious dreams, of which there were many, that left a resounding legacy. "[He] forged a new, American archtype," writes his biographer James Zug: "the heroic explorer."

The wanderlust that would define John Ledyard's life was evident early, when he dropped out of Dartmouth College after his first year and took a dugout canoe on a solo journey down the Connecticut River. It was a foolhardy venture for the inexperienced young man to explore a river no one had been recorded running before, and it nearly cost him his life when the canoe capsized close to the fifty-foot drop of Bellows Falls. Just before he was sent hurtling over, the sputtering youth was pulled to safety by villagers along the shoreline and resumed his adventure embarrassed but unbowed.

Ledyard returned home to Connecticut restless and without any real prospects. After a failed attempt to become a minister, he joined the crew of a merchant vessel that sailed to Europe, Africa, and the West Indies. "I allot myself a seven year's ramble more," he wrote to his cousin, "altho the past has long since wasted the means I had, and now the body becomes a substitute for Cash and pays my travelling expenses."

Unsatiated when he returned—it had only been a year into his "ramble," after all—Ledyard joined another crew and sailed to England in 1775. There he either enlisted with, or was forced into,[1] the British army. He wrote that he "was ordered to Boston

---

1. It was not unusual in the eighteenth century for military "recruiters" to force, or impress, able-bodied men into service against their will.

in New England [during the American Revolution]: to this your memorialist objected being a native of that country & desired he might be appointed to some other duty, which ultimately was granted." He was allowed to switch from the army to the navy and became a marine. It was in that capacity Ledyard sailed with Captain James Cook on one of the greatest voyages of discovery the world had ever known.

Cook had already completed two exploratory ventures around the globe, but this, his third, would be the most ambitious by far— the longest circumnavigation in history, and the one upon which he would meet his demise. The goal was to find the elusive Northwest Passage. But Ledyard saw the voyage as an excellent opportunity to "free himself forever from coming to America as her enemy," as he put it, as well as a way to satisfy his boundless curiosity.

The expedition set sail from Plymouth, England, on July 12, 1776, just eight days after Ledyard's countrymen declared their independence from Britain. It seems strange that at such a momentous time, a loyal American would be sailing under an enemy flag as a British marine, but Ledyard saw no incongruity. "For no State's, no Monarch's Minister am I," he later declared, "but travel under the common flag of humanity, commissioned by myself to serve the world at large."

Humanity's ambassador was in for an extraordinary trip: a four-year, 80,000-mile odyssey that took him from the beautiful beaches of Tahiti to the frozen Arctic. Along the way he met native peoples whose lives and customs fascinated him, and upon whom he looked with the kind of respect that was rare for the age. Many joyfully greeted the Cook party, though some in time turned on them with savage ferocity.[2] Beautiful women

---

2. Captain Cook was among a number of expedition members killed by native Hawaiians in 1779, after a brief skirmish over a stolen cutler. He was cut down on a beach at Kealakekua with iron daggers he had just traded to the Hawaiians. Only charred pieces of Cook were recovered for burial at sea.

gave themselves freely to the fair-haired Ledyard, and on more than one occasion left him with a wicked case of the clap.

During the journey, Ledyard became the first American citizen to visit Alaska and Hawaii, and described how it felt to be the first to step foot upon the west coast of the North American continent. "Though more than two thousand miles distant from the nearest part of New England I felt myself plainly affected: All the affectionate passions incident to natural attachments and early prejudices played round my heart, and indulged them because they were prejudices. It soothed a home-sick heart, and rendered me very tolerably happy."

The pelts the expedition collected in the Pacific Northwest and then sold in China at exorbitant prices inspired Ledyard with dreams of a lucrative fur trade in the East. The idea eventually became an obsession, and Ledyard later formed various partnerships with Revolutionary financier Robert Morris and naval hero John Paul Jones to establish a trading company. Nothing ever came of the efforts, but James Zug and others credit Ledyard's ambition for the eventual launch of the China trade and the opening of the Pacific for the United States.

After four years at sea and a world of discovery (though not of the Northwest Passage), Ledyard and the other surviving members of the Cook expedition returned to England in October 1780. A year later the navy sent him to America, where he promptly deserted and set about documenting his grand adventure in the popular book *A Journal of Captain Cook's Last Voyage*. The work is notable for the relatively enlightened and balanced accounts of the native cultures Ledyard encountered, as well as for establishing the size of North America for the first time. It also inspired American copyright protection after Ledyard asked the Connecticut assembly for "the exclusive right of publishing this said Journal or history in the State for such a term as shall be thot fit." (Ironically, the book was heavily plagiarized from other sources.)

By 1784, Ledyard was off to Europe again. A master of self-promotion, he took to calling himself "John Ledyard the Traveler," and cut a rather eccentric figure with his exotic clothes (which he could ill afford) and his sometimes manic disposition. But it was his intellect that most impressed people. Thomas Jefferson, then serving as U.S. ambassador to France, called him "a man of genius" and "a person of ingenuity and information. Unfortunately," he added, "he has too much imagination." Yet in spite of that express reservation, it was Jefferson who enthusiastically backed Ledyard's most outlandish ambition of all: to walk around the world. The plan was to go from Europe through Siberia and then across North America. It was the opportunity to explore his native land that seemed to excite Ledyard most:

> I die with anxiety to be on the back of the American States, after having either come from or penetrated to the Pacific Ocean. There is an extensive field for the acquirement of honest fame. A blush of generous regret sits on my Cheek to hear of any Discovery there that I have not part in, & particularly at this auspicious period: The American Revolution invites to a thorough Discovery of the Continent and the honor of doing it would become a foreigner. But a Native only could feel the pleasure of the Achievement. It was necessary that a European should discover the Existence of that Continent, but in the name of Amor Patria. Let a native of it Explore its Boundary. It is my wish to be the Man. I will not yet resign that wish nor my pretension to that distinction.

At the end of November 1786, John Ledyard the Traveler set out on his quixotic march. The first leg of his journey was miserable. "Never did I adopt an Idea so fatal to my happiness," he wrote after the brutal two-month trek through northern Sweden and Finland in the bitter cold. Yet he was unstoppable. "The

bruises, the sleeplessness, the dirty-fingernail poverty, the sweat
and mud-soaked clothes were real," James Zug writes of Ledyard's astonishing resilience. "Yet it was if his sufferings were
happening to another person. Staggeringly buoyant, he brushed
aside his pains and talked of trying again. He would leave on a
moment's notice. He would promise a new destination, despite
the lack of money, clothes, prospects or good sleep. His imagination remained unassailable."

Ledyard was without a doubt stalwart, but by the time he
reached St. Petersburg in March 1787, it was clear that his dream
would have to be modified. The vast stretches of Siberia that lay
before him would take years to walk, and Ledyard lacked the
money to support such an extended venture. Instead, he would
travel in a Russian coach known as a *kibitka*. "Kabitka travelling
is the remains of Caravan travelling," he wrote. "It is your only
home—it is like a ship at sea."

During the next four months Ledyard covered most of Russia's
enormous expanse, more than five thousand miles since he left
St. Petersburg. He was now tantalizingly close to the Pacific Ocean,
just five hundred miles away, and the next leg of his journey across
North America. But in the frontier town of Yakutsk, three hundred miles below the Arctic Circle, he was stopped in his tracks.
Winter made it impossible to go any farther. And it wasn't just the
elements that conspired against him. Catherine the Great, empress
of Russia, had denied Ledyard passage through her realm when
he applied for a passport, and he had defied her. Now he had to
pay the price. On February 1, 1778, while waiting for the winter
weather to pass, he was arrested in the town of Irkutsk, ordered
to be escorted under guard back across Siberia, and left at the Polish border with the warning never to return to Russia. Ledyard's
wandering spirit flagged under confinement.

"Loose your liberty but once for one hour, ye who never lost
it, that ye may feel what I feel," he wrote. "Altho' born in the

freest Country of the World, Ideas of its exquisite Beauties & of its immortal Nature that I had never before. Methinks every Man who is called to preside officially over the Liberty of a free People should once—it will be enough—actually be deprived unjustly of his Liberty that he might be avaricious of it more than of any earthly possessions."

An ordinary man might have taken a good long rest after traveling fifteen thousand miles over mostly inhospitable terrain, but not John Ledyard. Almost as soon as he returned to London, one and a half years after he began his walk, he was enthusiastically planning an expedition to Africa with the famed naturalist Joseph Banks and other esteemed members of a society known as the African Association. It would be the ultimate adventure into regions thus far unexplored. Yet despite his pretense of vigor, Ledyard was not a well man. And he seemed to sense that this would be his last journey. His friend Henry Beaufoy, a member of the African Association, recalled his words of farewell:

> I am accustomed to hardships. I have known both hunger and nakedness to the utmost extremity of human suffering. I have known what it is to have food given me as charity to a madman; and I have at times been obliged to shelter myself under the miseries of that character to avoid a heavier calamity. My distresses have been greater than I have ever owned, or will own to any man. Such evils are terrible to bear, but they never yet had power to turn me from my purpose. If I live, I will faithfully perform, in its utmost extent, my engagement to the Society; and if I perish in the attempt, my honor will still be safe, for death cancels all bonds.

John Ledyard never did make it out of Africa. Indeed, his last great venture had barely begun when, on January 10, 1789, he succumbed to dysentery at age thirty-seven. Perhaps Jefferson was right when he said Ledyard had too much imagination, but that's what made him uniquely American. "It is that overflowing, unmanageable, penetrating, elastic imagination which places him at the core of a nation's psyche," writes James Zug. "Too much imagination is the American ethos."

9

Elizabeth Patterson Bonaparte: Royal American

"Nature never intended me for obscurity," Elizabeth Patterson Bonaparte announced to her father in 1815. Although she may have been a bit premature in that assessment, largely forgotten as she is today, few at the time would have disagreed. The beautiful native of Baltimore, Maryland, achieved the fame she craved when she married Jérôme Bonaparte, younger brother of the soon-to-be emperor Napoléon. Entry into the imperial family banished all the young woman's fears of anonymity and allowed her to bask in worldwide celebrity. Unfortunately, it was quickly doomed, as the union clashed with Napoléon's own ambitions.

Elizabeth met Jérôme in September 1803, when the dashing but spoiled lieutenant in the French navy visited Baltimore during a tour of the American East. The attraction was immediate, and the couple soon made plans to wed. The only hitch was Elizabeth's father William, one of Baltimore's wealthiest citizens, received an anonymous letter detailing Jérôme's "profligate" ways. He had "ruined" many a young lady, the letter warned, and would marry Elizabeth only "to secure himself a home at your expense" until he returned to France, after which time he would "laugh at your credulity." Needless to say, William Patterson found this somewhat disturbing. He cancelled the wedding and sent Elizabeth away to stay with relatives in Virginia.

Love wasn't quenched so easily, however. Elizabeth pined for her prince, declaring that she "would rather be the wife of Jérôme Bonaparte for one hour than the wife of any other man for life." Her father relented when Elizabeth threatened to run away with Jérôme, and the couple was married on Christmas Eve. The mayor of Baltimore, James Calhoun, performed the civil ceremony, and John Carroll, the first Catholic bishop in the United States, performed the religious rite. In a bow to contemporary French fashion, the bride wore a rather flimsy wedding dress that one guest noted "could have been put in [his] pocket."

The newlyweds were eagerly received in the highest social circles, while the masses who read of the couple's every move in daily newspaper reports clamored to get a glimpse of them. They were stars, and Elizabeth certainly dressed the part. The revealing French fashions she had previewed at her wedding both shocked and titillated. At a party given for the couple in Washington, D.C., for example, she wore a gown described by one guest as "so transparent that you could see the color and shape of her thighs, and even more!" Another wrote that "her appearance was such that it threw all the company into confusion, and no one dared look at her but by stealth." Elizabeth ignored all warnings that her unconventional fashion sense would adversely affect her social standing, believing instead that the bold styles, combined with her notoriety, would gain her entrée almost anywhere. She was right. "Knowing how important these public occasions were," writes historian Charlene Boyer Lewis, "Elizabeth never shrank from the attention, as well-mannered ladies were supposed to do, and she always carefully dressed for them. Her clothing helped her maintain the celebrity status that she not only loved, but also considered a necessary part of her life."

While Elizabeth's daring dresses created quite a stir in the United States, her marriage had a seismic impact in France. Napoléon, then first consul, was enraged when he heard the news. He had great dynastic plans for his siblings, intending to marry them into some of the royal houses of Europe, and Jérôme had just thwarted his ambitions by taking an American nobody as a wife. He refused to recognize the marriage and ordered his brother home immediately—without Elizabeth. "If he brings her with him," Napoléon fumed, "she will not set foot on French territory. If he comes alone, I will overlook his error." Jérôme, every bit as stubborn as his mighty brother, refused his summons.

President Thomas Jefferson and Secretary of State James Madison had anticipated Napoléon's negative reaction to the wedding, and sent diplomatic reassurances that even the president of the United States was powerless to prevent a marriage. The Louisiana Purchase was at stake, and Jefferson could ill afford to alienate the French leader. Meanwhile, Jérôme's brother Lucien sent word that the Bonaparte clan was thrilled with the union. "Tell Monsieur Patterson [Elizabeth's brother] that our mother, myself, and the entire family unanimously and fully approve of the marriage," he wrote. "The Consul does not agree with us for the moment, but he must be considered the sole dissenting voice in the family." Napoléon's may have been the lone voice, but it was the only one that mattered. And he was implacable. He would never accept "Miss Patterson," as he insisted upon calling Elizabeth, and prohibited any French civil authority to recognize the union under penalty of prison.

Jérôme deluded himself into believing that Napoléon's heart would thaw once he met his charming bride. Accordingly, he and Elizabeth, now pregnant, set sail for France in the fall of 1804 after learning that Napoléon had declared himself emperor. They planned to attend his coronation, but their ship was beset by a fierce storm as it left harbor and sank. The couple barely escaped with their lives, and all their wedding gifts and other possessions, including several thousand dollars in gold, were lost. Desperate to share in the glory of the coronation, they hired another brig, but it was turned back by British warships. They missed the ceremony. Finally, William Patterson provided one of his own ships to sail them across the Atlantic. When they arrived in Lisbon, however, an emissary from Napoléon informed them that "Miss Patterson" would not be permitted to disembark on European soil. "Tell your master that *Madame Bonaparte* is ambitious and demands her rights as a member of the imperial family," Elizabeth reportedly responded—to no avail.

Faced with the emperor's unbending will and far-reaching power, Jérôme and Elizabeth decided that she would sail on to Amsterdam to have the baby, and he would proceed to Milan, where Napoléon was crowning himself king of Italy. There Jérôme would confront his brother. "My good wife, have faith in your husband," he wrote soothingly. "The worst that could happen now would be for us to live quietly in some foreign country. . . . My dearest Elisa, I will do everything that must be done." She never saw him again.

Jérôme had been given a powerful ultimatum: Either renounce his "mistress," or face ruin. Napoléon threatened to strip his brother of all ranks and titles, remove him from the line of succession, and abandon him to his staggering debts. Furthermore, Jérôme would be banished from France and all its territories (which then included Holland, Belgium, Italy, Spain, and Portugal), and would never receive another franc from the government or from the Bonaparte family.

Steadfast and true, Jérôme agreed to abandon his wife. The emperor was delighted. "Mon *frère*," he exclaimed, "there is no fault you could commit that would not be overlooked by your repentance. . . . Your marriage thus annulled at your own request, I should like to offer you my friendship." Napoléon gave Jérôme the kingdom of Westphalia to rule, and married him—bigamously— to Princess Catherine of Württemberg.

While her husband was busy renouncing her in Italy, Elizabeth was stuck at port in Amsterdam. Officials there, fearing the emperor's wrath, refused to let her off the ship, and she was forced to sail to England. There, for the first time in fourteen weeks, she finally touched solid ground. And on July 7, 1805, gave birth to a baby boy she named Jérôme-Napoléon Bonaparte. "Rest assured, your husband will never abandon you," brave Jérôme wrote. "I would give my life for you alone, and for my child." The British secretary of legation in the United States, Sir Augustus Foster, later recalled Elizabeth's dramatic declaration that she would rather be the wife of Jérôme Bonaparte for one hour than the wife of any other man for life, and noted wryly, "She did not know she was so near the real event."

Abandoned by her husband, Elizabeth returned to Baltimore with her baby, who she called Bo. Yet despite her rejection, she retained all her royal pretensions and continued to cultivate her celebrity. She ordered a coach with the Bonaparte family crest painted on its doors, and unfailingly reminded people of her imperial connections. Madame Bonaparte, as she styled herself, still wore her outrageous dresses and remained a sought-after guest. "The state of nudity in which she appeared [at a presidential dinner] attracted the attention of the Gentlemen," one guest reported, "for I saw several of them take a look at her bubbies when they were conversing with her."

In 1808, Jérôme, now king of Westphalia and married to Catherine of Württemberg, wrote Elizabeth and asked her to send him their son. She refused. Several years later, he asked again, offering to set Elizabeth up in her own castle. Again she refused, declaring that she would never relinquish her son, adding that Jérôme's kingdom was "not quite large enough to hold *two queens*."

Eventually she accepted a yearly pension from Napoléon, and obtained a divorce from Jérôme in the Maryland legislature. Soon after, Napoléon's empire collapsed and all the ruling Bonapartes were booted from their thrones.

With the collapse of the empire, Elizabeth felt free to return to Europe in 1815. Though once forbidden to step foot on the continent, she was now warmly welcomed by the European elite, and believed she had found her rightful place in the world. "I get on extremely well," she wrote her father, "and I assure you that altho' you have always taken me for a fool, it is not in my character here. In America, I appeared more simple than I am, because I was completely out of my element. It was my misfortune, not my fault, that I was born in a country which was not congenial to my desires. Here I am completely in my sphere . . . and in contact with modes of life for which nature intended me."

For the next twenty-five years, Elizabeth spent most of her time in Europe and became increasingly contemptuous of American mores and culture. In other words, she became French. Surrounding herself with aristocrats, artists, and intellectuals, she reveled in the attention lavished upon her and fancied herself a member of the nobility. She maintained friendly ties with the Bonapartes in exile, as she considered the family connection advantageous for her son, who she believed was born for greatness. And though she continued to call Baltimore home, she returned only occasionally to attend to her financial affairs. It was impossible, she sniffed, "to be contented in a country where there exists no nobility."

One of Elizabeth's primary obsessions as her son grew older was to marry him into an aristocratic European family. "Bo has rank," she informed her father. "His name places him in the first society in Europe." She was devastated, therefore, when she learned in 1829 that the young man had wed a girl from Baltimore. "When I first heard my son could condescend to marry anyone in Baltimore I nearly went mad," she wrote. Elizabeth's sense of nobility was offended by her son stooping so far beneath him. She had married "the brother of an emperor," and had not the "meanness of spirit to descend from such an elevation to the deplorable condition of being the wife of an American." But, she conceded in resignation, she and her son were different people. The young man, "not having my pride, my ambition, or my utter abhorrence to vulgar company," had the "right to pursue the course he prefers." She had done all she could "to disgust him with America," and "give him the ideas suitable to his rank in life."

Eventually Elizabeth settled back in Baltimore, among the masses she so disdained. She wasn't happy. "There is nothing here worth attention or interest," she wrote a friend, "except the money market." She returned to Europe one last time in 1860, when Jérôme died and left no provision for their son in his will. In a celebrated lawsuit against the surviving Bonapartes, she vainly sought to have Bo recognized as a legitimate heir. Defeated, she returned home and settled in a boarding house where she lived as an imperial relic until her death in 1879.

10

Stephen Pleasonton:
The Clerk Who Saved
the Constitution
(and the Declaration of Independence, Too)

The Founding Fathers are revered for having created two of history's most enlightened testaments: the Declaration of Independence and the U.S. Constitution. But no one seems to remember poor Stephen Pleasonton, who rescued the precious documents from almost certain destruction.

The sweltering languor of August in Washington gave way to a spreading panic in 1814. It was two years into America's second war with Britain, and the enemy was marching ever closer to the heart of her former colonies. Local residents, having heard of the terrible destruction already inflicted by the British on a number of towns along the Chesapeake Bay, were eager to escape the coming onslaught. The dusty roads leading out of the capital were filling with citizens carting out their most valued possessions, while the few government workers not serving in the local militia struggled at the same time to save what they could of the young Republic's most vital records and irreplaceable treasures.

It was in this atmosphere of escalating fear and tension that Pleasonton, a State Department clerk, went to work saving the Declaration and the Constitution from destruction. The War of 1812 was essentially a second declaration of independence, this time from British interference in U.S. trade and sovereignty, and Pleasonton ensured that these unique parchments of American principle would not become spoils of war—even if the nation's capital did. He was acting on instructions from his boss, Secretary of State James Monroe, who was out scouting British positions. Observing the enemy's advances and fearful of what lay ahead, Monroe sent a courier back to the department asking that someone attend to the safety of the historic books and papers kept there.

The task fell to Pleasonton. After purchasing quantities of coarse, durable linen, the clerk ordered the material made into book bags. He then gently packed the scrolled documents and prepared to haul them to safety. Before leaving the State Department, however, Pleasonton encountered Secretary of War John Armstrong, an officious character who had been stubbornly insisting for weeks that the British posed no threat to the capital. Just a month earlier, in fact, Armstrong had berated William Winder, the head of Washington's militia, for expressing concerns over enemy reinforcements sailing up the Chesapeake Bay.

"By God," Armstrong bellowed, "they would not come with such a fleet without meaning to strike somewhere. But they will not come here! What the devil will they do here? No! No! Baltimore is the place, sir. That is of so much more consequence."

The secretary of war had apparently not changed his opinion when he came across Pleasonton going about his task; he rebuked the clerk for being unnecessarily alarmed about the threat to the capital. "He did not think the British were serious in their intentions of coming to Washington," Pleasonton later wrote to Winder. "I replied that we were under a different belief, and let their intentions be what they might, it was the part of prudence to preserve the valuable papers of the Revolutionary Government."

After taking leave of Armstrong, Pleasonton ordered all the valuable papers he had collected sent two miles up the Potomac River to an abandoned gristmill on the banks of Virginia. But he was still uneasy. The mill was just across the river from Henry Foxall's Foundry, a munitions factory that had been supplying the nation's cannons and other heavy armaments throughout the War of 1812. If the British did attack Washington, Pleasonton reasoned, surely they would target the foundry that was less than a mile away from Georgetown. It would be only a matter of loose lips or deliberate treachery for the British to then discover the priceless hoard hidden at the mill. Determined to avoid this possibility, Pleasonton later reloaded the cargo onto several carts and took it farther inland, to Leesburg, Virginia. There the linen bags were locked in an empty house, the keys for which were given to the town sheriff. "Being fatigued with the ride, and securing the papers," Pleasonton wrote, "I retired early to bed."

Washington burned as he slept.

Earlier on that day of August 24, British forces had routed the Americans at the Battle of Bladensburg just outside Washington, scattering the city's defenders with a blizzard of heavy artillery and panic-inducing Congreve rockets. When they stormed the capital that same evening, the invaders found "the metropolis of our country abandoned to its horrible fate," as navy clerk Mordecai Booth later wrote. The navy yard was already in flames, preemptively torched by U.S. officials who did not want its rich supplies to fall into enemy hands. With a veneer of civility that barely concealed their relish in laying waste to the American capital, the British assured those few residents remaining in the city that private property would be respected. Public buildings, on the other hand, were most assuredly to be destroyed. They started with the Capitol.

The magnificent structure rising high above the city still in its infancy was the pride of the new Republic. Enormous care and expense had been lavished on its design, construction, and artistic detailing—from the ancient Virginia freestone hauled in from an island on Aquia Creek to the crimson silk curtains, fluted Corinthian columns, and the fine marble statue of Liberty sitting on a pedestal in the House chamber. Now a great fire roared through both wings of the building, consuming not only the House and Senate chambers but also the Library of Congress and the Supreme Court, which were then housed at the Capitol. It was, Mordecai Booth wrote, a sight "so repugnant to my feelings, so dishonorable, so degrading to the American character, and at the same time so awful."

With the U.S. Capitol now an inferno lighting up the night sky over Washington, the British marched down Pennsylvania Avenue to the President's House. They hoped to capture President Madison, but found the mansion empty. A table was still set for the evening, evidence of how quickly the building had been abandoned, and food and drink were abundant. The vandals gorged themselves. "Never was nectar more grateful to the palates of the gods than the crystal goblets of Madeira and water I quaffed off at Mr. Madison's expense," Captain James Scott, a British officer, wrote in his memoir. After eating and drinking their fill, the soldiers ransacked the exquisitely appointed home, snatching souvenirs and setting small blazes. Soon the entire structure was engulfed, joined later by the Treasury Building next door. With all the fires that had been set, the eerie orange and red glow of the capital's skyline could be seen as far away as Baltimore. "You never saw a drawing room so brilliantly lighted as the whole city was that night," one witness wrote. "Few thought of going to bed—they spent the night in gazing on the fires and lamenting the disgrace of the city."

The destructive fury of the invaders had not been sated by the next morning, even as the city's finest buildings lay in smoldering ruin. The pillage continued throughout the day. Though Georgetown and Foxall's Foundry were not attacked as Stephen Pleasonton had feared, the State Department from where he had rescued the Declaration of Independence and the U.S. Constitution was put to the torch, along with the War Department that adjoined it on the west side of the President's House. As the British rampage continued, American onlookers seethed. "If General Washington had been alive, you would not have gotten into this city so easily," one shouted at Admiral George Cockburn, who led the invasion. "No, sir," Cockburn replied haughtily. "If General Washington had been president, we should never have thought of coming here."

Twenty-four hours after storming the city, Cockburn and his army marched out. The goal of humiliating the upstart Americans by destroying their capital had been achieved. Returning residents were then confronted with the wreckage of their city. "I cannot tell you what I felt on re-entering it," First Lady Dolley Madison wrote to a friend. "Such destruction—such confusion." Richard Rush, a friend of Madison's, called it "the most magnificent and melancholy ruin you ever beheld."

Many in Congress argued that the cost of rebuilding would be too great and that the capital should be moved back to Philadelphia. Ultimately, though, the battered and humbled city prevailed, and it was to there that the great documents Stephen Pleasonton had saved were returned.

The State Department clerk's mission had been heroic, but his name and deeds were lost in obscurity for almost two centuries until historian Anthony Pitch stumbled upon them in a little-read scholarly journal from 1907 while researching his book *The Burning of Washington: The British Invasion of 1814*. Though he hoped to create a full portrait of Pleasonton, Pitch found details of the unsung patriot's life frustratingly sparse. What is certain is that honor and fame eluded him,[1] and that he was forced in his later years to beg to keep his government post in order to avoid an impoverished old age. "For saving these papers," he wrote to future president James Buchanan in 1853, "the British government, had that been done for it, would probably have given me many thousand pounds."

It remains unknown if Pleasonton got to keep his job, or if anyone even bothered to say thanks.

---

1. The only people who seem to have any recollection of Pleasonton are lighthouse historians who regard him with disfavor because of his failure to adequately fund these navigational aids while serving as auditor for the U.S. Treasury.

11

Richard Mentor Johnson:
The Veep Who
Killed Tecumseh

An American vice president is practically guaranteed obscurity, unless he reaches the highest office. (And even then there's no assurance of lasting fame—just look at Chester Alan Arthur.) "My country has in its wisdom contrived for me the most insignificant office that ever the invention of man contrived or his imagination conceived," the first vice president, John Adams, wrote ruefully. John Nance Garner, Franklin Roosevelt's veep, put it a bit more bluntly: The vice presidency, he said, "isn't worth a bucket of warm piss." That was a sentiment no doubt shared by Richard Mentor Johnson, whose once promising political future—not to mention his place in history—was all but extinguished when he was elected to serve under a president with his own overlooked legacy, Martin Van Buren. Yet while Johnson is now mostly forgotten, his life was really quite memorable.

The future vice president was born under fire, in a hastily constructed fortress on the Virginia frontier, near what became Louisville, Kentucky. The Revolutionary War was still raging in 1780, and the frontier was under fierce Indian assault. Johnson family lore held that a flaming arrow landed in baby Richard's cradle and that he was only saved when his older sister Betsey pulled it away. The incident, if it really happened, foreshadowed a time when Richard Johnson would make his name fighting Indians in another war with the British, some three decades later.

The Johnsons emerged from the Revolution as a family of great wealth and influence. Richard's father was one of the largest landowners in Kentucky, with numerous commercial interests, and two of his brothers served in the U.S. House of Representatives. Trained as a lawyer, Richard preceded them to Capitol Hill in 1806. Amiable and hardworking, if undistinguished, the young congressman was described by Washington socialite Margaret Bayard Smith as "the most tender hearted, mild, affectionate and benevolent of men . . . whose countenance beams with good will to all, whose soul seems to feed on the milk of human kindness." Nice qualities, but hardly sufficient to build an enduring reputation. That would take a war.

Tensions between the fledgling United States and its former motherland had been festering for years over Britain's oppressive interference with American shipping and its encouragement of Indian hostilities toward settlers in the Northwest frontier.[1] Johnson joined other vociferous young congressmen like Henry Clay and John Calhoun, known collectively as "the War Hawks," who demanded an aggressive response to the British outrages. What resulted was the War of 1812. Not wishing "to be idle during the recess of Congress," as he wrote, Johnson raised two regiments of Kentucky volunteers, and in the fall of 1813 led them north to join the army of his future rival, General William Henry Harrison. Their quarry was British general Henry Procter and his Indian allies under the leadership of the famed Shawnee chieftain Tecumseh. "Oh, how I did want to catch that fellow [Procter],"

---

1. The 260,000-square-mile territory included the modern states of Ohio, Indiana, Illinois, Michigan, Wisconsin, and parts of Minnesota.

Johnson later wrote. "I never thirsted for a man's blood but Procter was a monster."

The fateful clash came along the Thames River on the lower Ontario peninsula. Procter had been attempting to retreat after an American naval victory on Lake Erie made his position untenable, but Tecumseh shamed him into making a stand. On October 5, 1813, British forces were formed in a line of battle at Moraviantown, while Tecumseh's warriors took up flanking positions along a swamp on the British right. Johnson's brother James smashed through the British line, which sent Procter scurrying away to safety, but Tecumseh remained in position and kept fighting. It was then that Richard Johnson led a group of volunteers, known as "the Forlorn Hope," into a nearly suicidal assault on the Indian flank. Tangled in briar and under a relentless volley, fifteen members of the Forlorn Hope were killed instantly and four more were wounded. Johnson himself was shot through the hip and thigh, but pressed on with the rest of his regiment. He received several more wounds and had his horse shot from beneath him, yet he still managed to kill Tecumseh[2] and thus break the back of the Indian confederacy that had long plagued the Northwest Territory.

Richard Johnson returned to Congress in 1814 as a war hero, with the wounds that disabled him for the rest of his life to prove it. The Battle of the Thames had been one of the most decisive in the War of 1812, and Tecumseh's death boosted his political fortunes considerably. "Rumpsey, Dumpsey, Colonel Johnson killed Tecumseh!" his supporters would chant during many campaigns to come. Johnson's newfound status probably saved him from the furor that erupted over a bill he sponsored in 1816 that granted members of Congress an annual salary. (They were previously paid

---

2. The deed is memorialized in the Rotunda of the U.S. Capitol, though some historians question whether it was actually Johnson who killed Tecumseh. The evidence is inconclusive, but Johnson remains the most likely candidate.

only for the days when Congress was in session.) Many of his colleagues lost their seats in the aftermath of the unpopular measure, and Johnson himself repudiated it the next year. He was also left unscathed by what historian Robert V. Remini called a "colossal boondoggle" involving the construction of a series of fortresses along the Missouri River to the Yellowstone. Johnson, who was chairman of the House Committee on Expenditures in the Department of War, secured for his brother James the contract to supply materials for the new outpost. Only problem was, the steamboats James Johnson had built to transport men and supplies couldn't navigate shallow water. The ill-fated venture cost the government a fortune, but as President James Monroe noted, "the people of the whole western country" considered the project a worthy measure "to preserve the peace of the frontier." The Johnsons were celebrated rather than derided.

Throughout the rest of his term in the House, which lasted until 1819, and then in the Senate, Johnson's popularity was enhanced by his consistent advocacy of veterans and war widows relief, as well as his efforts to end imprisonment for debtors. In a speech before the Senate in 1823, he declared, "the principle is deemed too dangerous to be tolerated in a free government, to permit a man for any pecuniary consideration, to dispose of the liberty of his equal." Johnson's principles drew him to a coalition emerging under the leadership of Senator Martin Van Buren that eventually became the Democratic Party. And to its future standard-bearer, Andrew Jackson, he offered his unswerving loyalty. Johnson vigorously defended the Hero of New Orleans over charges that he had overstepped his authority by invading Spanish Florida in 1817, and supported him in the 1824 presidential election, which was decided in favor of John Quincy Adams in the House of Representatives, despite Jackson winning the popular vote.

Four years later Old Hickory defeated Adams to become the first "populist" president. Johnson lost his Senate seat at the same time, but was promptly reelected to the House, where he served as a powerful ally of the administration throughout both of Jackson's terms in office. Having "the rare quality of being personally liked by everyone," as John C. Calhoun's biographer, Charles M. Wiltse, notes, Johnson often found himself in the role of mediator— particularly in the disputes between Jackson and Vice President Calhoun over such issues as nullification.[3] But it was in a social-political fracas dubbed by Secretary of State Martin Van Buren as "the Eaton Malaria" that his conciliatory talents were most sorely tried.[4]

Essentially, the society women of Washington decreed that Margaret "Peggy" Eaton, wife of Secretary of War John Eaton, was a woman of questionable virtue and thus unfit for their company. Men of the day were expected to follow their wives' decisions on such matters and ostracize whomever they were told to ostracize. Accordingly, most of Jackson's cabinet, as well as Vice President Calhoun, rejected Mrs. Eaton. This enraged the president, who personally liked the shunned woman and also viewed the social assault on her as a political attack on him—a conspiracy to make John Eaton's position in the cabinet untenable, therefore destabilizing the administration and undermining his decisions.

Silly as it all may seem now, the Eaton Malaria consumed the first two years of Jackson's presidency and had tremendous political ramifications. The president was determined to have Peggy

---

3. Jackson and Calhoun had strongly opposing views on the role of government. The vice president was a proponent of a state's right to nullify federal laws deemed not to be in its interest. The president, while a believer in states' rights, saw this concept as a dangerous threat to the stability of the Union. Their differences on the nullification issue became glaringly apparent at a Washington dinner in 1830 when President Jackson exclaimed in a toast, "Our Union; it must be preserved," while staring straight at Calhoun. The vice president then responded with a toast of his own: "The Union. Next to our liberty, the most dear." The clash over nullification and other issues eventually led to Calhoun's resignation.

4. For a full treatment of the Eaton Malaria, see the author's *A Treasury of Great American Scandals: Tantalizing True Tales of Historic Misbehavior by the Founding Fathers and Others Who Let Freedom Swing.*

Eaton welcomed into society and sent Johnson as an emissary to three of his more recalcitrant cabinet members. Johnson, on friendly terms with all three, cordially advised them that Jackson was in earnest and was prepared to fire anyone who continued to snub John Eaton's wife. This would be persuasive enough, or so Johnson believed. He was stunned, therefore, when his diplomatic entreaties were rejected. Even the president of the United States could not force them into company their wives had determined was unworthy, the cabinet members declared. Defeated, Johnson went back to the president, who, he noted, was "like a roaring lion" upon hearing the news. In the end, the entire cabinet was dismissed—the only such event in American history.

Given his own domestic situation, Johnson's role in the Eaton affair is interesting. He was all but married to one of his slaves, a woman named Julia Chinn, with whom he had two daughters. They were his family, and he wanted them accepted as such. But that was asking way too much in the antebellum South. It was one thing to sleep with a slave, which many a master considered a perquisite of ownership, but to try to introduce her or the offspring of such miscegenation into white society was simply intolerable. George Prentice, editor of the *Louisville Journal,* reflected the hypocrisy of such standards when he lambasted Johnson in an editorial. "If Col. Johnson had the decency and decorum to seek to hide his ignominy from the world, we would refrain from lifting the curtain," Prentice wrote. "His chief sin against society is the publicity and barefacedness of his conduct; he scorns all secrecy, all concealment, all disguise."

Notwithstanding his unusual living arrangements, Johnson enjoyed wide support in the West (which then extended only to the Mississippi River), as well as among workingmen in the urban centers. Furthermore, he was close to the president and had every reason to expect that Jackson would select him as his running mate in the 1832 election after John Calhoun resigned from the vice presidency. This would in effect make Johnson the president's heir apparent. But Jackson chose Martin Van Buren. "The Little Magician," as Van Buren was sometimes called, had cast his spell over the president and had made himself indispensable.

Though deeply disappointed, Johnson still had faith in his own political future. Just a month after Jackson's second inauguration, the *Political Register* reported that "the western States are flooded with handbills nominating Col. *Richard M. Johnson,* of Kentucky, as a candidate for the Presidency in 1836." That same year William Emmons published his political hagiography, *The Authentic Biography of Colonel Richard M. Johnson,* which was followed by the laudatory play, *Tecumseh, or the Battle of the Thames, a National Drama in Five Acts.* After attending one well-received performance of the play, Johnson happily exclaimed, "I have now more friends than ever by the hundreds."

Certainly Johnson was well regarded in some quarters, but Van Buren was still Jackson's man and the one chosen to inherit his mantle. "It didn't strike [the president] as odd that he, the champion of the people's right to choose their leaders, should essentially appoint his own successor," writes historian H. W. Brands. Van Buren would be the Democratic candidate, but as a sop to the ever-loyal Johnson, Old Hickory bestowed upon him the second spot on the ticket. It wasn't a universally acclaimed decision: "I pray you to assure our friends that the humblest of us do not believe that a lucky random shot, even if it did hit Tecumseh, qualifies a man for the Vice Presidency," John Catron, chief justice of the Tennessee Supreme Court, wrote to Jackson. Catron predicted that "the very moment Col. J. is announced, the newspapers will open upon him with facts, that he had endeavored often to force his daughters into society, that the mother in her life time, and they now, rode in carriages, and claimed equality."

Delegates at the 1835 Democratic convention in Baltimore did as Jackson demanded and nominated Van Buren for president.

But some balked at Johnson for vice president. Virginians wanted William Cabell Rives, who had served as minister to France during Jackson's first term, and withheld their votes in protest. That left Johnson without the required two-thirds majority. Because Tennessee had not sent any delegates to the convention, the problem was solved when a random Tennessean by the name of Edmund Rucker was plucked off the street to deliver that state's fifteen votes to Johnson. Virginia's delegates "hissed most ungraciously," according to one report, and stormed out of the convention. It was an unpleasant preview of the bitter campaign to come.

Just as John Catron had predicted, Johnson's open relationship with Julia Chinn became the target of venomous Whig attacks. "It may be a matter of no importance to mere political automatons whether Richard M. Johnson is a *white* or a *black* man," wrote Duff Green in the *United States Telegraph*, "whether he is *free* or a *slave*—or whether he is married to, or has been in connection with a jet-black, thick-lipped, odoriferous negro wench, by whom he has reared a family of children whom he has endeavoured to force upon society as . . . equals. . . . But thank God, to the great majority of the people of the United States we may with safety address ourselves on this subject, with a full conviction that in their breast we shall find a response to . . . patriotic feelings."

Van Buren narrowly prevailed over the leading Whig candidate, William Henry Harrison, Johnson's commander at the Battle of the Thames. But, in an echo of the Democratic convention, Johnson fell short of the electoral votes needed to win the vice presidency. Virginia cast its votes for William Smith of Alabama, which caused the election to be thrown to the Senate, as dictated by the Twelfth Amendment. Richard Mentor Johnson thus became the only vice president ever elected by that body. It was a hollow victory, for his daughter Adeline had just died. Some believed it was from despair over the ugly campaign smears against her father. She was, he said, a "lovely and innocent child ! . . . a source of inexhaustible happiness and comfort to me. She was a firm and great prop to my happiness here—but she is gone where sorrow and sighing can never disturb her peaceful and quiet bosom."

Like so many vice presidents (that is, until Dick Cheney came along), Johnson found his largely ceremonial position frustrating. President Van Buren rarely, if ever, consulted with him, and though he did cast fourteen tie-breaking votes as the Senate's presiding officer, he was stifled by the constitutional limits placed upon the office. Quite simply, he was bored, and spent much of his time lounging around the Senate doing nothing. Journalist Henry B. Stanton described him as "shabbily dressed, and to the last degree clumsy." Indeed, the vice president was a rather eccentric presence around Washington. The English author Harriet Martineau sat across from him at a dinner party and observed that "if he should become President, he will be as strange-looking potentate as ever ruled. His countenance is wild, though with much cleverness in it; his hair wanders all abroad, and he wears no cravat. But there is no telling how he might look if he dressed like other people."

When he wasn't in the Senate, which was quite often, the vice president devoted much of his time to his various business ventures back home in Kentucky. These included the Choctaw Academy, which he established to "civilize" Native American boys, and a hotel and tavern he operated at White Sulphur Springs. Amos Kendall, a close associate of Andrew Jackson's, reported to President Van Buren that he found Johnson "happy in the glorious pursuit of tavern keeping—even giving his personal superintendence to the chicken and egg purchasing and water-melon selling department." Kendall also reported with some consternation details of the vice president's love life. Julia Chinn had died of cholera in 1833, and now Johnson was seeing "a young Delilah of about the complexion of Shakespeare's swarthy Othello." She was "said to be his third wife," Kendell continued; "his second, which he sold for her infidelity, having been the sister of the present *lady*."

By the time Martin Van Buren prepared to run for reelection in 1840, Democratic strategists had come to view Johnson as a major liability. They feared his unconventional personal life was too incendiary at a time when slavery was emerging as a national issue. Even the vice president's old friend Jackson urged Van Buren to drop him in favor of James K. Polk of Tennessee. "I like Col. Johnson but I like my country more," Old Hickory wrote, "and I allway go for my Country first, and then for my friend." Johnson did have some valuable assets, however. William Henry Harrison, the victor of Tippecanoe, was again the Whig candidate, and the Democrats needed their own military hero on the ticket to counter his appeal. In a rather spineless move, Van Buren decided to leave the selection of his running mate to the state party organizers, who ultimately settled on Johnson when Polk withdrew from consideration. The vice president campaigned hard, even touching off a riot in Cleveland when he attacked Harrison. Yet the Whigs prevailed, and Van Buren was swept from office.

Johnson was finished politically after the defeat, though he didn't know it at the time. He ran unsuccessfully for the Senate several times and waited expectantly for a call from his party to run for president. It never came. "He is not now even what he formerly was," noted one observer. "It may be there was never so much of him as many of us were led to suppose." Johnson did get elected to the Kentucky state legislature in 1850, but he was slipping mentally, and it proved to be a sad coda to his career. *The Louisville Daily Journal* reported that "it is painful to see him on the floor attempting to discharge the duties of a member." Soon after, on November 19, 1850, Richard Mentor Johnson died of a stroke.

He was remembered in a eulogy delivered by state senator Beriah Maggofin as "the poor man's friend. . . . Void of ostentation, simple in his taste, his manners, and his dress—brave, magnanimous, patriotic and generous to a fault, in his earliest years he was the beau ideal of the soul and chivalry of Kentucky." Then he was forgotten.

12

Zilpha Elaw:
An Unlikely Evangelist

The crowd gathered more out of curiosity than from any spiritual compulsion. For there, in the heart of the antebellum South, stood a black woman preaching the gospel. Though she had come from the North, where she was born and raised free, Zilpha Elaw knew she might be arrested at any moment and sold as a slave. Local law allowed that. Overcome by fear as the white fingers pointed at her, she retreated to a corner of the church. Yet as she sat nearly frozen, she remembered her calling. "My faith then rallied and my confidence in the Lord returned," Elaw later wrote, "and I said, 'Get behind me Satan, for my Jesus hath set me free.'" With that, she came forward again and resumed her sermon.

★

Zilpha Elaw was part of a forgotten minority of American women—both black and white—who, during the first decades of the nineteenth century, defied convention, as well as the scriptural admonition that their sex "keep silence in the churches," by preaching the gospel. Although they had entered a domain usually reserved for men, they were not quite protofeminists seeking to shake up the established order. Rather, they were women driven by evangelistic fervor during an era of Protestant revivalism known as the Second Great Awakening. The women were tolerated, even embraced for a time by newer sects such as the Methodists and Free Will Baptists, who needed them to minister to their ever-growing flocks. But as these denominations became more firmly established, the female preachers were gradually shunted aside, and in time were almost entirely written out of their churches' histories.

Some women like Zilpha Elaw, who actually preached without the sanction of any denomination, published testimonials of their spiritual rebirths and subsequent missions to spread the word of God. Most are out of print now, and the yellowed and brittle copies that survive (as well as the few that have been reprinted) are the only evidence that these women ever existed—let alone touched and transformed so many thousands of lives.

★

The call from God, as Elaw related it, wasn't subtle. She was an orphaned teenager living with a Quaker family in Pennsylvania when Christ himself silently appeared before her as she milked a cow. She swore on her own salvation that it happened that way, and, she wrote, "The peace of God which passeth understanding was communicated to my heart." Soon after that vision, in 1808, she joined the Methodists and "enjoyed a delightsome heavenly communion." Yet, she claimed, God had greater plans for her than a simple conversion. He wanted her to preach the gospel. For a poor black woman at the time, this call had almost overwhelming implications. Feeling unworthy, Zilpha resisted, despite what she said were obvious signs of the Divine will. It wasn't until she attended a frontier camp meeting—one of the great cultural phenomena of the era—that she finally gave in to God.

Millions of Americans (a third of the U.S. population, by some accounts) attended various camp meetings across the country each year. Part religious revival, part carnival, these mass assemblies held on the forested fringes of civilization lasted for days and drew all manner of people, from zealots to hucksters to those merely curious to see the sacred spectacle. The frontier observer Timothy Flint described the camp meetings he witnessed as "the most brilliant theatre in the world." Against a backdrop of lamp-lighted trees, preachers exhorted repentance while the faithful fell into fits of spiritual ecstasy.

As the time for a meeting approached, Flint wrote, "coaches, chaises, wagons, carts, people on horseback, and multitudes traveling on foot" hurried from every direction to the forested area that had been selected for the encampment. There tents were pitched "and the religious city [grew] up in a few hours under the trees, beside a stream" that offered an ample supply of fresh water for the enormous congregation.

Zilpha Elaw attended a number of these frontier camp meetings, where, she wrote, "the hardest hearts are melted into tenderness; the driest eyes overflow with tears, and the loftiest spirits bow down." At one meeting, compelled by the Spirit, she preached for the first time. "After I had finished my exhortation," she wrote, "I sat down and closed my eyes; and there appeared a light shining round me as well as within me, above the brightness of the sun." It was out of that light that she reported hearing a voice that said, "Now thou knowest the will of God concerning thee; thou must preach the gospel; and thou must travel far and wide." As if anticipating her readers' skepticism, Elaw added that the miraculous experience she described "did not occur in the night, when the dozing slumbers and imaginative dreams are prevalent, but at mid-day, between the hours of twelve and two o'clock."

Transformed and sanctified by what she believed was the hand of God, Elaw's status as a lowly black woman no longer mattered. What she called "the extraordinary directions of the

Holy Spirit" empowered her to begin her journey as an independent evangelist without the sanction of any established church and in defiance of all social convention. "Once she had been reborn," writes historian Catherine A. Brekus, "she was no longer an ordinary black woman, but a Christian who was superior to all the women—and men—who had not yet been saved."

Elaw's ministry took her all around the country and eventually to England, where she spent at least five years. And though she reported many obstacles along the way—including a husband who discouraged her, dismissive male ministers, and occasionally hostile crowds—she not only prevailed but often redeemed. This was particularly true in the South. After visiting Alexandria, Virginia, for example, she wrote: "I abode there two months, and was an humble agent, in the Lord's hand, of arousing many of His heritage to a great revival; and the weakness and incompetency of the poor coloured female but the more displayed the excellency of the power to be of God." So profound was Elaw's impact in the South, where the danger of arrest and enslavement loomed constantly, that she counted members of Robert E. Lee's family, as well as the secretary of the navy, Commodore John Rodgers, and his wife among her followers.

Although Zilpha Elaw sought to save souls, not necessarily to reform society, she did suffuse her narrative with running commentary on the racism and sexism that deeply permeated her era. She wrote of whites "who readily sacrifice their intelligence to their prejudices," and of "men whose whims are law" in the church. Her sardonic characterizations of certain male ministers' "august dignity" and "lordly authority" were not a call to overthrow the established order, however. "Woman is dependent on and subject to man," she wrote sternly. "Man is not created for the woman, but the woman for the man." These principles, she declared, "lie at the foundation of the family and social systems, and their violation is a very immoral and guilty act." Ultimately,

Elaw believed that all freedom flowed from God. Hers was "a gospel of human liberation," writes William L. Andrews in his introduction to her reprinted memoir, "addressed particularly to the spiritually enslaved."

The narrative ends abruptly in 1845, when Elaw was still in England. Whether or not she ever returned home, and what she did with the rest of her life, is lost to history—much like her ministry would have been had she not written it down.

13

Edwin Forrest: American Idol

He was America's first superstar, rising to fame in the century before cinema, when mass entertainment was found only on the stage and the greatest actors shared an unparalleled intimacy with their audiences. Theatergoers marveled at Edwin Forrest's muscular performances and the uniquely American way in which he inhabited the most complex characters, from Othello to Lear, in an arena where English actors had been thought to be naturally superior. But the passionate response to Forrest coincided with an ugly nativist trend in the United States, and it all culminated with a bloody theater riot in 1849 that left thirty-one people dead.

From the moment he first stepped on stage in a small role at the age of eleven, Forrest's course was set. He traveled the country as a teenager, taking any part he could get while living in near poverty. Along the way he befriended unforgettable characters, including the great frontiersman and knife duelist, James Bowie, who inspired him with the spirit of the young nation. And as he honed his craft in insignificant plays and divertissements, the young man's ambition became steadily focused. "He must become a serious tragedian," writes Richard Moody, Forrest's biographer, "an actor whose physical power would reflect the sublime sweep of his native land, whose spirit would be imbued with the fresh, free air of the young democracy. The American stage had been overrun with effete copyists of the British. It was time a home-grown, able-bodied, high-spirited American actor took over."

Forrest did indeed take over. Though he was not particularly tall, his well-developed frame, thunderous voice, and vigorous stage movements left audiences awed by his presence. "What a mountain of a man!" exclaimed the English actress and abolition-ist Fanny Kemble. The actor's physical gifts were matched by the fresh spirit he infused into the characters he played. He made classic roles his own and, as he became more successful, commis-sioned American playwrights to create new, heroic ones for him to inhabit. Each was approached in a precise, exacting way. "He heightened here and mellowed there," one writer noted, "rounded this and smoothed that, long after the average actor would have ceased to see that there was room for betterment."

Authenticity was Forrest's constant quest, and he took ex-traordinary measures to achieve it. To capture the essence of King Lear's madness, for example, he visited numerous insane asylums and was inspired by the carefully observed delusions of Senator Henry Clay's son Theodore, who believed he was George Washington, as well as the dignified insanity of Benja-min Rush's son John—the very personification of the tragic king, Forrest later said. Theater critic Alfred Ayers wrote in 1901 that "Forrest, probably, made the greatest part that ever has been written—the part of King Lear—more effective; got more out of it, than any other actor ever has gotten out of it, which rightly gives him the first place among the players of all time." Forrest unabashedly agreed.

Not all critics were quite so laudatory; some thought him a

bit bombastic and overwrought at times.[1] But the masses adored their homegrown hero, and they were the ones who brought in the box office receipts that made him a very wealthy star. "No other actor could churn up their emotions as Forrest did with his stormy renderings of Shakespeare's tragic heroes or with his passionately patriotic impersonations of any one of a half-dozen freedom-loving zealots struggling against tyrannical oppression," writes Richard Moody. "He was the first actor who refused to subscribe to the nation's cultural inferiority complex." In so doing, Forrest brought prestige to the American stage and made the people proud. His native appeal, however, would have tragic consequences.

A haughty English actor named William Macready watched Forrest's rapid rise to fame with increasing bitterness. He considered himself the master thespian and was dismayed that someone with Forrest's obvious limitations could achieve such widespread acclaim—especially as his own star was slowly dimming. Macready blamed boorish American audiences. "In this country, the masses, rich and poor, are essentially ignorant or vulgar," he wrote, "utterly deficient in taste and without the modesty to distrust themselves." Macready managed to conceal his jealous contempt for Forrest and the two actors remained cordial for years. Ill will eventually burst forth, however, and the very public feud that resulted set the stage for what became known as "the Astor Place Riot."

It all started with a hiss. Forrest, who was convinced that Macready had tried to sabotage his appearances on the London stage in 1845, was in the audience the following year, when Macready played Hamlet in Edinburgh. Evidently he didn't approve of a mannered dance Macready introduced into the performance

---

1. In one review from 1847, the New York *Courier and Enquirer* found "his whole style rough, unrefined, heavy, and laborious. His gentlemen are not such as Shakespeare drew; they are great roaring boys that cry like fat babies, and puff and blow like sledge men."

and made his feelings known with the unmistakable sound of displeasure. Macready was appalled. "I do not think that such an action has its parallel in all theatrical history!" he stormed melo-dramatically in his diary. "The low-minded ruffian! He would commit a murder, if he dare." For his own part, Forrest freely acknowledged the hiss. "The truth is," he wrote in a letter to the London *Times,* "Mr. Macready thought fit to introduce a fancy dance into his performance of 'Hamlet,' which I thought, and still think, a desecration of the scene, and at which I evinced that disapprobation." And so the great clash of egos commenced.

Had Macready been content to stay in England and stew in his grievances, the Astor Place Riot would have been averted. But his career was declining in his native country, and in the fall of 1848 he arrived in America to revive his fortunes. It was a fateful move. Though Macready had enjoyed successful tours of the United States in the past, Forrest was now at the peak of his popularity and clearly had public sentiment on his side. He was the rugged giant of the American stage who had put the spindly, aristocratic Englishman in his place. The public feasted on the actors' spat as newspapers gleefully reported every ex-changed barb. And when it was announced that each would be performing the role of Macbeth on different stages, the people were ready. "During the last thirty-six hours the excitement among the theatre-going people has been rising to fever heat in this atmosphere," the *New York Herald* reported on May 7, 1849. "Forrest plays at the Broadway, Macready at the Astor Place. . . . The excitement began in the green room, and has been generating for some time, in consequence of the public attitude of the two great tragedians of the age towards each other, and their appearance in this city at the same time, in the same characters, at different theatres."

Macready got a sobering preview of the mayhem to come

during his opening performance that night at the Astor Place
Theater (or Opera House, as it was also called). He was greeted
with a cacophony of groans and hisses when the curtain rose—
"an alarming outbreak that defies description," according to one
account of the evening. That rousing welcome was followed by
a barrage of "eggs of doubtful purity, potatoes, a bottle of pun-
gent and nauseating asafoetida, old shoes, and a copper coin."
Macready picked up the coin, the report continued, "placed it
in his bosom with dignity," and with "mock humiliation bowed
to the quarter of the galley from which the visitation had descended." He gamely continued through the first two acts of
the tragedy, though not a word from the stage could be heard
over the din as he dodged rotten vegetables and other unsavory missiles. But by the third act, when Macbeth came out as
the new king, the crowd went crazy and began hurling chairs
onto the stage. It was clearly too dangerous to continue, and the
curtain fell. "Three groans for the English bulldog!" members
of the audience chanted triumphantly. "Nine cheers for Edwin
Forrest!"

Macready was sufficiently frightened by his reception to immediately book passage back to England. But a reassuring letter
from prominent citizens like Washington Irving and Herman
Melville, as well as editorials condemning the night's events,
convinced him to stay and perform again at the Astor Place on
May 10. "The English actor was certain that the 'best citizens'
and all the forces of law and order were exercising themselves
in his behalf," writes Richard Moody, "and that to play out his
engagement would establish once and for all his superiority to
the American scoundrel [Forrest] and all his ill-bred supporters."
If he only knew.

A loose confederation of rabble-rousers from various gangs
and nativist organizations like the Order of United Americans

(forerunner of the anti-Catholic, anti-immigrant Know-Nothing Party) papered the city with calls to rally at the "English Aristo-cratic Opera House" on the night of May 10 and to stand up for Forrest and America. In anticipation of a disturbance, the windows of the theater were barricaded, and New York mayor Caleb Woodhull ordered a large contingent of police to be pres-ent at the scene. The military was also put on alert. No one thought to cancel the show, however, and thus all the elements of the unfolding tragedy were in place.

Macready seemed blithely unaware of any impending trou-ble. "I went gaily, I may say, to the theatre," he reported in his diary, "and on my way, looking down Astor Place, saw one of the Harlem cars on the railroad stop, discharge a full load of policemen; there seemed to be others at the doors of the theatre. I observed to myself: 'This is good precaution.' I went to my dressing room, and proceeded with the evening's business."

While Macready primped backstage, an enormous crowd be-gan to gather outside the theater. All day there had been a scramble for tickets and as curtain time approached for the sold-out perfor-mance, people began to rush for the doors. Policemen struggled against the surge and blocked the entrances before the theater was completely filled, leaving some ticket holders outside with the growing mob. Inside, the curtain rose and the first two scenes were played without incident. But the theater loudly erupted when Macready first appeared in the third. All action stopped on stage for fifteen minutes, and even as the play resumed, not a word could be heard through the continuous storm of groans and shouts of abuse. The police stationed in virtually every corner of the the-ater made no move against the demonstrators until the final scene of the third act, when they arrested a particularly rowdy group and ushered them away. It made little difference. Others in the audi-ence continued the disruption, while the mob outside, almost as if on cue, launched an assault on the building. The barricades put in place earlier proved useless against the onslaught.

"As one window after another cracked," the *New York Tribune* reported, "the pieces of bricks and paving-stones rattled in on terraces and lobbies, the confusion increased, till the Opera House resembled a fortress besieged by an invading army rather than a place meant for the peaceful amusement of a civilized community." Through it all, the report continued, "the obnoxious actor went through his part with perfect self-possession, and paid no regard to the tumultuous scene before him." Indeed, Macready was quite taken with his own performance. "The fifth act was heard," he pompously recorded in his diary, "and in the very spirit of resistance I flung my whole soul into every word I uttered, acting my very best, and exciting the audience to a sympathy even with the glowing words of fiction, while these dreadful deeds of real crime and outrage were roaring at intervals in our ears, and rising to madness all around us."

Police surrounding the theater were quickly overwhelmed, and many fell injured under the barrage of bricks and stones hurled by the increasingly ferocious crowd. "About 8 o'clock I reported to the Chief that I thought it would be impossible to retain our position much longer, as the lines had been broken," Benjamin Fairchild, captain of the Eighth Ward police, later reported. "I was directed to rally the men and make another effort. There was a space cleared in front of the theatre, the people having left to avoid the stones. After this I went again on the 8th street side, and found one or two hundred young men and boys stoning the building. I attempted to make an arrest of one and was beaten back by the mob and had to run for my life."

As the assault mounted in intensity, it was apparent that military reinforcement would be necessary, and the troops were called in. The mob was unmoved by this display of strength, however. Like the police, the soldiers were mercilessly stoned. According to General Charles Sandford, "Every man was more or less hurt and the horses were rendered almost unmanageable. A dense mob extended as far as I could see to the Third Avenue. The mounted men, being conspicuous marks, received most of the stones, and were finally driven off the ground. I dismounted, returned through the mob, and took charge of the infantry, who were halted in line across the open space beyond the theatre, with a dense mob on both sides, who were assailing them with all sorts of opprobrious epithets and frequent volleys of stones."

A volley of warning shots was fired, at which the crowd scoffed. "They've got leather flints and blank cartridges," some shouted, while others, according to one account, "commenced wresting the muskets from the soldiers' hands" and "pelting stones as large as your double fist like a shower of hail." Another series of shots had more fatal consequences and the desired effect. As people lay dead and dying, many of them innocent bystanders, the mob began to disperse. In the end, at least thirty people were killed, and many more suffered debilitating injuries. Macready, meanwhile, had concluded his performance; soon after the first shots were fired, he snuck out of the theater in disguise and found refuge in the home of Robert Emmet, nephew of the famous Irish patriot. He left New York the next day.

While the riot raged at the Astor Place, Edwin Forrest was at the Broadway performing before a wildly cheering crowd one of his signature roles: the heroic, defiant Spartacus in Robert Bird's *The Gladiator*. (Forrest's and Macready's simultaneous renditions of Macbeth had already taken place several nights before.) Although some editorials blamed Forrest in part for encouraging the mayhem at the Astor Place, his career was hardly compromised and he remained so much an American icon that a *Harper's* columnist was shocked to meet a man in 1862 who had never seen Forrest. "If he had said he had never seen Trinity Church, or the Astor House, it would have been strange; but to aver that he had never seen Forrest was to tax credibility."

How surprised, then, would that writer have been had he known that one day Edwin Forrest, and the riot he inspired, would be a mere footnote. To Forrest, though, it was entirely expected. "The actor's popularity is evanescent," he once said; "applauded today, forgotten tomorrow."

14

Rose O'Neale Greenhow:
A Spy of Grande
Dame Proportions

Allan Pinkerton found himself in an awkward position outside the home of Rose O'Neale Greenhow, one of the most prominent hostesses in Washington, D.C. The head of the famed detective agency—imported from Chicago by the Union to track and capture rebel subversives operating around the capital—stood barefoot in the pouring rain, balancing himself on the shoulders of two associates, trying to see and hear what he could through a second-story parlor window.

American counterespionage was in its infancy in 1861, but Pinkerton's quarry was no beginner. From her home on Sixteenth Street, which was noted by Confederate General P. G. T. Beauregard as being "within easy rifle-range" of the White House, Greenhow was running a spy ring meant to undermine the Union war effort. "To this end," she later wrote, "I employed every capacity with which God had endowed me, and the result was far more successful than my hopes could have flattered me to expect."

While she may have overestimated her achievements, her efforts on behalf of the South were relentless. "She did a better job than most in infiltrating the political and military elite of Washington," Tyler Anbinder, associate professor of history at George Washington University, said in 1999. "She flattered men into revealing sensitive information."

The nation's capital has been home to plenty of covert operatives, as well as highly connected grandes dames. But Greenhow, "the Rebel Rose," managed to unite the two professions within herself; in the process she added a unique chapter to the city's long history of deeply held Southern sympathies. As a young girl, she was sent from Rockville, Maryland, to live at the Old Capitol with an aunt who ran an inn there. This building, on the site now occupied by the U.S. Supreme Court, was constructed as a temporary home for Congress after the original Capitol was burned during the War of 1812. Years later, after the Old Capitol was converted to a prison during the Civil War, Greenhow would reside there again—this time as one of the Union's more celebrated captives.

With her charm, intellect, and ambition, as well as through her husband, Robert, a State Department official whom she married in 1835, Rose Greenhow came to know virtually everyone of importance in Washington. Dolley Madison, Daniel Webster, and President James Buchanan were among her many friends and intimates. No one was closer to her, however, than John C. Calhoun, the powerful statesman from South Carolina who served as senator, secretary of state, and vice president. As one of the great intellectual progenitors of the Southern Confederacy, he won Greenhow's eternal admiration and devotion. "I am a Southern woman," she wrote, "born with revolutionary blood in my veins, and my first crude ideas on State and Federal matters received consistency and shape from the best and wisest man of this century." As her idol suffered through his final illness at the Old Capitol in 1850, Greenhow was in constant attendance. Calhoun's memory remained sacred to her, and fueled her increasingly fanatic devotion to the Southern cause as the Civil War approached.

An uncomfortable chill swept through one of her dinner parties in the winter of 1859 when Abigail Adams, wife of presidential scion Charles Francis Adams, professed sympathy and admiration for the radical abolitionist John Brown, who recently had been hanged. With sectional feeling festering just below the surface, polite society in Washington assiduously avoided the topic of John Brown as simply too hot for discussion. Greenhow, however, had no hesitation in challenging Adams. "I have no sympathy for John Brown," she snapped. "He was a traitor, and met a traitor's doom." While Greenhow later professed to have regretted this breach of gracious hostessing, she would never temper or compromise her fierce Southern loyalties.

It was this fervor, along with her many intimate connections in the capital, that made the forty-four-year-old and widowed Greenhow a prime rebel recruit in April 1861, when the Civil War finally broke out. She proved her worth as a spy in a very short time, supplying to General Beauregard the information that Federal troops would be advancing on Manassas, Virginia, in mid-July. Her courier, a young woman named Betty Duvall, rode out of Washington dressed as a country girl. Meeting General Milledge L. Bonham at the courthouse in Fairfax County, Virginia, Duvall advised him that she had an urgent message for General Beauregard. "Upon my announcing that I would have it faithfully forwarded at once," Bonham later recalled, "she took out her tucking comb and let fall the longest and most beautiful roll of hair I have ever seen. She took then from the back of her head, where it had been safely tied, a small package, not larger than a silver dollar, sewed up in silk." As author Ishbel Ross noted in her book *Rebel Rose,* "Greenhow had ciphered the message. Greenhow had sewn it in silk. Greenhow had obtained the information."

Though historians debate the ultimate impact of her messages on the First Battle of Bull Run, both Beauregard and Confederate president Jefferson Davis honored her for her contribution to the rout of the Northern army in this opening conflict of the Civil War. "Had she not leaked word [of the Northern advance], I don't think anything would have happened differently," said Anbinder. Beauregard had a number of sources of information, he said, "but it served to embarrass the North that a woman could obtain such sensitive information." Indeed, Greenhow's covert activities did attract unfavorable attention in Washington, and soon enough Allan Pinkerton was peeping into her windows. "She has made use of whoever and whatever she could as mediums to carry out her unholy purposes," the detective reported. "She has not used her powers in vain among the officers of the Army, not a few of whom she has robbed of patriotic hearts and transformed them into sympathizers with the enemies of the country which made them all they were. . . . With her as with other traitors she has been most unscrupulous in the use of means. Nothing has been too sacred for her appropriation so as by its use she might hope to accomplish her treasonable ends."

Despite the fact that she was being watched, and was well aware of it, Greenhow continued to operate with bold defiance. She soon found herself under arrest. "I have no power to resist you," she declared grandly after challenging Pinkerton's authority to seize her, "but had I been inside of my house, I would have killed one of you before I had submitted to this illegal process." The dramatic flair she demonstrated when captured would characterize much of her time in captivity.

Under house arrest, she grew indignant that her home was being ransacked in the search for incriminating evidence and that she was subject to constant surveillance. "She wants us to know how her delicacy was shocked and outraged," Civil War diarist Mary Chestnut recorded. "That could be done only by most plainspoken revelations. For eight days she was kept in full sight of men—her rooms wide open—and sleepless sentinels watching by day and by night. Soldiers tramping—looking in at her leisurely by way of amusement. . . . She says she was worse used than Marie Antoinette when they snatched a letter from the poor queen's bosom."

Other female prisoners were sent to Fort Greenhow, as Rose's home came to be known—most of them "of the lowest class," as she called them. During her home confinement, Greenhow managed to continue her secret communications with the South. A letter she had sent to Secretary of State William H. Seward complaining of her mistreatment, in fact, was published in a Richmond newspaper. Because of all the leaks, Fort Greenhow was closed in early 1862, and Rose was transferred to the Old Capitol Prison, along with her eight-year-old daughter, Little Rose. Ironically, they were confined in the very same room in which Greenhow had comforted her dying hero, Senator Calhoun, more than a decade earlier.

Unpleasant as it was, Rose's imprisonment was ultimately her greatest service to the South—far more useful than the information she secretly provided. "They made her a martyr in the eyes of the Southern people," said historian James McPherson. "The brutal Yankees who would imprison a mother and child provided ammunition for the Confederate propaganda mills." In the squalid (yet hardly brutal) confines of the Old Capitol, Greenhow played the role of martyr for all it was worth. Mary Chestnut commented sardonically on this in her diary, while a fellow prisoner named Augusta Morris wrote, "Greenhow enjoys herself amazingly."

"This is the gloomiest period of my life," Rose wrote. "Time dragged most heavily. I had absolutely nothing to occupy myself with. I had no books, and often no paper to write on, and those who approached me appeared entirely oblivious of the mental as well as physical wants of a prisoner. . . . [I was] chafing against my prison bars, with the iron of the despot eating into my soul."

In March 1862, Rose was brought up on charges of espionage. The prisoner was defiant throughout the hearing. "If I gave the information you say I have," she taunted, "I must have got it from sources that were in the confidence of the government. . . . If Mr. Lincoln's friends will pour into my ear such important information, am I to be held responsible for all that?" With little accomplished at the hearing, and a formal trial thought to be too incendiary, the judge decided it would be best to exile the prisoner from Washington. He sent her south with the pledge not to return during the course of the war. She left the Old Capitol Prison draped in a Confederate flag, and when she arrived in Richmond, she was greeted as a hero by the local elite. "Had Madame Greenhow been sent South immediately after her arrest," opined *The New York Times*, "we should have heard no more of the deeds of Secesh women which she has made the fashion."

After a brief stay in Richmond, Greenhow was sent to Europe by Jefferson Davis to generate vitally needed support for the Confederacy. "It was highly unusual, perhaps unprecedented, for a president to send a woman to represent her country in a foreign land, even in an unofficial capacity," writes Rose's biographer Ann Blackman. Napoléon III and Queen Victoria both received her, and, according to Blackman, she "buttonholed anyone who would listen to her arguments for recognition and her defense of slavery." Her book, *My Imprisonment and the First Year of Abolition Rule at Washington,* was published in Britain, where it became a bestseller.

Tragedy struck, however, as Greenhow returned home in 1864. Her ship ran aground along the North Carolina coast, and Rose, fearing capture by Union ships blockading the area, demanded that she be taken ashore in a smaller boat. The ship's captain reluctantly agreed to let her go, despite a raging storm, and she carried with her several small mailbags, presumed to be secret dispatches from Europe, as well as a large quantity of gold. But the little boat capsized in the darkness and rough surf, and Rose Greenhow was lost. Her body subsequently washed ashore and was found by a Confederate soldier, who discovered the gold and snatched it before pushing the body back into the water. When the corpse was rediscovered and identified, the soldier was reportedly overwhelmed by guilt and returned the gold.

Rose O'Neale Greenhow was buried with full Confederate military honors in Wilmington, North Carolina. The inscription on her tomb reads in part: "A bearer of dispatches to the Confederate Government."

"Her death," wrote Ishbel Ross, "had the epic touch in which she herself would have gloried."

15

Clement L. Vallandigham: Copperhead

Several hours past midnight on May 4, 1863, a contingent of soldiers from the 115th Ohio made their way along the darkened streets of Dayton to the home of Clement L. Vallandigham, two-term U.S. congressman and relentless critic of President Abraham Lincoln. Three days earlier, Vallandigham had appeared at a Democratic rally in Mount Vernon, Ohio, where, before a wildly cheering crowd, he denounced the tyrannical rule of "King Lincoln" and his aggressive war policies that were designed, he claimed, to liberate the black man and enslave whites. By delivering the fiery speech, the former congressman deliberately defied an order recently issued by General Ambrose Burnside, which stated in part that "the habit of declaring sympathies for the enemy will no longer be tolerated in this department [Ohio]." Now Burnside's men were about to deliver the general's response to Vallandigham's remarks.

Upon reaching the residence at 323 First Street, the soldiers quickly cordoned off the property. Captain Charles G. Hutton then rang the doorbell. Vallandigham appeared at an upstairs bedroom window in his nightshirt and demanded to know what the soldiers wanted. Hutton informed him that he was to be arrested under orders from General Burnside and suggested that he surrender peacefully. "If Burnside wants me," Vallandigham shouted scornfully, "let him come up here and take me."

Several more requests to come downstairs were ignored. Instead, Vallandigham shouted for the police and insisted he wasn't properly dressed. Hutton assured him that he would be given time to make himself presentable, but still Vallandigham resisted. Finally the captain ordered his men to force open the front door. As they attacked it with bars and axes, Vallandigham fired three pistol shots out of his window in a final attempt to alert the police or sympathetic neighbors. It was in vain. Hutton and his men succeeded in entering the home through the back door and felt their way in the darkness to the second floor, where Vallandigham had barricaded himself behind two bedroom doors. After smashing through both, the soldiers found the former congressman standing in the middle of the room, his wife and sister-in-law both cowering behind him and shrieking in terror.

"You have now broken open my house and overpowered me," Vallandigham said sarcastically, "and I am obliged to surrender." With that he was led away to face trial and a most unusual sentence, decreed by Lincoln himself: banishment to the Confederate States of America.

★

Vallandigham's arrest came at a time when Lincoln faced fierce resistance from many Democrats in the North, the most rabid of whom were known derisively as "Copperheads." They vigorously opposed the president's prosecution of the war, his emancipation policies, and the powers he took upon himself to suppress rebellion, such as the suspension of the writ of habeas corpus. Lincoln despaired of these malcontent Copperheads, who, he believed, undermined the Union and in some cases actively conspired against it. "The enemy behind us," he said in frustration during the grim winter of 1862–63, "is more dangerous to the country than the enemy before us."

Of all the president's foes within the Union, Vallandigham was among the most prominent. His sharp attacks against Lincoln and the war began while he still served in the U.S. House of Representatives. "The Richmond Government could not have planted a readier spokesman than it had in Congress at Washington in Clement L. Vallandigham," wrote Lincoln's biographer Carl Sandburg. The new president had barely taken the oath of office before Vallandigham pounced on his inauguration speech. "It was not written in the straightforward language expected from the plain, blunt honest man of the Northwest," he declared, "but with the forked tongue and crooked counsel of the New York politician [William H. Seward], leaving thirty millions of people in doubt whether it meant peace or war."

Civil conflict was an anathema to the congressman, even in the face of secession. The Union could never be preserved by bloody coercion, he stated repeatedly, and insisted that he would never "vote one dollar of money whereby one drop of American blood should be shed in a civil war." In a blundering effort to avoid war and preserve the Union, Vallandigham proposed to amend the Constitution by dividing the nation into four sections, giving each area a veto on the passage of any law or the elections of presidents or vice presidents, and allowing each state the right of secession on certain specified terms. It was a supremely unworkable solution, worthy of a man who, according to his biographer, Frank L. Klement, "possessed a self-confidence bordering on audacity." With his silly idea shelved and the nation violently divided, Vallandigham's only recourse was to prick the government at every opportunity.

On January 14, 1863, after nearly two years of civil conflict and shortly before he left office in defeat, Vallandigham took to the floor of the House and delivered his most impassioned speech yet against the war and the president who waged it. "Tall, bearded, sonerous, he was," Sandburg wrote, "his self-righteousness gave him personal exaltation; he was chosen to be the vocal instrument of absolute justice." For nearly two hours the Chosen One spoke, declaring that Lincoln's effort to restore the Union by force was an "utter, disastrous, and most bloody failure," and insisting that immediate peace, with the aim of eventual reunion, was the only solution.

"On the 14th of April [1861] I believed that coercion would bring on war, and war disunion," he told the assembled congressmen and other observers. "More than that, I believed, what you all in your hearts believe today, that the South could never be conquered—never. And not that only, but I was satisfied . . . that the secret but real purpose of the war was to abolish slavery in the States . . . and with it . . . the change of our present democratical form of government into an imperial despotism. . . . I do not support the war; and today I bless God that not the smell of so much as one drop of blood is upon my garments. . . . Our Southern brethren were to be whipped back into love and fellowship at the point of the bayonet. Oh, monstrous delusion!"

Reaction to Vallandigham's speech was ferocious, both in Congress and in many Republican newspapers. "The people of the Northwest spurn him," wrote Isaac Jackson Allen of the *Ohio State Journal,* "and spit upon his detestable dogma." But there were some, particularly in Vallandigham's home state of Ohio, who celebrated what he had to say. "It is a speech," wrote James J. Faran in the Cincinnati *Enquirer,* "which would add to the fame of a Clay, or a Webster, or a Burke, or a Chatham."

The enthusiastic response to Vallandigham in the Midwest reflected the discontent many of its Democrats felt about the war, which had taken an enormous human and economic toll on the region, and especially about the Emancipation Proclamation that they feared would result in a disastrous influx of freed slaves. "Ohio," one Copperhead wrote, "will be overrun with negroes, they will compete with you and bring down your wages, *you* will have to work with them, eat with them, your *wives* and *children* must associate with theirs and your families will be degraded to their level." The anti-administration sentiment ran so strong in the region that John A. McClernand, a leading Illinois Democrat, warned Lincoln in 1863 of "the rising storm in the Middle and Northwestern States," and predicted "not only a separation from the New England States but reunion of the Middle and Northwestern States with the revolted [Southern] States."

The president was inclined to believe such threats and moved to suppress dissent he considered dangerous. It was in this unsettled atmosphere that General Burnside, commander of the Department of the Ohio, issued General Order No. 38—an ill-conceived measure made by a man still smarting from his crushing defeat at the Battle of Fredericksburg and suffering from a scorching case of diarrhea. The order prohibited not only acts that benefited the enemy, which was reasonable enough, but also stated that treason, "express or implied," would not be tolerated. This was a far-reaching clause that, Lincoln biographers John Nicolay and John Hay wrote, "may be made to embrace, in its ample sweep, any demonstration not to the taste of the general in command." The order, with its disturbing constitutional implications, caused an immediate uproar—even among loyal Republicans. One of Burnside's own staff officers warned President Lincoln that the general's order had "kindled the fires of hatred and contention." Clement Vallandigham was determined to defy it.

On May 1, 1863, he delivered the speech that doomed him to exile. Along with his usual rhetorical lashes against Lincoln, the war, and abolition, Vallandigham declared that Burnside's

General Order No. 38 was a base usurpation of arbitrary power that he despised, spat upon, and trampled under his feet. Standing among the crowd roaring its approval, two of Burnside's men, dressed as civilians, took careful notes on the address. Three days later Vallandigham was arrested at his home in Dayton and taken by train to a military prison in Cincinnati. From his cell he issued a widely published statement to the Democrats of Ohio:

> *I am here in a military bastile for no other offense than my political opinions, and the defense of them, and the rights of the people, and of your constitutional liberties. Speeches made in the hearing of thousands of you, in denunciation of the usurpation of power, infractions of the Constitution and the laws, and of military despotism, were the causes of my arrest and imprisonment. I am a Democrat—for the Constitution, for law, for Union, for liberty—this is my only crime.*

While Vallandigham wrote from Cincinnati, riots broke out in Dayton. The offices of the *Dayton Journal,* a Republican newspaper, were torched; in the resulting inferno a number of other businesses were also destroyed. And the outrage wasn't limited to Ohio. Editorials across the nation condemned the arrest. The *New York Atlas,* a Democratic paper, asserted that "the tyranny of military despotism" exhibited in Burnside's actions demonstrated "the weakness, folly, oppression, mismanagement and general wickedness of the administration at Washington." A huge protest rally was held in New York, during which one speaker warned that if Vallandigham's arrest wasn't rebuked, "free speech dies, and with it our liberty, the Constitution and our country." Another pointedly noted that Vallandigham hadn't spoken out against the war nearly as vociferously as Lincoln had against the Mexican-American War when he was a congressman.

Several days after his arrest, Vallandigham was brought before a military commission that he insisted had no right to try him. He was not part of the land or naval forces of the United States, he said, nor in the militia; therefore he was subject only to the civil courts. Furthermore, he asserted that the alleged offense itself was not known to the Constitution, or to any law. "The Vallandigham case did indeed raise troubling constitutional questions," writes historian James M. McPherson. "Could a speech be treason? Could a military court try a civilian? Did a general, or for that matter a president, have the power to impose martial law or suspend habeas corpus in an arena distant from military operations where the civil courts were functioning? These questions went to the heart of the administration's policy for dealing with fire in the rear."

The military tribunal was seemingly untroubled by these constitutional concerns. Vallandigham was convicted and sentenced to close confinement in a fortress of Burnside's choosing. His lawyers immediately applied to the U.S. Circuit Court for a writ of habeas corpus, which was denied. Burnside himself had sent a written statement to the court in which he argued against the writ and defended the actions he had taken against Vallandigham: "If I were to find a man from the enemy's country distributing in my camp speeches of their public men that tended to demoralize the troops, or to destroy their confidence in the constituted authorities of the Government, I would have him tried and hung, if found guilty, and all the rules of modern warfare would sustain me. Why should such speeches from our own public men be allowed?"

The quick succession of Vallandigham's arrest, trial, and sentence took President Lincoln "somewhat by surprise," according to his biographers Nicolay and Hay, "and it was only after these proceedings were consummated that he had an opportunity to seriously consider the case." The historians concluded that the president would probably not have allowed the events to go forward had he been consulted in advance. As it stood, though, Lincoln was determined to support Burnside; to do less, he believed, would only encourage the subversive elements in the Northwest. The president declined the general's offer to resign in the midst of the uproar surrounding the case. "When I shall wish to supersede you I will let you know," he wrote to Burnside. "All the Cabinet regretted the necessity of arresting . . . Vallandigham, some doubting there was a real necessity for it; but, being done, all were for seeing you through with it."

Though Lincoln upheld Burnside, he went against the general's advice and commuted Vallandigham's sentence from imprisonment to banishment behind enemy lines. This, he believed, would remove an irksome martyr around whom the Copperheads could rally. Thus, under order of the president, Vallandigham was escorted to the headquarters of General William S. Rosencrans in Murfreesboro, Tennessee, and from there into the hands of the Confederates.

"Why, sir, do you know that unless I protect you with a guard my soldiers will tear you to pieces in an instant?" Rosencrans reportedly said to Vallandigham.

"That, sir, is because they are just as ignorant of my character as yourself," the prisoner responded, his considerable self-regard still very much intact. "But, General, I do have a proposition to make. Draw your soldiers up in a hollow square tomorrow morning, and announce to them that Vallandigham desires to vindicate himself, and I will guarantee that when they have heard me through they will be more willing to tear Lincoln and yourself to pieces than they will Vallandigham."

The exile received a mixed reception in the South. Many welcomed him for what he represented. "The Government in Richmond saw it as a promise of counter-revolution in the North," wrote Nicolay and Hay, "and some of the Confederate generals built upon it the rosiest hopes for future campaigns." But because Vallandigham maintained his allegiance to the United States and his desire for reunion, some viewed him as an enemy of Southern independence who had no place in their midst. "Unless he intends to renounce his allegiance to our enemies," wrote one editor of the Richmond *Sentinel,* "he owes it to himself and us not to stay here."

As it turned out, Vallandigham had no intention of staying. When Confederate president Jefferson Davis requested a formal statement of his "guest's" intent and status, Vallandigham replied that he was in the South under compulsion and wished to leave. "My most earnest desire is for a passport, if necessary, and permission to leave as soon as possible through some Confederate port . . . for Canada, where I can see my family, and as far as possible, transact my business unmolested." His wish was granted; after just twenty-four days in the Confederacy, he was on a ship that managed to avoid a Union blockade and take him to Bermuda. From there he sailed to Canada.

While Vallandigham was maneuvering his way out of the South, in the North Lincoln continued to face hostile Democrats and even some loyal Republicans. It was an era when presidents, by tradition, did not directly court public opinion, but, writes historian David Herbert Donald, "by mid-summer of 1863, it was desperately important that the administration's policies should be understood. On no issue was this need so great as on the abrogation of civil liberties." The president had been waiting for an appropriate time to address his critics, and found it when a group of New York Democrats sent him a series of stinging resolutions they had adopted in Albany that strongly condemned the treatment of Vallandigham. It was, they declared, a "blow . . . against the spirit of our law and Constitution" and an assault on "the liberty of speech and of the press, the right of trial by jury, the law of evidence, and the privilege of habeas corpus."

Lincoln's response, which he considered the best state paper he had written up to that time, was sent on June 12, 1863, with a copy delivered to the influential *New York Tribune* so that the nation at large could read what he had to say. The president began on a cordial note, thanking the Albany protesters for their "eminently patriotic" resolve "to maintain our common government and country, despite the folly and wickedness, as they may conceive, of any administration." He then went on to explain that the suspension of certain liberties guaranteed in the Constitution during times of peace was vitally necessary in this time of peril, when those who wished to destroy the Union would use those very liberties "to keep on foot amongst us a most efficient corps of spies, informers, suppliers, and aiders and abettors of their cause in a thousand different ways."

Furthermore, he argued, the Constitution itself provided for the suspension of habeas corpus "in cases of Rebellion or Invasion, [when] the public Safety may require it." This, he wrote, "is precisely our present case." Lincoln rejected the argument that the measures taken in this time of war might continue after peace was restored, suggesting that it would be akin to saying "that a man could contract so strong an appetite for emetics during temporary illness, as to persist in feeding upon them through the remainder of his healthful life."

As for the specific charges the Albany protesters made in regard to Vallandigham, the president emphasized that he was not arrested for criticizing the administration, "but because he was damaging the army, upon the existence and vigor of which the nation depends." Lincoln reminded the petitioners that he had the right and the duty to sustain the armies by punishing deserters, and then poignantly asked them, "Must I shoot a simpleminded soldier boy who deserts, while I must not touch a hair of the wily agitator who induces him to desert?" Having presented his defense of the actions taken against Vallandigham, the president made a rather remarkable concession to fallibility:

> And yet let me say that in my own discretion I do not know whether I would have ordered the arrest of Mr. Vallandigham. While I cannot shift the responsibility from myself, I hold that, as a general rule, the commander in the field is the better judge of the necessity in any particular case. . . . It gave me pain when I learned that Mr. Vallandigham had been arrested—that is, I was pained that there should have seemed to be a necessity for arresting him—and it will afford me great pleasure to discharge him so soon as I can, by any means, believe the public safety will not suffer by it.

Lincoln's letter, reprinted and read by an estimated ten million Americans, received an enthusiastic response in many circles. "The right word has at last been spoken by the right man, at the right time, and from the right place," wrote John W. Forney of the *Washington Chronicle*. "It will thrill the whole land." But many Democrats, including the Albany protesters, were decidedly unimpressed, and their attacks on the administration continued unabated. Less than one month after the missive was printed, former president Franklin Pierce weighed in at a rally in New Hampshire: "Here in these free states it is made criminal for that noble martyr of free speech, Mr. Vallandigham, to discuss public affairs in Ohio—ay, even here, in time of war the mere arbitrary will of the president takes the place of the Constitution, and the president himself announces to us that it is treasonable to speak or to write otherwise than he may prescribe."

Copperheads in Ohio had already shown their contempt for the administration by nominating Vallandigham, still exiled in

Canada, as the Democratic candidate for governor. It was a worrisome turn of events for the president. Though he found it difficult to believe that "one genuine American would, or could, be induced to, vote for such a man as Vallandigham," he nevertheless understood that the Ohio gubernatorial election could be used by his enemies as a means to repudiate him. Therefore, as he told Gideon Welles, he watched it with "more anxiety . . . than he had in 1860 when he was chosen."

Prominent supporters of the president were sent to Ohio to rally around the Republican candidate, John Brough, in the exceedingly nasty race, while Vallandigham did his best to inspire his adherents from his base in exile at Windsor, Ontario. In one typically grandiose letter, dated July 15, 1863, the Copperhead candidate addressed the faithful: "Six weeks ago, when just going into banishment, because an audacious but mostly cowardly despotism compelled it, I addressed you as a fellow-citizen. Today and from the very place then selected by me, but after wearisome and most perilous journeyings for more than four thousand miles by land and upon the sea—still in exile, though almost in sight of my native state—I greet you as your representative."

Lincoln was elated when Vallandigham lost the key election in a landslide. It had been a referendum on his administration, and he had been vindicated. "Glory to God in the highest," he reportedly telegraphed John Brough. "Ohio has saved the Nation." As far as the president was concerned, the Copperhead had essentially been defanged. Indeed, Vallandigham had become so inconsequential that Lincoln barely reacted the next year when he learned that his nemesis had, in disguise, quietly slipped back to the United States. Carl Sandburg recounted the rather ignoble return:

On the night of June 14, 1864, a man in his room in the Hiron's House in Windsor, Canada, stands before a mirror

and in an amateur way arranges himself in disguise. On his
unshaven upper lip he smoothes down a large mustache, over
the close-trimmed beard of his chin and jaws a long luxuriant
flowing set of whiskers. He blackens his reddish eyebrows.
Under trousers and vest he buttons a bed pillow.

Nobody bothers him as he rides the ferry from Her Maj-
esty's domain to Detroit and the U.S.A. A customs officer
punches him lightly in the stomach asking what he's got there,
and lets it go at that. A policeman in Detroit is suspicious,
takes him to a street gaslight, looks him over and lets him go.
On a train out of Detroit a passenger bends down to whisper
in his ear, "I know your voice but you are safe from me."
Snuggled in the berth of a sleeping car he rides safely over-
night to Hamilton, Ohio.

Though he continued to agitate against Lincoln and the war
after his return, it was apparent that Vallandigham had lost most
of his luster. A secret Democratic order known as the Sons of
Liberty did draft him as their "Grand Commander." But considering its membership was drawn from what one editor described
as an "an assorted lot of ninny-hammers and zanies . . . whose
heads are emptier than an idiot's skull," it was hardly a crowning achievement. Plus, their silly rituals annoyed and embarrassed their chosen leader. Vallandigham was further humiliated
at the 1864 Democratic National Convention in Chicago when
the peace platform he put forth was virtually ignored by the
party's nominee for president, General George McClellan. And
Lincoln's sweeping victory in the election that followed left the
nation's leading Copperhead with little to do but slither back to
his law practice in Dayton. Seven years later, while defending a
client on murder charges, he accidentally shot himself dead as he
demonstrated to the jury how the murder weapon might have
been used.

Vallandigham always believed that history would vindicate him and hold him in high regard, but it was his enemy, "King Lincoln," who remains enshrined in the nation's consciousness. Still, "the wily agitator" did leave a legacy of sorts, serving as the inspiration for Edward Everett Hale's 1863 classic short story "The Man Without a Country."

16

Mary Surratt:
The Mother of Conspirators?

It was July 7, 1865. Mary Surratt was led to the gallows of the Washington Arsenal Penitentiary. Debilitated by fear and barely able to walk, she was practically carried up the steps to the scaffold. There, gently swaying in the hot breeze, four ropes awaited her and the three men who were also condemned. As the noose was adjusted around her neck, she could see her own coffin and a freshly dug hole in the ground yawning to greet her. She swooned at the sight and begged her captors, "Don't let me fall," just before the floor dropped from beneath her and the rope snapped her neck.

★

It is said that a person who dies violently under the shadow of unresolved circumstances is remanded to a certain purgatory—a disturbed spirit in the realm of the living, waiting for a time when the truth behind his or her death is revealed. If so, Mary Surratt qualifies as a ghost of exceeding prominence.

She was the first woman executed by the U.S. government, a forty-three-year-old widow hanged as a conspirator in the assassination of Abraham Lincoln. Yet nearly a century and a half after her death, proof of her guilt or innocence remains stubbornly elusive. And, some say, her spirit is restless. There have been numerous reported sightings of her ghost, including at her execution site in Washington, D.C., where a black-clad figure, bound hand-and-foot as Mrs. Surratt was at her death, now moves effortlessly, her hooded head drooping unnaturally close to her shoulder.

The portraits of a stern, hardened woman in the few photographs of Mrs. Surratt known to exist seem to reflect her character—a person who had lived a difficult life and who thought in extremes. Sent as a young, fatherless girl to be educated by the Sisters of Charity in Alexandria, Virginia, she became a convert and a relentless Roman Catholic proselytizer. She also had an abiding kinship with the South all of her adult life—an association that, justly or not, would lead to the noose.

At age seventeen she married John Harrison Surratt, a rabid secessionist and debt-ridden drunk. They purchased 287 acres in Prince George's County, Maryland, and built a home they also used as a tavern, a hostel, a post office, and a polling place in a town that would become known as Surrattsville (now Clinton). Located in a county with deep-seated Southern sentiments (Lincoln received just one vote there in the 1860 election), and with John Surratt's vocal opposition to Union policies (he owned seven slaves), the establishment became a speakeasy for those sharing similar attitudes. There is also ample evidence that the Surratt residence, just twelve miles outside the nation's capital, became a safe house for the flourishing Confederate underground.

When John Surratt died in 1862, his wife was left with the burdens of an encumbered farm and other legacies of her ne'er-do-well husband. With her elder son, Isaac, serving in the Confederate Army, and with John Surratt Jr. occupied as a Confederate courier, it proved nearly impossible for Mary to keep the family business afloat. She decided to rent the Surrattsville property to a former D.C. policeman, John Lloyd, and move to a boardinghouse in Washington that had been acquired by her husband years earlier. It was a fateful move.

John Wilkes Booth was a frequent visitor at Mrs. Surratt's. The impassioned, secessionist actor had allied himself with John Surratt Jr., and they set about forming a plot to kidnap the president. The boardinghouse became a meeting place for those recruited to carry out the plan they hoped would effect a better settlement for the South near the end of the Civil War. The kidnapping scheme, a rather inept effort, failed miserably, and Booth's intentions soon turned to murder. It was carried out on the night of April 14, 1865, as President and Mrs. Lincoln enjoyed a performance of *Our American Cousin* at Ford's Theatre.

The recently unified nation—North and South—was stunned by the assassination, and an immediate restoration of stability was the paramount goal of Secretary of State Edwin Stanton. He sought swift justice for the ghastly crime. Booth, the lead actor, was already dead—shot in a barn by Union troops who had tracked him down to Bowling Green, Virginia, after his dramatic escape from Ford's Theatre. The government quickly pressed its case against the supporting cast.

By some accounts Mary Surratt was a bit player swept up in the frenzy. To others, however, she was the "mother of conspirators," as one newspaper called her. According to Judge Advocate General Joseph Holt, who served as the lead government prosecutor, she was "the master spirit among them all." Lincoln's successor, Andrew Johnson, declared that she had "kept the nest that hatched the egg" of murderous conspiracy. And the military tribunal he ordered to try Mrs. Surratt and seven others ensured that his view would prevail.

The trial opened on May 8, 1865, less than a month after Lincoln died. A quick, decisive resolution appeared to be its primary concern; a fair hearing trial for the defendants certainly wasn't. "Here the government made its own rules," writes historian Michael W. Kauffman, "shared them with no one, and changed them as it saw fit." For example, Joseph Holt, who served as legal adviser to the commission in addition to his role as lead prosecutor, recommended that the trial begin in secret, whether or not the defendants had representation. They had to scramble for lawyers, and Mary Surratt was stuck with a pair of neophytes who harmed her case immeasurably.

The testimony against her was damning, particularly that of John Lloyd, the former policeman who rented her property in Surrattsville, and Louis J. Weichmann, a tenant at her Washington boardinghouse. Lloyd testified that Mary had come to Surrattsville on the day of the assassination, delivered a pair of field glasses, and told him to have them ready, along with some guns previously hidden at the property, as they would be called for that night. Sure enough, Booth and coconspirator David Herold came to Surrattsville for the supplies after Lincoln's murder, just as she had said they would. Weichmann testified that a number of the accused conspirators met frequently at Mrs. Surratt's Washington boardinghouse, which was just a few blocks away from Ford's Theatre, and were warmly welcomed there. He also claimed that after she returned from Surrattsville, she and Booth conferred privately in her living room only hours before the assassination.

Lawyers more experienced than Mrs. Surratt's might have effectively argued that both Lloyd and Weichmann were suspects in the plot to kill Lincoln, and that their testimony was perhaps prompted by an effort to save their own skins. But as it stood, her attorneys bungled their way through the whole trial. Prosecutors openly ridiculed them and lectured them on their inadequacies. On one occasion, when Mrs. Surratt's lawyer Frederick Aiken asked for some leeway on a particular point by arguing that he hadn't objected to other issues as he could have, prosecutor Henry Burnett lacerated him:

"It is certainly a very weak argument for counsel to say that he permitted illegitimate matter, and therefore illegitimate matter should be permitted for him. It is his duty, under his oath, to see that his client has the rights of law, and it is an admission that I certainly would not make to the court, that I had not maintained the rights of my client. He is to blame, and no one else, if such has been the case."

Inept lawyers aside, the hasty trial was indisputably biased in favor of the prosecution, which sought to link the defendants inexorably with the crimes of the Confederacy. "If ever Justice sat with unbandaged, blood-shot eyes, she did so on this occasion," said trial witness Henry Kyd Douglas, author of *I Rode with Stonewall*. Mary Surratt, along with three of her codefendants, was convicted and sentenced to hang. (The four other defendants were given life sentences.) Though few at the time doubted her guilt, almost no one believed she would actually die on the gallows given her sex and age. It was a surprise, then, that President Johnson's expected commutation of her sentence never came— even after the filing of a writ of habeas corpus and a clemency petition signed by five members of the military tribunal that had convicted her. Johnson later claimed he never saw the petition, and Holt was accused of withholding it from him—a charge he vigorously denied.

The trial left unanswered many questions that a more judicious, accountable proceeding might have resolved: Was Mrs. Surratt really an active participant, or merely at the periphery of the plot? If she was involved in the abortive kidnapping scheme, did that make her liable for Booth's subsequent decision to murder? Could it be that she was charmed by the handsome actor, a genuine superstar in his day, and unwittingly assisted him? Did she meet with some of the conspirators with malicious intent, or, as some supporters have claimed, simply as a gracious hostess to associates of her son's who were guests in her home? Lewis Powell, the Booth cohort who grievously wounded Secretary of State William Seward in an attempt to kill him on the night of Lincoln's assassination, attested to her innocence. On the other hand, George Atzerodt, who was supposed to kill Vice President Johnson that night, stated that she was fully involved. Both hanged with her.

And what of those accused conspirators who escaped the noose? Was Samuel Mudd, the doctor who set Booth's broken leg, really less culpable than Mary Surratt? He was given a life sentence and pardoned four years later. John Surratt Jr., a prime mover in the kidnapping plot, escaped to Canada after the assassination and was later captured in Egypt. He was tried and acquitted in a civilian court on charges nearly identical to his mother's. Then there was John Lloyd, the prime witness against Mrs. Surratt. Why wasn't he charged in the plot? After all, he provided Booth with guns and other supplies during his escape.

Mary Surratt's guilt or innocence still preoccupies historians and other interested folk. "It's addictive," said Laurie Verge, a historian for the Maryland-National Park and Planning Commission, which oversees the restored Surratt home and business in Clinton. "Everyone is looking for that one bit of evidence that will settle once and for all the big question."

In the meantime, the ghost smolders.

17

Tunis Campbell:
Pillar of Reconstruction

A small group of freed slaves found a rather inhospitable new home when they first landed on Georgia's Sea Islands in April 1865. The abandoned plantations were overrun with weeds and infested with snakes. Anything of value had already been looted by marauding Union soldiers, and the small cabins once occupied by slaves were in crumbling disrepair. Nevertheless, this land at the heart of the South's rice-growing empire was now theirs. And for their leader, Tunis Campbell, it was where his dream of a free society for those once enslaved would be built, and then—all too soon—destroyed.

★

He was a northerner who never suffered the bonds of slavery, yet when Tunis Campbell went south after the Civil War to help freed blacks achieve equality, he ended up in chains. It was a devastating blow to a movement that began with so much promise, and symbolized in its way the collapse of all that Reconstruction promised. Nevertheless, Campbell's impact had been enormous.

For a brief period of time, against implacable white resistance, he showed those who had once been enslaved what it meant to be truly free.

Reared among whites, including twelve years of education as the only person of color at an Episcopal school in Babylon, New York, Campbell grew up to believe himself equal to any man. As a committed abolitionist and activist against the movement to colonize American blacks in the African country of Liberia, he strove to lift the oppressed members of his race to the same level. His efforts received government sanction in 1863 when Secretary of War Edwin Stanton commissioned him to work with General Rufus Saxton in the resettlement of freed slaves in South Carolina.

"I was sent down . . . to organize civil government," he wrote, "to improve the colored people in the South wherever I could do it, and . . . to instruct and elevate the colored race."

Historian Russell Duncan has noted that Campbell's experiences in South Carolina prepared him well for his future as a leader of freedmen in Georgia. Not only did he meet former slaves and hear firsthand about their hopes and aspirations, he learned from the missionaries, politicians, soldiers, and others he encountered as they worked to facilitate the transition from bondage. He also witnessed numerous abuses by whites, both northern and southern, as they sought to profit from the chaos of the war or to sabotage any strides made by blacks to establish themselves. Campbell absorbed it all, and in 1865 he was given the opportunity to put his practical education to use.

General Saxton, now an assistant commissioner of the recently established Freedmen's Bureau, appointed him to oversee the settlement of liberated blacks on the Sea Islands along Georgia's coast—right in the heart of a region where the "barbarous aristocracy" of rice planters, as abolitionist Fanny Kemble called them,[1] once held absolute dominion over other men. On these abandoned island plantations Tunis Campbell would found a society based on the basic American principles of freedom and equality for a group of people who had never known any such thing.

As the Civil War drew to its close, Campbell led the first group of settlers to the islands that had been set aside for them as part of a larger program prompted by General William Tecumseh Sherman's order—issued after his famous march through Georgia— that freed slaves be given land to call their own, without any white interference. Campbell was permitted to operate the settlement on the Sea Islands the way he saw fit, and immediately set about drafting a constitution modeled on that of the United States. There would be a legislature, with eight senators and a twenty-member House, a judicial system topped by a supreme court, and an executive branch, with Campbell himself serving as president.

Land ownership was fundamental in a free and democratic society, Campbell believed, and so the former plantations were parceled into individual farms and distributed. Education was key as well, particularly for people who had been systematically deprived of it. Using his own funds, Campbell imported teachers from the North and invited his family to help as well. "Bring the sons down," he wrote to his wife, Harriet. "We're going to establish the schools. We're on an island of our own. There are no white people here and we're going to lift up children. Bring all the primers you have, and please join us."

---

1. Kemble, an English actress and author, was married to Pierce Butler, a member of this "barbarous aristocracy," from 1834 until their divorce in 1849. The horrors of human bondage that she observed firsthand at her husband's Georgia plantation, and later wrote about, inspired her antislavery activism. "I have sometimes been haunted with the idea that was an imperative duty, knowing what I know, and having seen what I have seen, to do all that lies in my power to show the dangers and the evils of this frightful institution," she wrote to a friend a year after leaving Butler. Her diary was published twenty years later.

Campbell hoped the inhabitants of the coastal islands—his microcosm of America, albeit an all-black one—would one day be integrated into the white world and thrive there. But he thought it essential that the races be kept separated at first, and he formed a militia of citizen soldiers to ensure it. "The freedmen needed time to grow," writes Russell Duncan, "to be instructed in democratic ways, to develop a true feeling of equality, to learn self-sufficiency, and to establish nuclear families free from the watchful eye, instructions, and intimidations of still-hostile whites. Campbell believed that separation for strength was the quickest way to transform the freedmen into free men."

By the end of 1865, the new colony appeared to be well on its way. Nearly one thousand people had been settled, and, despite the meager rations provided by the Freedmen's Bureau, they were able to sustain themselves on the islands' bounty as well as on their own labor. But the project was doomed. Andrew Johnson had succeeded Lincoln after his assassination, yet inherited little of the late president's wisdom or benevolence. A Southern Democrat, his vision for a reunited nation was to restore confiscated plantations to their owners and thus force freedmen back to their subordinate positions as slaves in all but name.[2] A colony of self-sustaining blacks claiming ownership of property that belonged to white men simply did not fit with this president's idea of Reconstruction.

In short order, Rufus Saxton, Campbell's supporter and protector, was fired and replaced by Davis Tillson, who forced the islands open to white planting interests. Many blacks were manipulated into inequitable labor contracts, which Campbell vehemently denounced. As a result, baseless charges of malfeasance were leveled against him, and he was removed from his position as a bureau agent. Though he continued to promote the move-

2. "Whatever else this man may be," Frederick Douglass remarked after first meeting the president, "he is no friend of our race."

ment toward independence and self-sufficiency on the islands, it was soon clear that he would have to base his dream elsewhere.

A plantation owner ruined by the war agreed to sell Campbell his 1,250-acre property on the Georgia mainland, with payments to be made in installments and rent due until the price was paid in full. Here Campbell planned to reestablish his island colony as a cooperative community. The land would be divided into individual farms and owned by members who would raise crops both for sustenance and profit. Each would contribute to the payments due on the land, as well as toward the reimbursement of the Freedmen's Bureau for the initial rations and supplies it provided. And, most important, they would all work in various capacities, from sweepers to sheriffs, for the general good of the community. Upon arriving, members made the following promise: "We hereby pledge ourselves, our interest[s] and our labor to the successful issue of this permanent [organization] for our welfare and hope thereby to merit the approbation of our friends who have assisted us and the disappointment of our enemies who seek our downfall."

Establishing the new community, called BelleVille, proved difficult. The settlers arrived to find no shelter and land that had been left unplowed for years. Yet Campbell's adopted son, E. E. Howard, expressed their greatest hopes: "Soon will this place teem with the fruits of the people's labor and . . . this land, now almost impenetrable with weeds and underbrush, having grown up so profusely during the year, laid out into little farms of from ten to twenty acres, and what is better still, the people who thus labor will be able to claim it as their 'home,' where under their own vine and fig tree they may contemplate the goodness of God."

Torrential rains and a cotton blight dampened expectations at BelleVille somewhat, yet as the new community struggled to establish itself in Georgia, radical changes were taking place in Washington. The Republican-controlled Congress repudiated

President Johnson's Reconstruction agenda and launched one of its own. In addition to passing the Civil Rights Act of 1866 (over Johnson's veto) and drafting the Fourteenth Amendment that made blacks full citizens of the United States, Congress enacted harsher measures against the South—again, over the president's veto. The rebellious states were divided into five military districts and had to meet certain conditions before they would be readmitted to the union. They were forced to rewrite their constitutions and to adopt the Fourteenth Amendment. Most odious of all, for many southerners, was the requirement that men they regarded as chattel be registered to vote. As blacks began to occupy state legislatures and even the U.S. Congress, Tunis Campbell saw opportunities for empowerment that extended far beyond BelleVille.

★

Georgia crackled with expectation as Radical Reconstruction took hold, and in this atmosphere General John Pope appointed Campbell to the three-man board of registration for the state's Second District. With all the passion of the preacher he had once trained to be, Campbell extolled the power of the ballot and the virtues of the Republican Party. He also traveled throughout the state promoting black rights, and on Independence Day 1867 he represented McIntosh County at the Republican State Convention in Atlanta.

"The colored men of the Convention . . . met the white on equal ground, feeling that it was no disgrace to be black," one newspaper reporter wrote. "They argued well and showed themselves men of ability and task. Take, for instance, the conduct of Mr. Campbell, who won favor everywhere, than who none was more honored and respected . . . [and who was one of] the leading spirits of the Convention."

Following his success in Atlanta, Campbell was elected as a delegate to the state convention that drafted the most liberal constitution in Georgia's history. He then ran for the Senate and became one of three blacks to win office. These were heady times indeed, but Campbell would not sit securely. Conservatives who believed that only whites were fit to serve in the General Assembly were outraged by the presence of men they considered inferior beings. On September 12, 1868, the Senate voted that blacks had no right to hold office and expelled Campbell and another senator (a third had been forced to resign a month earlier). Campbell's protest was recorded in the *Senate Journal:*

> *You have this day decided by your vote, declared us not eligible to seats on this floor.*
>
> *Sirs, by a very large majority of all the votes cast in our several districts, and by the right guaranteed us both in the Constitution of the United States and of the State of Georgia, as well as in the Reconstruction laws of Congress; we claim to be the legally elected representatives of a very large portion of, and nearly one-half of the legal electors of the State of Georgia.*
>
> *Sirs, the Constitution and the laws of Georgia strictly provide that no law shall be made or enforced which shall abridge the privileges or immunities of citizens of the United States, or of this State, or deny to any person within its jurisdiction, the equal protection of its laws.*
>
> *Therefore in behalf of ourselves, our constituents, and also in behalf of nearly five hundred thousand loyal citizens of this State, we do enter our solemn protest against the illegal, unconstitutional, unjust, and oppressive action of this body, based on the Senator from the 35th Senatorial District, declaring us ineligible on account of color.*
>
> *And we respectfully request that this, our protest, be spread upon the journals of the Senate.*

Campbell may have lost his Senate seat, but he remained justice of the peace for the predominately black McIntosh County. And from that position he built a political power base—not for his own aggrandizement, but for the advancement of his race. With severe labor shortages in the South, he counseled blacks on how to use the situation to their best advantage and how to avoid being exploited. He met with them frequently, coalesced them into a vigorous community, inspired them with possibilities, and, with other blacks who held positions of authority in the county government, protected their interests.

"They gaze upon him as having no part in their humanity," wrote one observer, "a demi-god whose wonderful attributes are quite beyond their comprehension and whose wisdom is past finding out, and they almost worship him and follow withersoever he leads."

While Campbell helped shield the black people of McIntosh County, others in the state suffered from continuous, often violent coercion and intimidation from the Ku Klux Klan and other racist organizations. As a result, Congress reinstated military rule over Georgia late in 1869, and, under order of the new commander, Campbell and the other black legislators who had been deprived of their seats were reinstated. They were not warmly welcomed back. Democratic papers called Campbell "the Congo Senator," and referred to one of his speeches against unfair polling practices as "the gorilla's insolent harangue." The sentiments were deep-rooted, and in time, those who were behind them would crush Tunis Campbell.

★

Radical Reconstruction was faltering in the South, and those who wished to see white supremacy restored—"Redeemers," as they were known—were on the rise. By 1872 they controlled the governor's office and the legislature in Georgia, but Campbell continued to impede their total domination. The *Savannah Morning News* declared that because of that "monkey-faced evil spirit, Tunis G. Campbell and his ready vassalmen," McIntosh County remained "one of the strongholds of Radicalism and Grantism [a reference to the Republican president] in Georgia." The Redeemers fumed over the influence Campbell had over black laborers, his frequent trips to Washington to agitate against white abuses, and, most insidious of all, the power he wielded with the backing of an armed militia. Many feared an armed insurrection. "I never slept without a loaded pistol by my bed," one planter reported. Yet Campbell was too prominent to kill outright without repercussions from Washington. He would be destroyed instead by a vast conspiracy that reached into the highest levels of government.

As the climate in Georgia became increasingly hostile to blacks, some proposed leaving the state and resettling in Arkansas. Campbell vigorously resisted. "I propose to sink or swim, live or die, right here, and not ask any man if I can stay here," he declared. "Let our wives and children know they have husbands and fathers [and] that we are able and willing to defend them in this state. I am opposed to any plans of emigration. I repeat, sink or swim, live or perish, Georgia is to be our home."

Campbell probably never fathomed just how inhospitable his home would become. He hoped to live in a color-blind society where all men were treated equal, but his idealism gradually gave way to cold realism as he came to understand that few whites in Georgia would ever share his vision. If they couldn't be coaxed toward fairness, he concluded, they would have to be forced. He used his office as justice of the peace to that end, and never hesitated to arrest anyone who mistreated his people. "He makes up his mind and pursues his course, whether right or wrong," said Judge William M. Sessions after Campbell was attacked for being overzealous in his position. "He professes to look, and his acts show that he does look, very closely to [blacks'] rights as citizens." To many whites, that made him a "lawless nigger," as the

Savannah Morning News called him. His decisions as justice of the peace would be one way they would use to bring him down.

Another weapon was an act passed by the state Senate that established an unelected board of commissioners to control McIntosh County. "Not only did the law provide for an all-white county government with the authority to create and control patronage positions," writes Russell Duncan, "but it also threatened to destroy Campbell's position. He saw five years of black progress imperiled." Naturally he opposed the law, calling it "the most iniquitous, unjust, and diabolical thing ever attempted on citizens of a free country," and he encouraged blacks in the county to resist it—violently, if necessary. The Redeemers pounced, charging Campbell with inciting the populace.

"His influence is a blight on the community," wrote William Robert Gignilliant, the man who had taken Campbell's seat when he was ousted from the Senate in 1868. "If he could be arraigned before the Senate and dismissed for malpractice as a Justice of the Peace, his expulsion from that body would necessarily follow. As he lives only by his office he would then be obliged to quit the County or starve."

A Senate investigation found Campbell "guilty of using disrespectful and slanderous language towards the Senate . . . guilty of trying to excite an insurrectionary spirit among the people of his district by advising them to resist a public law of the State with the bayonet," guilty of being "a general disturber of the peace and order . . . [and] guilty of malpractice in the office of Justice of the Peace." Despite the conclusions, no action was taken against Campbell—Duncan theorizes that it was out of fear of retaliation from Washington and the restoration of military control in the state. But the Redeemers were far from finished.

Campbell lost his bid for reelection to the Senate in 1872 after the votes in two key precincts were tossed out because of "irregularities." Election fraud similarly undid his bid for the

House two years later. Meanwhile, he was bombarded with bogus charges arising from his activities as justice of the peace. In 1872, for example, he was arrested for marrying a mixed-race couple four years earlier. "Last Tuesday Senator Campbell was arrested and incarcerated in jail," Henry McNeal Turner wrote in a letter to the *Savannah Journal* that charged there was a state-wide conspiracy to jail black leaders. "The senator is handcuffed as though he was a murderous desperado and hurried off to Atlanta. And what is all this for? Why manacle, shackle, and gyve this senator with such unusual ferocity? Is it because he married that couple four years ago? No! It is because they mean to get him out of the senate and defeat his re-election."

The judge who heard the case called it a "broad farce," and Campbell was released after trial. But there was no such judicial restraint when a staunch Democrat and Confederate veteran named Henry B. Tompkins was appointed to preside over the superior court of McIntosh County in January 1875. That same month Campbell was indicted for the false imprisonment of Isaac Rafe, whom he had arrested in 1873 for breaking into the homes of two blacks. Campbell had fined Rafe $100 and ordered him to keep the peace for six months, but Rafe refused to pay the required court costs or bond and was ordered to jail. According to Campbell, he ran away and never spent a minute behind bars.

Under pressure from Judge Tompkins, the jury in the case returned a guilty verdict, but recommended mercy. Tompkins wouldn't hear of it. He stripped Campbell of his office as justice of the peace and sentenced him to one year of hard labor. When Campbell's attorneys appealed for a bond, Tompkins snapped that he "would not take a bond for the sum of a million dollars." He also repeatedly put off the hearing on a motion for a new trial until Campbell was finally hauled away to a labor camp. Though Tompkins was eventually forced to release him on a $2,000 bond, the Redeemers were delighted with his tactics. "Everybody at the capitol is jubilant over the initial exploits of your new Judge in the administration of criminal law in the negro bestridden County of McIntosh," wrote a correspondent to the *Savannah Advertiser*. "He has rid the County of . . . the Senior Campbell."

While Campbell was free on bail in the Rafe case, the ever-zealous Tompkins had him arrested for another case dating back to 1871. Campbell had jailed one John Fisher for contempt and was later found guilty of falsely imprisoning him. The Georgia Supreme Court had reversed the case, but now Tompkins saw fit to revive it. A grand jury—hardly comprised of his peers— indicted Campbell, after which Tompkins ordered a $3,000 bond. When he was unable to pay, the sheriff's men tried to take him to jail. But outside the courthouse hundreds of armed blacks had gathered and demanded Campbell's release. When the city marshal went out to the crowd and tried to disperse it, an ex-change of gunfire ensued. As a result Campbell was kept at the courthouse overnight, and by the next evening was taken away by steamer. "Goodbye Mas Jesus," the crowd cried mournfully, "goodbye."

Judge Tompkins's persecution of Campbell and other blacks was reported to President Grant, along with requests for his inter-cession. An investigation followed, and Tompkins was found un-worthy of holding judicial office. Assistant U.S. Attorney George S. Thomas, who conducted the investigation, wrote to Attorney General Edwards Pierrepont after discussing Tompkins with sev-eral local judges: "Judge Russell very frankly told me that he was a Democrat and opposed to Campbell politically, but that candor compelled him to state that he (Campbell) was being shamefully persecuted by Judge Tompkins and others for the purpose of rid-ding McIntosh County of his presence and influence . . . and that he was satisfied that Judge Tompkins's prejudices against Mr. Campbell on account of his race and color were such to disqualify him from giving Mr. Campbell justice, and that he looked upon

Judge Tompkins's conduct toward Mr. Campbell as a disgrace to the judicial position he occupied."

The conclusions did little to help Campbell. While George Thomas was trying to get the Fisher case moved to federal court to ensure a fair trial, the Georgia Supreme Court declined to hear the appeal on the Rafe case because of a technicality. It was returned to Judge Tompkins, which doomed Campbell. After waiting in jail for nearly nine months pending the Fisher trial, he was now ordered to serve his sentence for the Rafe case by working on a plantation as part of Georgia's convict-lease law. He later described his first day of bondage:

> On or about the 12th of January, 1876, the guard from the state prison came, about 7 o'clock a.m., and handcuffed me, and, with a chain about twelve feet long, dragged me along the streets of Savannah to the Central railroad, and then took me one hundred and forty miles from Savannah, to a prison camp on the plantation of Colonel Jack Smith's, in Washington County, State of Georgia. The weather was very cold, and they took me up in a wagon. I was helpless when we got there, at 1 o'clock in the night—my hands being chained together.

After a year of labor, Campbell was released from Smith's plantation at age sixty-four. "We think it very doubtful if the old man ever comes back to Darien [the seat of government in McIntosh County] to live anymore," gloated the editor of the *Timber Gazette*. He was right. Assured that he would be jailed again if he remained in Georgia, Campbell moved to Washington, D.C., where he continued the struggle for justice and equality, but to little effect. Radical Reconstruction was dead in the South, and so, it seemed, were Tunis Campbell's dreams.

18

Sarah Winnemucca:
"Paiute Princess"

The Great White Father in Washington seemed indifferent to the Northern Paiute woman who had traveled across the continent to plead for her obscure and suffering tribe. "Did you get all you want for your people?" President Rutherford B. Hayes asked somewhat dismissively. "Yes, sir," Sarah Winnemucca tentatively replied, "as far as I know." With that, the brief interview ended and the powerful man in whom Sarah had placed so much hope swept out of the room. Though she had been given a written guarantee from Secretary of the Interior Carl Schurz that the sorry lot of the Northern Paiutes would be improved, so many whites had broken their promises before. Only the near-mythic president of the United States could truly help her people, Sarah believed, and she found that he didn't care. Dejected, she returned to her homeland in the western Nevada desert and saw soon enough that Secretary Schurz was yet another in a long list of whites who wouldn't keep their word.

One hundred and twenty-five years after Sarah Winnemucca's disappointing journey to Washington in 1880, she was given a place of honor among other great Americans in the U.S. Capitol.

Though not as recognizable as some of the carved figures enshrined there, it was a fitting tribute to a dynamic woman who defied the limitations placed upon her sex to lead a most extraordinary life. She was the first Native American woman to write a book, and one of the few to have had national influence. A compelling speaker with a sharp tongue and ready wit, she lectured in countless halls and was invited to testify before Congress.

Hers was a life of contrasts—a brave heroine with a weakness for bad men; an advocate for peace with a violent temper when it came to her own honor; a firm believer in the superiority of the native culture criticized by her own people for assimilating too far into the white world. But Sarah's overriding legacy was her tireless, often frustrated efforts on behalf of the Northern Paiutes[1] and other native tribes in the face of relentless white encroachment onto their lands and sometimes barbaric abuse of their people. "They came like a lion," she wrote, "yes, like a roaring lion, and have continued so ever since."

When Sarah was a young girl, with the given name of Thocmetony (meaning "shell flower"),[2] these encroachers were called "white owls" because of their bearded faces and pale eyes. The white invasion of the Paiute homeland in northwestern Nevada had barely begun when she was born around 1844. Even then, however, the white owls were striking terror. They were known to shoot Indians on sight, and were believed to be cannibals after reports that a group of white travelers had resorted to eating one another while stranded in the Sierra mountains. It was this fear that informed one of Sarah's earliest memories. A party of white

---

1. The Northern Paiutes of the Great Basin in western Nevada, northeastern California, and southeastern Oregon are a distinct group from the Southern Paiutes of northern Arizona, southern Nevada and Utah, and adjacent areas of southeastern California. The simplified term Paiutes to describe Sarah and her people in the rest of the text should be taken to mean Northern Paiutes.

2. Although she never said when, Sarah was probably given her adopted name at an early age by whites unable (or unwilling) to pronounce her real name.

men was heard to be approaching her camp, but she and a cousin were too frightened to run. Their panicked mothers, saddled with other children on their backs, had no choice but to bury the little girls before fleeing themselves. Only their faces were exposed and hidden under sagebrush to protect them from the desert sun. "With my heart throbbing and not daring to breathe, we lay there all day," Sarah later recalled. "It seemed that the night would never come."

Despite the Paiutes's fear of whites, Sarah's revered grandfather Truckee encouraged friendship with them. Indeed, he demanded it, for he believed the future of his people lay in the white world. The tribal leader had served as a guide for expeditions into California and was awed by the technological wonders he witnessed there. He also fought with General John Fremont's army in the 1846 Bear Flag Rebellion to wrest control of California from the Mexicans, and one of his most prized possessions was a letter he received from Fremont requesting that all who read it treat him well. Truckee called the letter his "rag friend," and described its amazing powers to his people: "This can talk to all our white brothers, and our white sisters, and their children. . . . The paper can travel like the wind, and it can go and talk with their fathers and brothers and sisters, and come back to tell what they are doing, and whether they are well or sick." Although Truckee's abiding faith in the goodness of his "white brothers" was sorely tested, particularly when a group of them killed his son, it never wavered. His granddaughter, on the other hand, would always be ambivalent.

She had seen the wonders of the white world when Truckee took her to California as a young girl and when she was later sent to live with a white family, where she learned English. But she had also seen its innumerable cruelties. The gradual influx of white settlers into her homeland became a flood after gold was discovered in the region. The native people, scorned by the newcomers as subhuman, were pushed from the land they had occupied for thousands of years and deprived of the meager resources the desert provided. An early Indian agent noted that "the encroachments of the Emigrant have driven away the game upon which [the Paiutes] depend for subsistence. They cannot hunt upon the territories of other tribes, except at the risk of their lives. They must therefore steal or starve."

Rampant disease and starvation among the displaced people were punctuated by periodic cycles of violence. While the Indians sometimes killed settlers, far more often they were the victims. White fear and greed inspired genocidal tendencies. The *Humboldt Register* declared that killing Indians on sight was the "only sane" policy to control them, and the *Gold Hill News* advocated a "final solution of the great Indian problem: by exterminating the whole race, or driving them forever beyond our frontier." The violence touched Sarah personally on a number of occasions, perhaps most notably in 1865 when her mother and baby brother were slaughtered in what became known as the Mud Lake Massacre.

"The soldiers rode up to the encampment and fired into it, and killed almost all the people that were there," she wrote. "Oh, it is a fearful thing to tell, but it must be told. Yes, it must be told by me. It was all old men, women and children that were killed. . . . After the soldiers had killed all but some of the little children and babies still tied up in their baskets, the soldiers took them also, and set the camp on fire and threw them into the flames to see them burn alive."

Soon after the Mud Lake Massacre, Sarah moved to a reservation that had been established in the area surrounding Nevada's Pyramid Lake. There she shared the extreme deprivations of her people and found the cause that would consume her for the rest of her life. "She would not withdraw as some did," writes Sarah's biographer Sally Zanjani, "nor would she accept in silent misery what she had no power to change. Before her spirit finally broke, she would rage with all the eloquence at her command in print and in lectures against the reservation system, and she would carry her appeals to men of power."

The corrupt agents appointed to the Pyramid Lake Reservation were the frequent targets of her sometimes caustic tongue. She denounced them for the meager food and clothing they provided, for profiting from their positions, and for their Christian hypocrisy. After one agent made a great show of presenting a ton of flour to the Shoshone Indians for the benefit of their agent, his superior, Sarah confronted him. "I said, 'You come up here to show off before this man. Go and bring some flour to my people on the Humboldt River, who are starving, the people over whom you are agent. For shame that you who talk three times a day to the Great Father in Spirit-land should act so to my people.' This man called himself a Christian, too."

After about a year at the Pyramid Lake Reservation, during which time her uncle was murdered by a group of whites who coveted his land, Sarah moved north to Camp McDermit on the Oregon border to serve as an interpreter. There she wrote her first letter pleading for the cause of the Paiutes. It was sent to Major Henry Douglas, superintendent of Indian Affairs for Nevada, who forwarded it to the commissioner of Indian Affairs in Washington, D.C. The letter brought Sarah national recognition when it was excerpted in *Harper's Weekly* as part of a profile on her, and later in Helen Hunt Jackson's popular book, *A Century of Dishonor*. The agents at Pyramid Lake were once again the subjects of her scorn. "If we had stayed there, it would only be to starve," she wrote. "If this is the kind of civilization awaiting us on the Reserves, God grant that we may never be compelled to go on one, as it is much preferable to live in the mountains and drag out an existence in our native manner."

Sarah apparently enjoyed life at Camp McDermit, where the Paiutes were well provided for and where she basked in all the attention accorded her. "She was fully aware of her charms and lost no opportunity to display them," wrote Fanny Corbusier, the wife of an army surgeon at the post. "With a flourish which I have never seen duplicated in any show, she would gallop across the parade ground—supple, but erect in perfect balance—her quirt hand lifted in a queenly salute. Between the barracks and across the parade ground again, and she would be gone amid the lusty cheers of the men. Or, on occasion she would dismount just long enough to receive their plaudits—be remounted by some gallant soldier, and be off."

The soldiers at Camp McDermit proved to be good company for Sarah. She drank, gambled, and caroused with the men, and ended up eloping with one of them. Lieutenant Edward Bartlett became the first in a succession of ne'er-do-well white husbands whom she found irresistible. "His example would ruin the best company in the service," Bartlett's commanding officer observed of him. He was a handsome rogue with a drinking problem who narrowly avoided a court martial on charges of defrauding the government. Sarah was smitten. She defied her father, Winnemucca, chief of the Paiutes, to marry Bartlett, but within a month she returned to her family. It seems her new husband had deserted her after the novelty of an Indian wife had worn off.

A Paiute woman who dared question Sarah's virtue after the demise of her ill-fated marriage perhaps did so without realizing the consequences of casting such aspersions on her character. In full fury, Sarah attacked the woman, beat her mercilessly, then triumphantly bounced on top of her. With each bounce she issued a sharp slap across the face. "There," she exclaimed, "talk so about me to white folks, will you!" Sarah's wrath, when aroused, did not discriminate between the sexes, either. Two weeks after the brawl with the unfortunate Paiute woman, she clashed with a hotel waiter in what a *Humboldt Register* headline called A BLOODY COMBAT. The waiter ended up with a black eye, but Sarah fared worse, slipping into a coma from which it took her several days to emerge. Later, when a man named Julius Argasse tried to rape her, she slashed him across the face with a penknife. Usually such an assault on a white man, no matter how well justified, would result in serious punishment. Fortunately, Sarah had a good lawyer who produced an impressive list of character witnesses, and the charges were dropped.

In 1875 Sarah went to work as an interpreter at the Malheur Reservation in southeastern Oregon. The agent there, Samuel B. Parrish, was one of the few ever to earn her approbation. He treated the Indians with kindness, encouraging them to work the land and to keep the rewards of their labor. "The reservation is yours," Parrish told them. "The government has given it all to you and your children." While the Indians enthusiastically dug irrigation ditches and planted crops, Sarah served as an assistant to Parrish's sister-in-law when she opened a school at Malheur in the spring of 1876. "Oh, how happy we were!" she wrote. "We had three hundred and five boys, twenty-three young men, sixty-nine girls, and nineteen young women. They learned very fast, and we were glad to come to school. Oh, I cannot tell or express how happy we were."

The idyll at Malheur was not destined to last, however. To the Indians' great dismay, Parrish lost his position and was replaced by William V. Rinehart, a tyrannical figure who despised his charges. He advised them that everything they produced at the reservation belonged to the government and that they would be paid a small fee for their labor. After expenses for their care were deducted, this came to nearly nothing. When the Indians appealed to him with the promises that had been made to them, Rinehart was unmoved. "Nothing here is yours," he snapped. "It is all the government's. If Parrish told you so, he told you lies." Rinehart's gross abuses prompted Sarah to petition against him to various authorities. This resulted not only in the loss of her job at Malheur, but in Rinehart's enduring enmity as well. He would hound her for years to come.

★

The Northern Paiutes weren't the only tribe in the region to suffer from the influx of white settlers. The Bannocks, who shared a common language with the Paiutes but who were far more aggressive, long bristled under the many injustices heaped upon them. By 1878 they were ready for war. Several bands of Paiutes joined the Bannocks and their allies when hostilities commenced, a turn of events that distressed Sarah. Like other members of her family, she believed a war against the whites could not be won and would only spell doom for her people. Therefore, she determined to work with the army to help stop it. "Sarah never doubted her course of action," writes Sally Zanjani. "She would follow the path on which Truckee had propelled her since she was a small child. She believed that acting for the army to bring an early peace was the best way to serve the Paiutes." Her courage throughout the crisis was remarkable.

With the approval of General Oliver O. Howard, Sarah pursued a daring plan: She would find the Bannock camp and persuade the Paiutes there to come over to the army in exchange for protection and rations. The mission was fraught with danger, but she was undaunted. "There is nothing that will stop me," she declared. Some officers on Howard's staff weren't so sure. "I have little idea that she will succeed," wrote Major Edwin C. Mason. Nearing the Bannock camp, Sarah and her two companions met her brother Lee, who advised them that Winnemucca and his band had been captured by the Bannocks and were being held prisoners. "They have treated our father most shamefully," Lee told her. "They have taken from us what guns we had, and our blankets, and our horses. They have done this because they outnumber us." Lee warned his sister of the great danger she faced and pleaded with her not to enter the camp, to no avail. "I must save my father and his people if I lose my life in trying to do it, and my father's too," she said. "That is all right, I have come for you all. Now let us go."

With Lee's help, Sarah disguised herself by unbraiding her hair, exchanging her dress for a blanket, and painting her face. The party then made their way over the steep mountain above the Bannock encampment and saw some five hundred warriors swarming below. Sarah later admitted that the sight made her feel "a little afraid," but she and her brother nevertheless went down to the valley and slipped into their father's lodge. "Have you come to save me yet?" exclaimed Chief Winnemucca. "My little child is in great danger. Oh, our Great Father in Spirit-land, look down on us and save us!" Sarah instructed the women in Winnemucca's band to pretend they were gathering wood for the evening and to make their escape that way. "Whisper it among yourselves," she ordered. "Get ready tonight for there is no time to lose." The men were told to gather as many horses as they could under cover of darkness and drive them to Juniper Lake on the other side of the mountain, where they would all meet. After they had all gone, Sarah and her father stole away later that night. Depleted from the difficult ride to the camp and from all the tension, Sarah could barely move. "It was like a dream," she recalled. "I could not get along at all. I almost fell down at every step, my father dragging me along."

The exhausted party barely had a moment to rest at Juniper Lake before Sarah urged them forward. The women were told to gather the food they had cooked and eat it on the ride, "for we must travel all night." At that point Lee announced he was going back to the Bannock camp for more people and would meet up with them later. The rest of the group proceeded to Summit Springs, which they reached the next morning. Sarah hadn't slept for two days and prepared to rest, but her father encouraged her to eat first. "I did not know what hunger was all that time," she wrote. "I had forgotten all about eating." Just then a rider approached and alerted her that the Bannocks were in pursuit. One band of Paiutes had been overtaken while making their escape, the rider said, and Lee had presumably been killed. (He wasn't, as it turned out.) Chief Winnemucca despaired over the news. "If my son is killed, I will go back and be killed by them too," he cried. "If we are to be killed off for what the white people have done to them, of course we cannot help ourselves." Sarah managed to persuade her distraught father to save himself and continue the flight, while she and Lee's wife, Mattie, rode ahead to General Howard for help.

"Away we started over the hills and valleys. . . . No water," she related. "We sang and prayed to our Great Father in the Spirit-land, as my people call God." When they finally reached Howard's camp, Sarah burst into tears of relief and exhaustion. She had endured a grueling ride of 220 miles over three days, and had saved at least seventy-five of her people. "I went for the government when the officers could not get an Indian man or a white man to go for love or money," she recalled with justifiable pride. "I, only an Indian woman, went and saved my father and his people." General Howard sent troops to bring Winnemucca and the rest to safety, and was so impressed with Sarah's fortitude that he retained her as a guide and interpreter for the rest of the Bannock War. "I had sufficient confidence in her story [about the size and location of the Bannock forces] to change my whole plan of movement," Howard wrote, "a change which afterward proved to be for the best."

Despite her heroism, rumors of her disloyalty were rife. Some even said that it was she who had incited the Paiutes to join the Bannocks and that she was now Howard's prisoner. Sally Zanjani suggests that Sarah's nemesis from the Malheur Reservation,

William Rinehart, was behind many of the suspicions that swirled around her. "After all," she writes, "he had blamed her rather than his own corruption and mismanagement for the troubles at Malheur, and now he badly needed a scapegoat. . . . Why not again blame Sarah?" Indeed, Rinehart had received some bad press when every Indian at the reservation abandoned it and a number of them joined the Bannocks.

The innuendo wounded her deeply. In one particularly troubling incident she was accosted by a woman serving her and several officers at an inn. "Why don't you take her and tie one part of her to a horse, and the other part of her to another horse, and let them go?" the woman demanded of the officers. "I would see the horses pull her to pieces with good grace." Though her companions tried to reassure her, Sarah was inconsolable. She couldn't eat after the scene and it was seared into her memory. "Dear reader," she later wrote, "this is the kind of white women that are in the West. They are always ready to condemn me."

With her knowledge of Indian customs and strategies, as well as her endurance and bravery, Sarah proved herself invaluable as she accompanied Howard's forces in pursuit of the Bannocks north through Oregon to their ultimate defeat in the last major Indian uprising in the Northwest. "She did our government great service," Howard wrote after her death, "and if I could tell you a tenth part of all she willingly did to help the white settlers and her own people to live peacefully together I am sure you would think, as I do, that the name of Toc-me-to-ne [Sarah] should have a place beside the name of Pocahontas in the history of our country." For Sarah, however, the victory was bittersweet. Certainly she had saved many lives, but her service to the army damaged her credibility among her own people, many of whom blamed her for the deaths of those Paiutes who had fallen in the conflict. And her standing would be eroded further still in the aftermath of the war.

She had promised those Paiutes who had not participated in the hostilities that they would be spared any punishment. "What need have you to be afraid?" she assured them. "You have not done anything. . . . General Howard knows all about you. None of you have fought the whites. You have all done your duty to the whites during the campaign." But General Howard and officials in Washington had other ideas. *All* the Paiutes who had left Malheur, regardless of their involvement in the war, were to be sent far from their homeland to the Yakama Reservation beyond the Columbia River in present-day Washington State. Sarah was devastated. "If you knew what I have promised my people, you would leave nothing undone but what you would try not to have them sent away," she pleaded. "My people will never believe me again."

Her service during the Bannock War would have spared her the banishment to Yakama, but she chose to endure it with her people. Thus, in the depth of the winter of 1879, the exiled Paiutes made the arduous 350-mile journey north. When they finally arrived at Yakama they were left on the fringes of the reservation, "as if we were so many horses or cattle," before they were finally housed in a makeshift shed. "Oh, how we did suffer with the cold," Sarah recalled. "There was no wood, and the snow was waist-deep, and many died off just as cattle or horses do after traveling so long in the cold." The agent at Yakama, James H. Wilbur, described them as "in the most destitute condition of any Indians I have ever known in this or any other country. Some of them were literally naked."

Like so many reservation agents, Wilbur was a religious missionary as well as a bigot. He saw Indians as savage heathens who needed to be civilized and converted, yet he grossly neglected the very people he sought to improve. He did nothing to stop the abuse of the Paiutes by the Yakama Indians who resented the intrusion onto their reservation, and the meager clothing he provided was almost laughable. Much of it was so thin that Sarah sardonically remarked that one could sift flour through the cloth. "Another Rinehart!" the Paiutes said of Wilbur. "Don't you see he is the same? He looks up into the sky and says something just like Rinehart."

Sarah had a keen eye for Christian hypocrisy, writing disdainfully of missionary agents who praised God while profiting off the people in their care. Nevertheless, she became a Methodist while at Yakama and worked to convert other Paiutes. At one point Agent Wilbur was planning for a religious revival at the reservation, during which important people from the East were to come and observe his work with the Indians. He told Sarah to keep the Paiutes out of sight during the revival, all too aware that their threadbare presence would belie the charitable message he hoped to convey. She ignored him, and at the meeting she directed the Paiutes to sit on benches reserved for Christian Indians. "I wanted all to see how well we were treated by Christian people," she explained.

The source of Sarah's conflict with Wilbur was his determination to prevent the Paiutes from leaving Yakama to return home. They were "woefully heart sick and grieving to death," her brother Lee reported. "They are continually brooding over their wrongs and pining to come back to their native country. They can talk of nothing else." Sarah hoped to raise public awareness of their plight with a series of lectures she gave in San Francisco late in 1878.

Her celebrity had increased after her exploits during the Bannock War were extensively chronicled in newspapers across the country; talks by the "Paiute Princess," as she was often called in the press, were eagerly received. "San Francisco was treated to the most novel entertainment it has ever known . . . in the shape of the address by Sarah, daughter of Chief Winnemucca, delivered in Platt's Hall," one columnist reported. "The lecture was unlike anything ever before heard in the civilized world—eloquent, pathetic, tragical at times; at others her quaint anecdotes, sarcasms and wonderful mimicry surprised the audience again and again in bursts of laughter and rounds of applause." She dazzled people with her proud bearing and stories about Paiute history, her childhood, the Bannock War, and the evils of the reservation system—particularly one of its cruelest representatives, William Rinehart. *The San Francisco Chronicle* noted wryly that "there was little left of the redoubtable Christian agent when she finished him."

After her successful tour of San Francisco, Sarah was invited by government officials to visit Washington, D.C. There, writes her biographer Gae Whitney Canfield, she "was to be confronted with a concerted effort to destroy her usefulness as a witness against the reservation system and the men who benefited from its bungling procedures." Sarah met several times with Secretary of the Interior Carl Schurz, who hoped to shut her up by making promises that would quickly be broken. He decreed that the Paiutes at Yakama would be allowed, but not compelled, to return home, and guaranteed that one hundred tents would be provided for those Paiutes still in Nevada. But he admonished her not to speak in Washington. "I don't think it will be right for you to lecture here after the government has sent for you, and your father and brother, and paid your way here," he said. "The government is going to do right by your people now. Don't lecture now; go home and get your people on the reservation; get them located properly; and then, if you want to come back . . . we will pay your way here and back again." After meeting with Schurz, Sarah had her disappointing encounter with President Hayes. Still, she managed to charm the capital, if not the Great White Father. "Dashing Sarah," wrote one reporter, "in intellect, grace and knowledge of the world, will compare favorably with many belles on Pennsylvania Avenue."

While Sarah was in Washington, William Rinehart was actively conspiring to ruin her reputation. He sent a petition and affidavits to the capital, signed by the "best men in the country," as he called them, but who were in reality his biased associates. "We have seen with amazement the charges brought against him [Rinehart] by an Indian woman calling herself Sarah Winnemucca," the petition read. It continued: "That her influence with the Indians has always been to render them licentious, contumacious and profligate. That this woman has been several times married, but that by reason of her adulterous and drunken habits, neither squawmen nor Indians would long live with her, that in addition to her character of Harlot and drunkard, she merits and possesses that of a notorious liar and malicious schemer." One of Rinehart's cohorts wrote that Sarah was "generally regarded by those who know her as a common prostitute and thoroughly addicted to the habits of drunkenness and gambling"; another stated that she "could be bought for a bottle of whiskey." Had Sarah been aware of these vicious smears, no doubt she would have confronted them. As it stood, though, Rinehart's campaign silently ate at her reputation like a cancer.

Sarah returned West to a hero's welcome from the Paiutes still in Nevada, who, she wrote, "came from far and near to hear of the wonderful father we had seen, how he looked and all about him." But the enthusiasm died when it became clear that the tents Schurz had promised would never arrive. In their eyes, Sarah had betrayed them. "What could we say?" she wrote. "We were only ashamed because we came and told them lies which the white people had told us." Adding to her shame, she learned upon her return that the *Silver State* had reported that she had been drunk at one of the lectures she gave before departing for the nation's capital. Sarah challenged the editor of the paper to a duel with pistols or knives "just to show him how a drunken woman can shoot." The indignant editor had her arrested, declaring,

"A drunken savage, who threatens to take the life's blood of a white person, should be given to understand that there is such a thing as jail in the community." The charges were eventually dismissed, but her troubles were far from finished.

She traveled to Yakama to bring the joyous news to her people that their exile was over, but encountered stiff resistance from Agent Wilbur when she arrived. He accused her of "putting the devil into [her] people's hands" and threatened to have her "put in irons and in prison." He then wrote to Washington and argued that the Paiutes should remain at Yakama lest their journey homeward be "the signal of warfare" to the settlers along the way. Schurz listened and his order was rescinded.

Sarah departed Yakama brokenhearted, but promised the Paiutes held there that she would work for them "while there was life in my body." General Howard offered her a position at Fort Vancouver in Washington, where she continued to agitate for her people and urged them to engage in what amounted to a strike. "Sarah Winnemucca finds frequent means to communicate with them," Wilbur reported, "urging them to take no steps and accept of nothing that can be contrived into a prospect of accepting this reservation as their home." While at Fort Vancouver, Sarah met again with President Hayes, who was visiting with his wife, Lucy. "I spoke to him as I done in Washington to the Secretary," she related, "and I said to him, 'You are a husband and father, and you know how you would suffer to be separated from your wife and children by force, as my people still are, husbands from wives, parents from children, notwithstanding Secretary Schurz's order.' Mrs. Hayes cried all the time I was talking, and he said, 'I will see about it.' But nothing was ever done that I heard of."

It would take Wilbur's resignation from Yakama for the Paiutes suffering there to finally gain their freedom. He was replaced in 1882 by the more humane Robert H. Milroy, who understood how miserable the Indians were at the reservation and how they would never consider it home. He looked the other way as they gradually escaped in small groups, and by the end of 1884, they were all gone.

In December 1881 Sarah married the last of her loser husbands,[3] a former soldier named Lewis H. Hopkins. Why she was so consistently attracted to white men remains a mystery. Sally Zanjani speculates that she was drawn to the exotic, as were the men she married. "Moreover," she writes, "for Sarah, who always cared deeply about her acceptance by whites and felt her repeated rejections so keenly, a white husband may have provided another item for her credentials, along with Methodism and her claim to a convent education."[4] There was also the fact that had she married within her race, she would have had to settle for the obscure domesticity of an Indian wife. "I would rather be with my people," she once told a reporter, "but not to live with them as they live." Whatever her reasons for marrying Hopkins, he would cause her no end of trouble.

The couple traveled to Boston in the spring of 1883. There Sarah came under the patronage of two elderly sisters, Elizabeth Palmer Peabody and Mary Mann, widow of the famed educator Horace Mann. The sisters encouraged Sarah to write about her experiences and helped prepare for publication *Life Among the Piutes: Their Wrongs and Claims*, the first book written by a Native American woman (and one of the earliest written by any Indian west of the Mississippi). "It is of the first importance to hear what only an Indian and an Indian woman can tell," Mann wrote. Through Peabody, who became her devoted friend, Sarah was introduced to many persons of influence, including Ralph

3. Her second husband was Joseph Satewaller, about whom little is known. She may have had more than three husbands, but the record is murky.

4. She claimed to have been enrolled in the San Jose convent school, though there is no record of her attendance.

Waldo Emerson and John Greenleaf Whittier. She also launched a wildly successful lecture tour of the East, speaking more than three hundred times in various cities. "She never repeated or contradicted herself once," Peabody wrote, "though it was obvious that except in the choice of some particular subject to be made her theme, she took no previous thought as to what she should say, but trusted that the right words would be given her by the 'Spirit Father,' whose special messenger she believed herself to be, and impressed her audiences to believe that she was."

The tour culminated in Washington, D.C., where Sarah met President Chester Arthur and Secretary of the Interior Henry Teller, both of whom proved no more helpful than their predecessors had been. "Their eyes aren't opened yet," she said at the time. She was also invited to testify before the House Subcommittee on Indian Affairs, where she eloquently pleaded for a permanent home for the Paiutes: "We have no reservation, no home, and now I ask you for my people to restore us and put us I do not care where as long as it is our own home, in the home where we were born, and that is all."

Casting a considerable pall over the otherwise successful tour was Sarah's husband Lewis Hopkins, who, before deserting her, disgraced her with his reckless gambling and by forging checks in the names of her supporters. She was forced to repay the money with funds raised for the Paiutes, leaving many with the impression that she was nothing but a huckster out to profit from her people's misery. "Poor dear Winnemucca," one New England supporter wrote to Elizabeth Peabody, "my heart aches for her, I fear that her husband's conduct will injure her *cause*. I hope that she . . . may find a quiet home under the protection of her brother out of the reach of her dishonest husband. I hope he will receive the imprisonment that his crime deserves that will make it impossible for him to follow her. . . . I fear her enemies will take advantage of his misconduct to prove that she is equally base & false."

Yet in spite of her husband's dishonesty, Sarah had accomplished much in the East. "Hers had been a remarkable journey," writes Zanjani, "walking out of the Stone Age where she was born into the parlors of the intellectual elite and the halls of Congress. In bringing the sufferings of a small and obscure Indian tribe to the attention of thousands, she had surely contributed to that sharp turn in American public opinion toward justice for Indians." Now all she wanted was to go home and teach.

Education for Indians at the time was based on a policy of eradication of the native culture and conversion to Christianity. "The Indian is DEAD in you," a commencement speaker at the Carlisle School in Pennsylvania said, expressing a general philosophy. "Let all that is Indian within you die! . . . You cannot become truly American citizens, industrious, intelligent, cultured, civilized until the INDIAN within you is DEAD." Sarah believed differently, and in 1885 she opened her own Native school on her brother's ranch outside the town of Lovelock, Nevada. She named it the Peabody Institute in honor of her friend Elizabeth, who devoted herself to raising funds for the school—a rather daunting task given the battering Sarah's reputation had taken courtesy of her husband, as well as William Rinehart's lingering campaign against her. Despite the difficulties, Sarah's humane and loving approach to education made the school a success. Louisa Marzen, a leading citizen of Lovelock, praised it after a visit in 1886. "When we neared the school shouts of merry laughter rang in our ears," she wrote to Elizabeth Peabody, "and little dark and sunburnt faces smiled a din of approval of our visitation." Marzen then went on to describe the accomplishments of Sarah's students:

Speaking in her native tongue [Sarah] requested the children to name all the visible objects, repeat the days of the week and months of the year, and calculate to the thousands, which they did in a most exemplary manner. Then she asked them to give a manifestation of their knowledge upon the black board, each in turn printing his name and spelling aloud. It is needless to say, Miss Peabody, that we were spellbound at the disclosure. Nothing but the most assiduous labor could have accomplished this work. But most amazingly did I rudely stare (and most of our party were quietly guilty of the same sin) when these seemingly ragged and untutored beings began singing gospel hymns *with precise melody, accurate time, and distinct punctuation. The blending of their voices in unison was grand, and an exceedingly sweet treat. We look upon it as a marvelous progression; and so gratified were we that we concluded to send this testimonial containing the names of those present, in order that you may know the good work [Sarah] is trying to consummate.*

As it was so often the case in Sarah Winnemucca's life, success was fleeting. Her school struggled from a lack of financial support by the government, which demanded assimilation in Indian education, and from her benefactors in the East, many of whom either distrusted her or had simply drifted to other causes. Furthermore, she lost her standing among her own people in favor of another Paiute named Wokova, who preached of the mystical Ghost Dance, which he claimed would bring the Indian dead back to life and restore the world to the native people. Many Paiutes withdrew their children from Sarah's school because of Wokova's prophecy that when the dead warriors returned, they would exterminate not only the whites but also those Indians who could speak or write English. Another blow was the sudden reappearance of Sarah's estranged husband, Lewis Hopkins. Before succumbing to tuberculosis in 1887, he stole the money earned from a bountiful harvest on her brother's ranch that might have saved the school. It wound up closing sometime in 1889.

Completely disillusioned, Sarah retreated to Henry's Lake, just south of the Idaho-Montana border near Yellowstone Park. There she died on October 17, 1891, at age forty-seven. The cause of her death remains a mystery,[5] and the precise location of her unmarked grave is unknown. "Let my name die out and be forgotten," she once said in despair, perhaps realizing that history has a tendency to do just that.

5. Some historians believe she died of tuberculosis; others that she killed herself. Sally Zanjani suggests that she may have been poisoned by her sister as a result of a romantic rivalry.

19

Alexander "Boss" Shepherd: The Man Who Made Washington "Worthy of the Nation"

The rat-hunting terriers stood at the ready on the night of September 3, 1872, eagerly waiting for the walls of the District of Columbia's Northern Liberties Market to come crumbling down. Despite vigorous protests by the people who made their living there, the decrepit and unsanitary old building at what is now Mount Vernon Square had been ordered demolished by Alexander "Boss" Shepherd, head of the city's Board of Public Works. No shopkeepers were going to stand in the way of progress. The Boss made certain of that. While his hastily assembled demolition crews set to work with their ropes and sledgehammers—releasing a horde of displaced rodents to the frenzied terriers—Shepherd was at his estate in the nation's capital entertaining the judge who might have otherwise issued an injunction against the work at hand. When the dust settled the next day, a sprawling eyesore was gone for good. But in the rubble were the corpses of a young boy, there to catch rats with his dog, and a butcher who had failed to clear out in time.

The human toll on this occasion was an aberration, but the incident was nevertheless typical of Shepherd's relentless—and sometimes ruthless—campaign to transform Washington, D.C., from muddy morass to grand metropolis. Just two months after the deaths at Northern Liberties Market, an unrepentant Shepherd orchestrated what was perhaps the most audacious move of his career. The Baltimore and Ohio Railroad had tracks running smack in the middle of improvement projects on Pennsylvania Avenue. Shepherd wanted them removed, but the railroad balked. Undaunted, he sent a crew of men to tear up the tracks under cover of night, and regrade the avenue to his specifications. "I did that without authority of law," Shepherd later recalled, "but it was the right thing to do, and the nuisance would not otherwise have been removed." John Garrett, B&O's president, was reportedly so impressed by Shepherd's nerve that he offered him a job as his vice president.

Boss Shepherd certainly knew how to get things done. During his tenure as head of public works and then as governor of the short-lived Territory of Columbia in 1873–74, the willful and imposing man almost unilaterally transformed the face of the nation's capital. With a wave of his hand, hills were leveled and gullies filled. Miles upon mile of sewers, sidewalks, and roads were laid. Street lamps were erected, new water mains and gas lines installed. City parks were created, and more than sixty thousand trees planted. The fetid Washington Canal, running along what is now Constitution Avenue, was mercifully filled, removing one of the city's most visible blights. Washington was on its way. "People who remember it as it was in the old days . . . can hardly believe that it has been transformed into the new and elegant city of today," one observor reported in 1875. "There is a constant demand for houses at increased rentage, while rents in other cities have fallen. New buildings are rising everywhere. . . . There is no question that the city of Washington is at the beginning of a long period of growth and prosperity, which in a few years will make it one of the most important, as it will be one of the most beautiful, cities in the Union."

★

Before Boss Shepherd came along, Washington was widely derided as one of the ugliest urban blights in the nation—"as melancholy and miserable a town as the mind of man can conceive," the English author Anthony Trollope wrote in 1860. Indeed, little had changed since another Englishman, Charles Dickens, slammed the city two decades before: "It is sometimes called the City of Magnificent Distances, but it might with greater propriety be termed the City of Magnificent Intentions . . . Spacious avenues that begin in nothing and lead nowhere; streets, miles long, that only want houses, roads, and inhabitants; public buildings that need but a public to be complete; and ornaments of great thoroughfares, which only lack great thoroughfares to ornament—are its leading features."

The Civil War had doubled Washington's population, but the city itself remained an unsightly backwater, with muddy streets, open sewers, and disease-ridden slums. William Tindall, a local official, later recalled that there were "in every part of the city . . . hog pens . . . many cow sheds . . . chicken, geese and cows roamed at large . . . Scavenger service offended both sense and sentiment, the most noisome kind of offal and refuse were dumped daily on the surface of the common."

One of the worst areas was around what is now Washington's monumental core. "Here crime, filth and poverty seem to vie in a career of degradation and death," one police report read. "Whole families are crowded into mere apologies for shanties, which are without light and ventilation."

Major Nathaniel Michler of the Army Corps of Engineers headed an office in charge of the city's public buildings and grounds after the war, and issued a report that criticized some of the more offensive aspects of the nation's capital—including the ones that Boss Shepherd would soon tackle. The Northern Liberties Market, for example, was "unsightly . . . an intolerable nuisance . . . on market days the most offensive matter accumulates in the adjoining streets, greatly detrimental to the health of the residents . . . vegetable matter . . . offal from the stall of the butcher . . . filth created by animals . . . causing a most disagreeable stench . . . engendering sickness." As for the streets that Shepherd would have paved, Michler wrote: "There is scarcely a street or avenue in the city over which one can drive with ease and comfort. . . . [Parts of Pennsylvania Avenue] become almost impassible, either from the effects of weather, or being cut up by the immense amount of travel over them."

Washington was in such sorry shape that there was talk, as after the burning of the city by the British in 1814, of moving the nation's capital. St. Louis, in fact, even held a convention in 1869 to vie for the honor. And proposals for a major Centennial celebration in the capital were greeted with howls of derision. Senator William M. Steward of Nevada called Washington "the ugliest city in the whole country," and declared, "The idea of inviting the world to see this town, with its want of railroads and its muddy streets, seems to me altogether out of the question."

Clearly it would take a man of enormous strength and will to make the city, as President Grant said before Congress, "worthy of the nation."

★

The boy who would be Boss was born January 31, 1835, in the city's Southwest quadrant, which was then cut off from the rest of Washington by that foul-smelling canal Shepherd would later have filled. Only thirteen when he was forced to drop out of school to help support his mother and six siblings after the death of his father, young Alexander worked a series of jobs, ranging from store boy to carpenter's apprentice, before landing a place

at the city's leading plumbing and gas-fitting firm at age seventeen. He quickly rose from head bookkeeper to partner to owner.
After a brief stint with a local militia during the Civil War, Shepherd married and then purchased a 300-acre estate at what is now
Northwest Washington's Shepherd Park neighborhood. He also
got very rich in real estate, building, by some estimates, 1,500
homes in about ten years. This gained him entree into the clubs
and saloons of the Washington elite. President Ulysses S. Grant
became a pal, local politics a passion.

In 1871 Congress created a territorial form of government for
the District of Columbia—a blend of local and federal partic-
ipation, with the most powerful positions subject to presidential appointment. Shepherd was hoping his friend Grant would
make him governor. Instead, he was appointed to the newly
created Board of Public Works, which he quickly made his personal kingdom. This coup of sorts was abetted by the fact that
Governor Henry D. Cooke, who also served as nominal president of the Board of Public Works, was otherwise preoccupied
by the banking business, taking little interest in the territory he
was appointed to run. "Why is Governor Cooke like a sheep?"
went a popular joke at the time. "Because he is led around by
A. Shepherd."

Using his new office to the best advantage, Shepherd immediately commenced massive improvement projects. The pace was
frantic, and money was no object. Hundreds of workers, many of
them friends and supporters, were added to the city payrolls. Huge
tax increases were ordered, to howls of protest. Construction
chaos often ruled. While streets were being leveled and graded,
for example, some houses were left sitting high above the road,
while others sank well beneath it, a situation that is still apparent
on some streets around the city today.

The board received plenty of complaints. Banker William
Corcoran, one of Washington's richest and most powerful men

(and benefactor of the art museum that today bears his name), was enraged when his home was damaged during the laying of sewer lines. In another case, a woman fell into a giant street hole on F Street NW. "I . . . was in an instant precipitated into the deep mud and water to my waist," she wrote in her complaint to Shepherd, "and the more I attempted to extricate myself, the deeper I got into the mire. . . . When I returned to the house I found all my clothing except my hat quite ruined."

Others were angered by Shepherd's high-handed, occasionally subversive methods of doing business. One newspaper even compared him to New York's infamous swindler, William "Boss" Tweed. Cronyism and corruption were rampant. It did not go unnoticed, for example, that the destruction of the Northern Liberties Market could only benefit Shepherd's own Central Market a short distance away. In addition, many complained that most of the great improvements were focused on the increasingly fashionable Northwest section, where Shepherd and his associates had substantial holdings.

Shepherd dismissed his critics, especially Washington's old-line property owners and unreconstructed Democrats, as political opportunists hoping to undermine President Grant and the Republicans through him. What he could not ignore, though, was Congress. His unchecked spending had not gone unnoticed, and he would have to answer for it on Capitol Hill.

A series of congressional investigations revealed the enormous sums that had been spent. Shepherd, who had been promoted to territorial governor in 1873, acknowledged that he had exceeded the city's debt limit, but had done nothing illegal. Congress, though outraged over all the money spent, took no action against him. One member of the investigating committee, Senator William Allison of Iowa, noted that while the territorial government was rife with mismanagement, he was "sorry that Shepherd was temporarily sacrificed as he had done so much for the city. He can afford to wait, however, as no stain is cast on his honor or integrity by the investigation or report." The District, on the other hand, lost whatever measure of independence it had gained when Congress abolished the territorial democracy in 1874. Home rule would not return for another century.

Despite Senator Allison's reassuring words, Shepherd's reputation in Washington had been sorely battered, and the specter of misused funds hung about him for years. He declared bankruptcy two years after leaving office. "I had failed," he later recalled, "and a man who is down cannot easily command the support of his friends. I concluded that I would endeavor to strike out anew."

In 1880 the fallen Boss and his family moved to Mexico, where he owned a failing silver mine. His legacy in Washington remained, however, garnering almost universal praise. *Harper's New Monthly Magazine* was particularly effusive in 1875, noting how the streets were "covered with the most noiseless and perfect pavements in the world, and embowered in the greenest borders of grass-plots, enclosed with panels of post and chain or graceful palings, and planted with trees. . . . At all points of junction new squares and circles appeared, their verdure relieved with flashing fountains, or bits of statuary, or effects in sodded terraces, all ready for the sculptor."

The city itself gave belated tribute to the man who had changed its fortunes when Shepherd was given a grand homecoming in 1887. Among the festivities were a parade up Pennsylvania Avenue and a reception for six thousand at the Willard Hotel. The *Evening Star* heralded him as "the man who redeemed and beautified Washington and came out of office a poor man." "It was a question of national pride," Shepherd said at the time, "but there were some old fogies here at the time who couldn't, or wouldn't, see it."

After Shepherd's death in 1902, further tributes came, capped by the unveiling of his statue on Pennsylvania Avenue. But as his fortunes fluctuated in life, so they did in death. After standing grandly in front of the District Building for seven decades, Shepherd's statue was removed in 1979 to make way for the refurbishment of the avenue. For years it was stored far away from the heart of Washington, in an obscure location near the city's sewage treatment facility. Finally, in 2005 the Boss was rightly restored to his place of honor in the capital he had helped make among the most magnificent in the world, and indeed "worthy of the nation."

20

Isaac C. Parker: "The Hanging Judge"

The crimes were heinous, even by the lawless standards of the Wild West. Daniel Evans, a young Texan, had shot his traveling companion in the head and made off with his horse, saddle, and boots. William Whittington slashed his friend's throat and robbed him of $100 while the victim's son watched in horror. Horse thief James Moore murdered a deputy marshal and boasted that the lawman was "the eighth man I've killed—niggers and Indians I don't count." Smoker Mankiller, an eighteen-year-old Cherokee, borrowed his neighbor's new Winchester rifle and then, for no apparent reason, shot him with it. Samuel Fooy robbed and killed an itinerant schoolteacher in the Cherokee Nation. And Edmund "Heck" Campbell resolved a dispute with one Lawson Ross by shooting the man and his mistress after a prayer meeting. All six murderers were condemned to swing together on the same gallows by Isaac C. Parker, the "Hanging Judge" who came to personify rough frontier justice.

"I sentence you to hang by the neck until you are dead, dead, dead," Parker reportedly said to Evans, the first man he ever condemned, as the judge's eyes filled with tears. To Smoker Man-killer he pronounced, "The sword of human justice is about to fall upon your guilty head." And in an address to Campbell, Parker stated in biblical tones, "Your fate is inevitable. . . . Let me, therefore, beg of you to fly to your Maker for that mercy and pardon which you cannot expect from mortals . . . and endeavor to seize upon the salvation of the cross." On September 3, 1875, before an estimated crowd of five thousand, the sentences were carried out on a gallows built for six at Fort Smith, Arkansas. Over the next two decades, seventy-three more men, in various combinations, would meet a similar fate under Parker's judicial maxim: "Permit no innocent man to suffer; let no guilty man escape."

The much-feared judge presided over a unique federal court at Fort Smith: the U.S. District Court for the Western District of Arkansas, known by some as "the Court of the Damned." Its jurisdiction encompassed a staggering seventy-four thousand square miles, the largest in the nation, and included not only eighteen counties in Arkansas, but the entire Indian Territory to the west in what is now Oklahoma. Because of its sheer size and remoteness, criminals of every kind found ample refuge in the territory that had been set aside for displaced Native Americans and divided into separate "nations" for the "Five Civilized Tribes": Creek, Cherokee, Seminole, Chickasaw, and Choctaw. The vast majority of offenses tried at Fort Smith were "crimes committed in the Indian country by . . . refugee criminals from every state in the Union," Parker later wrote. And though he labored for over twenty years to "establish the supremacy of law in the Indian country," he was ultimately unsuccessful. The job was simply too onerous. Parker did his best, though. Over the course of his tenure—from his appointment at age thirty-seven by President Ulysses Grant in 1875 to his death in 1896—more than 12,800 cases were docketed, most of them criminal. He may have exaggerated when he wrote that more "desperados, murderers and outlaws" had been "brought to merited justice . . . than in any other courts in the world," but he certainly proved himself a committed force for law and order.

Parker, a Civil War veteran and two-term congressman from Missouri, arrived at Fort Smith after his appointment as a man on a mission—not only to tackle the lawlessness that infested the Indian Territory, but to restore the reputation of the notoriously corrupt court over which he was to preside. Five marshals and three district attorneys had been removed from office during the prior eight years, and Parker's predecessor, William Story, had been facing impeachment when he resigned in 1874. Diligent attention to his duties and swift justice quickly earned the new judge respect from a skeptical community. Just a week after his arrival in May, Parker opened court and tackled the enormous backlog of cases left by the ineffectual Story. That September the first six convicted murderers were hanged together. Another batch of five soon followed, and the fearsome reputation of the Hanging Judge was launched.

Executions at Fort Smith were public affairs where thousands gathered, many from distant parts, to witness the grisly spectacle of death. A carnival-like atmosphere pervaded. People brought picnics; hawkers sold whiskey and souvenirs. The condemned were taken from the squalid prison in the courthouse basement known as "Hell on the Border"[1] and led in chains to the gallows.

---

1. Attorney General Augustus Hill Garland called it "the most miserable prison, probably, in the whole country." It was replaced by a new, much-improved facility in 1889, partly as a result of Parker's efforts. The judge, despite his harsh reputation, was a strong advocate for prison reform. The purpose of imprisonment should be "to lift a man up," he wrote, "to stamp out his bad nature . . . and so govern and direct him that he becomes a good citizen, of use to himself and his fellow man."

On the scaffold their death warrants were read, after which the doomed men were given the opportunity to speak their last words. Some were contrite; others defiant. James Moore, for one, surveyed the crowd in front of him and declared, "There are worse men here than me." Many were too paralyzed by fear to speak at all. As local clergy led the crowd in hymns and prayers, black hoods were placed over the heads of the condemned and the nooses adjusted around their necks by George Maledon, the so-called "Prince of Hangmen" who presided over nearly all the executions during Judge Parker's tenure. The trapdoor was then sprung.

Although Maledon took great pride in the skill and technique he brought to his job—importing handwoven hemp from St. Louis, which he oiled and impregnated with pitch to avoid slippage—not all the criminals were dispatched efficiently. Indeed, some struggled and convulsed for five minutes or more before they finally breathed their last. Nineteen men died in front of huge crowds before a wall was erected around the gallows to keep executions more private. Thus, potential onlookers were spared such ghastly episodes as the hour-long strangulation of Edward Fulsome in 1882, and the near decapitation of John Thorton a decade later. Still, newspapers could always be relied upon to report the lurid details of executions the public could no longer see.

Judge Parker has often been portrayed as a man who relished sending other men to the gallows, watching their executions with grim satisfaction from a courthouse window. Although he did hand down more death sentences than any other American judge, he presided over an enormous district where an extraordinary number of capital crimes were committed. The law mandated the ultimate punishment in cases of murder and rape, which left Parker no options in his sentencing, and at the end of his life he professed to favor the abolition of the death penalty—as long as there was "a certainty of punishment."

Until 1889, there was no appeal in capital cases from the Western District of Arkansas,[2] and the condemned could only hope for a presidential commutation or a pardon. Parker frequently supported applications for executive clemency, which suggests he may not have been as bloodthirsty as people believed. On the other hand, he was often indignant when clemency was granted against his wishes. And, if he really was opposed to the death penalty, he nevertheless seemed to favor the prosecution in those cases where it would be applied, particularly with his often biased jury instructions. "Juries should be led," he wrote. "They have a right to expect that, and if guided will render that justice that is the greatest pillar of society." Or, as his critics complained, that justice demanded by Parker.

Though Judge Parker's reputation rests largely on the capital cases he heard, they were only a small percentage of those that came through his courtroom—the busiest criminal tribunal in the federal system.[3] A small army of deputy marshals patrolled the Indian Territory and followed the judge's admonition to "bring [outlaws] in alive—or dead!" Many deputies were killed while performing their duties in the territory (a "Golgotha to [law] officers," as Parker once called it), and a few, like the infamous Dalton brothers, became criminals themselves. Among the horde of thieves, smugglers, bigamists, and embezzlers hauled into Fort Smith, one of the most notorious was the "Bandit Queen" Belle

---

2. This anomaly arose from a congressional oversight: When lawmakers established the Western Judicial District of Arkansas, they neglected to create a separate circuit court to rule on applications for new trials. Parker exercised this power and as a result was not inclined to grant motions for new trials that were based on his own district court decisions.

3. This court heard relatively few civil cases, mostly because the great distances potential litigants in the Indian Territory had to travel to bring suit in Fort Smith discouraged them. Parker himself expressed his contempt for "controversies between man and man" on a number of occasions: "Avarice," he said, "which is the curse of the age, has so poisoned the people that civil law for the protection of property concerns it more than the criminal law which protects life."

Starr, who frequently stood as a defendant before Parker (and with whom he reportedly participated in a mock stagecoach robbery during a local Wild West exhibition in 1886).

The rampant lawlessness in the Indian Territory was not caused by its legal Indian inhabitants, Parker always said, but by white interlopers who exploited them and their land. Indeed, the vast majority of crimes committed in the territory were violations of the Intercourse Act of 1834, which sought to protect Native Americans from whiskey peddlers, unauthorized hunters, coal thieves, timber poachers, and other such intruders. Tribal courts in the five Nations were not permitted to try whites, and Parker saw his court as the only shield against crime and exploitation that the Indians in his jurisdiction could rely upon. "The territory was set apart for the Indians in 1828," he said. "The government of that time promised them protection. That promise has been ignored. The only protection that has ever been afforded them is through the courts. To us who have been located on this borderland, has fallen the task of acting as protectors."

Yet while Parker maintained, with all the paternalism typical of the time, that his court had guarded Indian rights and "aided them in their journey along the pathway to civilization," many of his rulings demonstrated his conviction that the U.S. government held ultimate authority over them. "Time and again he ruled against the Five Civilized Tribes," writes historian Roger H. Tuller, "declaring that they could not prevent the construction of railroads across their lands, denying their rights to extradite criminals or to try adopted citizens. In fact, Parker contributed to the diminution of tribal self-determination and hastened the territorial status [of Oklahoma] that he stridently opposed by consistently undermining American Indian sovereignty." It was one of many peculiar contradictions in this remarkable judge. His allegiance to rule of law, and his apparent contempt for it, was another.

For the first fifteen years of his tenure at Fort Smith, Parker was the most powerful district judge in the nation. His decisions were final, and those sentenced in his court had no right to appeal. In 1888, however, a series of bills were introduced in Congress that would curb the judge's authority and allow appeals of capital convictions to the Supreme Court. Senator James K. Jones of Arkansas declared that "the commonest principles of humanity" demanded that "this anomaly in our judicial system" be changed to provide a "remedy for what seems to be an outrageous wrong." He was echoed by Senator George G. Vest of Missouri, an outspoken critic of Parker's, who said that "for years men have been executed without any right to ask the Supreme Court of the United States whether it be judicial murder or not." Although President Grover Cleveland killed one bill with a pocket veto, a nearly identical one passed in both Houses the following year and became law without the president's signature. Parker's nearly absolute power had been broken. Coinciding with this, his court's jurisdiction in the Indian Territory was gradually reduced until it was abolished altogether in 1896. For the judge who saw himself and his court as the only bulwark against chaos in the troubled region—and who had gotten rather used to operating with near autonomy—these developments were intolerable. And he lashed out fiercely at the system that imposed them.

Beginning in 1890, the Supreme Court remanded nearly two-thirds of capital appeals from Fort Smith for new trials, often because of the judge's leading jury instructions, which tended to favor the prosecution. This enraged Parker, who contemptuously ignored admonitions from his superiors in the Justice Department to modify his instructions, and decried the Supreme Court's "mania for reversing murder cases" as well as its ignorance of criminal matters. He viewed the appellate process as a hindrance to the imposition of law and order in his jurisdiction—his way. It destroyed the "effect of trial, conviction, and punishment," he wrote in one of his many screeds, and gave comfort to dangerous criminals.

The judge gave full vent to his anger and frustration in 1895, when an outlaw named Crawford Goldsby, better known as "Cherokee Bill," killed a guard while in prison awaiting a decision on the appeal of a murder conviction. The Supreme Court was responsible for the guard's death, Parker fumed in an interview with the *St. Louis Globe-Democrat*, as well as for the general upsurge in crime. The appeals process allowed condemned convicts a "long breathing spell" before the high court heard their cases, allowing murderers like Goldsby the opportunity to kill again. And, Parker charged, when the justices overturned convictions, they "always" did so "upon the flimsiest of technicalities."

Judge Parker's final years on the bench at Fort Smith were not happy ones. His rants in the press continued as what he perceived as his life's work was unraveled by a gradually shrinking jurisdiction and an appeals process that severely undermined "the certainty of punishment" he so valued. After one particularly vitriolic newspaper exchange with Solicitor General Edward B. Whitney, whom he called a "legal imbecile" who knew "absolutely nothing of criminal law," Parker was reprimanded by Attorney General Judson Harmon for his general conduct. "I do not doubt your ability or devotion," Harmon wrote, "but it is quite apparent that you are . . . disposed to be insubordinate and not yield fully to . . . the Supreme Court."

Despite Parker's best efforts for more than twenty years, crime continued unabated in the Indian Territory. On July 30, 1896, James C. Casharego became the seventy-ninth and last man to be hanged during the judge's tenure at Fort Smith. Casharego had killed his traveling companion in the Creek Nation, and tried to cover up the crime by dumping the body into a creek and setting a fire on the spot where the victim had bled to death. The earth was dry, however, and some of the blood had seeped into cracks. Deputies dug up several samples of the tainted soil, which were then introduced at Casharego's trial. He was duly convicted. "Even nature revolted against your crime," Parker told the condemned man. "The earth opened and drank up the blood, held it in a fast embrace until the time it should appear against you; the water, too, threw up its dead and bore upon its placid bosom the foul evidence of your crime."

Time and disappointment had not diminished Parker's voice of righteous indignation, and as if harking back to when the judge's sentences were final, the Supreme Court rejected Casharego's appeal. A month after the execution, the Western District's jurisdiction over the Indian Territory ended. Soon after that, on November 17, 1896, the Hanging Judge died at age fifty-eight. "I am glad to have the honor of knowing this alleged cruel judge," a reporter wrote shortly before Parker's death. "It is darkly, indeed, the press and people view him through the glass of distance."

21

Hetty Green:
"The Witch of Wall Street"

The elderly lady made her way from the sparsely furnished flat she rented in Hoboken to the ferry that would take her to New York. Beneath her faded, outdated black dress were newspapers she used as leg warmers and a revolver she carried for protection. Upon docking, she rode a streetcar to the Broadway offices of the Chemical National Bank, where she tended to her financial affairs. It was a routine that rarely varied. Sometimes she carried a pail of dry oatmeal to which she would later add water and heat over a radiator for lunch. Other days she ate at a local restaurant and, almost without fail, haggled over the price. She never tipped.

"Her appearance would never cause the uninitiated to think she was anything more than an old fashioned woman of moderate means and simple tastes," one newspaper reported. "Yet, if money is power, this same staid looking person is one of the most powerful human beings in the country."

Hetty Robinson Green was indeed the richest woman in America, and perhaps the world. With a vast real estate and railroad empire, her fortune rivaled that of Rockefeller, Vanderbilt,

Astor, and Carnegie. Yet while those giants of finance and industry gave the Gilded Age its name with their lavish spending,
Hetty Green's penuriousness was legendary. Here was a woman,
wealthy enough to have rescued New York City from financial
ruin, who once spent hours in search of a missing two-cent
stamp. Her real estate holdings stretched across the continent,
yet she lived in near squalor and dressed in such shabby, old-
fashioned garb that people dubbed her "the Witch of Wall Street."
Her meanness with money was rivaled only by her genius for
making it.

It was a fortune built on a rich inheritance. Hetty's father,
Edward Mott Robinson, had grown wealthy in whaling and
shipping, and it was at his feet that she learned the fundamentals
of finance. "When quite a child I was required to read reports of
the stock markets and of various business transactions to my father who would carefully explain to me those things I did not
understand," Hetty told *Harper's Bazaar* in 1900. "I was obliged
to keep a strict account of personal and household expenses. All
these things were most useful in forming the mind for business
responsibilities when it became necessary to assume them." When
he died in 1865 Edward Robinson left his daughter a large fortune and an enduring philosophy. "My father taught me never to
owe anyone anything," she said. "Not even a kindness."

Hetty also stood to inherit a significant amount of money from
her late mother's side of the family in the person of her invalid aunt
Sylvia. She was determined not to see one dime of it wasted. When
Sylvia decided at one point to put an addition on her home to
house the staff required to take care of her, Hetty went ballistic.
The young heiress, who saw the addition as an extravagant misuse
of *her* money, dropped to the floor in protest and, according to
one servant on the scene, "cried and boo-hooed the night out."
Her snit lasted for weeks; as she wrote in a letter, "It will take me
two years at least to get over the shock."

As offensive as the addition was to Hetty's miserly sensibilities, she was in for an even bigger jolt when Aunt Sylvia died and left a portion of her estate to her caretakers, as well as to various civic and charitable organizations. Hetty believed she was entitled to every penny and sued to have Sylvia's will overturned. Though she lost the celebrated case—during which she produced a codicil to the will supporting her claims, with Aunt Sylvia's allegedly forged signature fixed upon it—she was still left a very wealthy woman. In time she would make herself infinitely richer.

Both her father's and her aunt's estates were held in trust, which galled Hetty to no end, but the income they produced was substantial and allowed her ample opportunities for investment. She started buying up "greenback" notes printed in large quantities by the U.S. government after the Civil War to cover its enormous expenditures. Most people were apprehensive about the economic prospects of the newly reunited nation, and abandoned the government notes in favor of gold. "Here was an excellent chance for any far-seeing person to pick up government securities at half their value," wrote John T. Flynn in his book *Men of Wealth*. "All it required was a little faith in the nation that had just demonstrated in a most extraordinary way its ability to come through a terrible civil war." Hetty had faith few others shared. She gobbled up greenbacks as well as railroad bonds to finance that rapidly expanding enterprise, and quickly quadrupled her fortune. Soon she was wealthier than many banks, and when those institutions needed cash they sold Hetty loans they had made to people who often used property as collateral. Anytime a borrower defaulted, Hetty acquired the property, and in the process laid the foundation of her real estate empire.

The New York Times asserted in a 1909 article that most women made bad investors, except Hetty. She has a "masculine instinct for finance," the newspaper stated. "She has a broader grasp of finance than many men in the Street, and her views of the values of railroads and real estate are always worth having. She makes her investments in the logical way a man does, and she usually makes wise ones." Sexism aside, *The Times* was right. Hetty was a formidable figure in a man's world—a world in which she felt she had no allies and had to rely on her own strength and instincts. "She was a free agent in the truest sense of the term," writes her biographer Charles Slack, "and anyone going into a deal assuming he had Hetty Green in his corner, or that she could be pushed, harassed, or cowed into going along with a crowd, learned difficult and expensive lessons to the contrary."

Hetty's business prowess was vividly demonstrated in 1886, when a group of New York investors set out to take over the stagnating Georgia Central Railroad. They began buying up stock with the aim of installing their own managers and directors, but met with stiff resistance from the Georgians, who viewed the investors as a band of Yankee plunderers. Hetty learned of the takeover plan in its earliest stages and began to buy stock in the railroad at about $70 a share. Soon she held 6,700 shares, a significant voting block in the upcoming directors' election.

As the battle between the investors and the railroad became increasingly bitter, and the stock rose to $100 a share, Hetty remained aloof. She knew her shares would become more valuable as the election approached. Sure enough, the nervous investors feared a tight race and wanted Hetty's voting block to help ensure a victory. They offered her $115 for each of her shares, a hefty price for the already inflated stock, but she boldly countered at $125, confident that the investors needed her. They initially balked, but eventually agreed to her price—under the condition that the transaction would take place after the election and that Hetty would promise to vote their way. She would then get her money, regardless of the outcome of the election or the price of the stock. The investors believed it was an offer she would find irresistible, but they didn't know Hetty. "If I have to wait for my money," she declared, "the price is $130." Stunned by this stubborn woman, they countered at $127.50. She agreed and the deal was done. The investors won the election, while Hetty walked away with a fat profit.

Nothing was more important to Hetty Green than her fortune, not even her family. Her husband, Edward, learned this in 1885 when the bank where they both kept their money, John J. Cisco and Son, faced a financial crisis. Hetty demanded that her cash deposit of $550,000 be transferred immediately to another bank. Officials at Cisco demurred, however, informing their largest creditor that her husband happened to be the bank's largest debtor, owing in excess of $700,000. Outraged, Hetty argued that her husband's financial affairs were no concern of hers. She continued to demand her money and threatened to sue if she didn't get it. Unable to honor such a massive withdrawal, the bank closed its doors. Hetty now faced the implacable assignee of the failed bank, Lewis May. Though the millions in securities she kept at Cisco were not part of the bank's assets, May nevertheless held them hostage. He informed Hetty that he would be happy to release them as soon as she honored her husband's debt. In a scene reminiscent of the Aunt Sylvia episode, Hetty screamed, stomped, and cried, to no avail. Forced to concede at last, she gritted her teeth and wrote the check that freed her fortune but doomed her marriage: Like Cisco and Son, it collapsed. Edward Green's insolvency had effected her financially, and that was unforgivable.

Hetty's son, Ned, learned a painful lesson about the limits of his mother's love, too. He had injured his leg as a young boy, which caused a painful limp that grew steadily worse over the years. Ned's agony became so great that it briefly distracted his mother from the stock market. She was determined to find the best medical care for the young man—so long as it didn't cost her anything. Dressed as a pauper, as she customarily did when she wanted free medical treatment,[1] Hetty marched her limping son to all the free clinics in Manhattan and Brooklyn. Alas, she was recognized everywhere and was unceremoniously shooed away. Having exhausted all possibilities for medical charity, she was forced to call a specialist who advised immediate amputation of the now gangrenous leg. Hetty wasn't buying it.

"Mamma still felt there was a chance to save my leg," Ned later recalled, without apparent bitterness. "We both wanted this, of course. We didn't have much faith in doctors and believed, given time, the limb would heal itself." But Hetty's remedies of "oil of squills" and Carter's Little Liver Pills didn't do the trick, and the leg came off. The doctor determined that the limb might have been saved had the injuries been treated sooner. Fittingly, it was Hetty's banished, bankrupted husband who paid for the operation.

Hetty kept her son financially crippled as well. Though she decreed that her enormous fortune would go to Ned and his sister upon her death, which it did, she maintained absolute dominance over them while she lived. Even after she installed Ned as president of a Texas railroad, she still controlled the purse strings, as this rather pathetic letter attests: "Dear Mamma, I am 25 years old today. I think you might send me money so I could go to the [World's] Fair at Chicago in about two weeks before the fall rush comes. It would only cost about $200. I can get passes to Chicago and return. Let me know as soon as you can so I can get ready. I want to see the fair *so* bad. Please let me go."

---

1. A physician named J. H. Brudenshaw described Hetty's abuses of the system in an 1898 speech before the Medico-Legal Society that was quoted at length in *The New York Times:* "That woman put on an old gown and worked upon the sympathies of the attending physician to such an extent that out of sheer pity he advised her to come to his private office, where he could give her better treatment and save her the trouble of the long waits. She gladly accepted, and for a considerable time came to the physician's house, where he gave her the best of treatment absolutely free of charge!"

Hetty's tactics have been described by some of her more sympathetic biographers as a means to avoid being overcharged because of her wealth.

Poor Ned Green, along with his sister, Sylvia, finally inherited his mother's vast wealth when Hetty died in 1916 at age eighty-one. After years of deprivation, he lived lavishly and spent a good chunk of Hetty's carefully hoarded fortune before his own death in 1936. Neither Ned nor his sister left any heirs, and within a few generations most of the money was dispersed. Now all that remains of Hetty Green's legacy is the dubious distinction she received in the *Guinness Book of World Records* as the world's greatest miser.

22

Oliver Curtis Perry: Outlaw of the East

Some outlaws live forever as icons of wayward Americana. Others flare briefly in the collective imagination and then, for whatever reason, simply fade away. So it was with Oliver Curtis Perry, one of the boldest and most charismatic of these forgotten bandits, who captivated the nation at the end of the nineteenth century when he introduced a little of the Wild West to the otherwise civilized East.

On the night of September 29, 1891, the New York Central freight train known as the American Express Special was steaming toward the city of Utica when a hooded intruder suddenly appeared inside the so-called "money car," which contained cash, bonds, and other valuables protected by an armed guard. "It's money I'm after," shouted the bandit, brandishing two guns. "Quick, we're getting near to Utica!" With that he fired a shot past the guard, disarmed him, and ordered him to open one of the safes on board. He then stuffed a canvas bag full of loot and slithered back through the small hole he had cut to enter the car. The speeding train suddenly ground to a stop, its air-brake hose apparently severed by the brazen thief who escaped into the night with a fortune.

WILD WESTERN WAYS IN THE EMPIRE STATE! screamed a headline in the *New York Herald,* while Joseph Pulitzer's *New York World* expressed shock over the audacious crime: "A train held up right in the heart of the Empire State! And this on one of the most frequented roads in the Union—the New York Central! It seems almost incredible that such wild Western methods could be successfully practiced in the centre of civilization without a trace being left as to the perpetrators of such a daring deed; yet such is a fact."

The American Express Company, which owned the plundered money car, immediately retained the services of the famed Pinkerton National Detective Agency to catch the thief. The agency had plenty of experience dealing with train robbers in the West, but this case presented the Pinkertons with a unique challenge. "The man who committed the train robbery here is one of the nerviest I ever heard of," wrote George Bangs, the agency's New York manager, to Robert Pinkerton. "There are few if any men who possess the daredevil courage to accomplish what this train robber did yesterday."

After weeks of investigation the elusive outlaw was finally identified as Oliver Curtis Perry, a twenty-six-year-old railroad worker living in Troy, New York, and now a sudden celebrity on the run. People were fascinated not only by Perry's bold exploits, but by what kind of man he might be. Photographs circulated during the manhunt showed him to be quite handsome, with an expression that suggested an enigmatic mixture of troubled sensitivity and a certain roguish charm. Conflicting accounts of his character made him seem more mysterious. The Pinkertons described him as a ruthless criminal, yet some prominent citizens of Troy defended the man they had come to know as religiously devoted, hardworking, and determined to leave his difficult past behind.

Adding to his allure were unsubstantiated rumors of his munificence toward the poor, some of whom supposedly found stolen cash and jewelry left on their doorsteps. And he was gallant, too. When the guard on board the looted train was suspected of assisting in the crime, Perry wrote a letter to the authorities and declared himself solely responsible. The elusive thief was quickly becoming a legend.

"Perry became the object of the day-dreams and fantasies of men, women and children: a man you might want to be, or be with, or become," writes his biographer Tamsin Spargo. "Handsome, boyish, clever and honorable, he now became for some people a latter-day Robin Hood, a worthy successor to Jesse James, an eastern outlaw to rival any the west could boast." And he was about to strike again.

Just five months after pulling off the spectacular heist aboard the American Express Special, Perry did something even more astonishing: He hit the very same train! This time, however, the robbery didn't go quite so smoothly. He found there was no cash in the money car, only jewelry and silver that would be difficult, given his fugitive status, to sell. Furthermore, he wounded American Express guard Daniel McInerney in an exchange of fire, but not before McInerney was able to alert the conductor by pulling on an air-whistle cord. Now Perry had to make a quick escape, empty-handed. He climbed atop the roof of the train as it approached the town of Port Byron, then dropped off the side just before it reached the station. While the train was being searched, Perry kept hidden behind some stationary cars, replacing his hood with the gentleman's attire he had been wearing when he originally slipped aboard the Special in Syracuse. With the thief nowhere in sight and presumably long gone, the train departed Port Byron. Just before it did, Perry emerged from his hiding place and crept back on board. It was a brilliant ploy. And it almost worked.

When the Express arrived at its next stop at the village of Lyons, Perry jumped off on the opposite side of the station platform and snuck along the tracks away from the depot. Then, when he reached the road that led to the station, he turned around and casually walked back as if he was there to buy a ticket or meet a passenger. Only problem was, the Express conductor remembered the well-dressed young man after seeing him at the station in Syracuse and realized there was no way he could have made it to Lyons so quickly unless he were aboard the American Express Special, which didn't carry passengers. He had to be the thief, the conductor concluded, and alerted some railroad workers on the scene. They immediately rushed toward Perry, but abruptly stopped when he leveled his guns at them. An extraordinary chase ensued.

Perry backed away from the platform and onto the tracks, where a westbound coal trail awaited the signal to depart. Unhitching the train's engine, he ordered the engineer and fireman off the cab and then thrust it into motion. The railmen watching the scene were momentarily stunned, but quickly gathered themselves. One grabbed a rifle while the others uncoupled the Express engine to give chase. Several miles into the pursuit, the railmen were close to overtaking the engine Perry had commandeered. It was then that the desperate bandit slammed on the brakes, threw the cab into reverse, and started hurtling backward toward the Express. Guns blazed as Perry and his pursuers faced one another in a railroad duel. The trainmen ran out of ammunition, however, and rather than risk confronting the robber unarmed, they retreated back to Lyons. Their quarry then proceeded west, only to find he was quickly losing steam—he hadn't kept the engine stoked during the chase. Abandoning the cab at a place called Blue Cut, he raced up an embankment and set off into the countryside deeply covered in snow. Meanwhile, the police were alerted and began to descend on the area.

Perry tried to make his getaway by hijacking horses from local farmers, but the icy terrain proved extremely difficult to navigate. Exhausted and freezing five hours after his flight began, he barricaded himself behind a crumbling stone wall and was soon surrounded.

"Is there an officer in the crowd?" Perry shouted from his makeshift fortress.

"I am," a young deputy named Jeremiah Collins called back.

"If you drop your gun and come unarmed I'll talk with you," Perry announced, "but if you try to play me any tricks it will go hard with you."

Collins agreed and crossed the field toward Perry, who immediately asked about the guard he had shot in the American Express money car. He may have been genuinely concerned about the man, or perhaps he simply wanted to know if he was facing a murder charge. Collins assured him that Daniel McInerney was alive, then persuaded him to put down his gun.

"You might as well give in," the deputy said, "the whole country is after you and you are bound to be caught. Suppose you do kill a few people. It'll only be worse for you in the end."

"If I give up," Perry answered, "it means spending all my life in prison. Liberty is sweet to me and I'll sell it dear."

The trapped fugitive heard a noise behind him. When he turned around to see what it was, Collins seized the opportunity and leaped on top of him. As the two men struggled, Perry tried to bite the deputy's face, but he was soon overpowered and handcuffed. The great train robber of the East was in custody at last.

Perry seemed blithely unconcerned about the situation, cracking jokes and poking fun at the Pinkerton agents who had stumbled over themselves trying to find him. "I never saw anyone so cool," remarked an American Express agent who spoke to him in jail. The public's fascination with the charismatic outlaw remained undiminished, and Perry played to it like a veteran performer. He delighted reporters with exaggerated tales of his exploits, his misspent youth in the West, and of his redemption back in New York, where he struggled on the path of righteousness. Appealing to public sentiment, he suggested his crimes were motivated by callous railroad companies that exploited their workers, and by the love of a woman for whom he hoped to provide a better life. It was a one-man public relations campaign that happened to make terrific copy.

"Men and boys could imagine his wild cowboy days, as industrialization made the frontier seem more like a myth every day," writes Tamsin Spargo. "Radicals and reformers could identify with the working man who had finally snapped under the weight of social and economic injustice. Romantics could feel for the sensitive but proud man, torn between right and wrong as he fought to build a life with the woman he loved."

Perry was more appealing than ever, and he seemed to know it. Yet for all the wit and charm he used to seduce the people, his fate was leading inexorably toward something he truly dreaded—prison. Perhaps hoping for a lighter sentence, he surprised observers anticipating a lively trial by pleading guilty to all counts against him. He was given forty-nine years. "Perry received his sentence as meekly as an erring child receives a mother's kind reproof," one reporter noted. "The bravado had left him. The wild western spirit had died away and the most noted desperado of the East, perhaps of the country, quailed before the verdict of grim justice."

Prison ultimately broke Oliver Perry. Though he rebelled against the often brutal and dehumanizing system that confined him, he was really no match for it. Just twenty months after entering New York's Auburn facility he suffered a mental breakdown and was declared insane. Any lingering doubts about the diagnosis were settled in one horrifying instance when, in 1895, he repeatedly jammed two nails into his eyes. When that failed to completely blind him, he finished the job with a shard of glass. "I

was born into the light of day, against my will of course," he
wrote. "I now claim the right to put out that light."

Over the next thirty-five years, the thief who once dazzled
the nation lived in total darkness as he slowly faded from the
public memory. No one read the poetry he wrote or paid any
heed to the hunger strikes he staged to protest his treatment in
confinement. And when he died in 1930 at age sixty-four, he
was buried in an unmarked felon's grave. It was as though he had
never even existed.

23

Anna Jarvis:
The Mother of Mother's Day

Anna Jarvis was a woman of fierce loyalty and tireless enterprise. She was also a total raving lunatic. Childless herself, the spinster schoolteacher was consumed by twin obsessions that tore her apart: First, a relentless effort to establish a perpetual tribute to her dead mother, and later, an equally tenacious drive to destroy the very monument she had created.

Jarvis's attachment to her mother was reminiscent of a remora. The bond was so strong, in fact, that Lillie, the younger sister, felt a little left out. "It has been your aim to render me virtually motherless," Lillie complained in a letter to Anna. "Nothing would help and encourage me like your death."

When Mother Jarvis died in 1905, Anna's mission began. It started in her hometown of Grafton, West Virginia, with a memorial service she organized on the second anniversary of her mother's passing. She purchased five hundred carnations, her mother's favorite flower, one for each mother in her church's congregation. Then she began to lobby for a national holiday in her mother's honor, browbeating politicians, pestering bureaucrats, and generally making an awful nuisance of herself. It worked. Mother's Day became a popular cause. Americans' loyalties may have been deeply divided in those prewar days, but everyone had a mother.

It all culminated with a joint resolution in Congress, signed by President Woodrow Wilson in 1914, that established the second Sunday in May as a national holiday. But Anna Jarvis wasn't finished. She had barely begun. She quit her job and spent all her time writing foreign heads of state hoping to establish Mother's Day abroad. Her home became so cluttered with correspondence and mementos that she purchased the house next door and filled that up, too.

Then it started to get ugly. Mother's Day was becoming a crassly commercial bonanza for florists, card shops, and candy makers. Jarvis lost it. She railed first against the vile floral profiteers making a killing off her mother's beloved carnations. One of her press releases read: "WHAT WILL YOU DO to rout charlatans, bandits, pirates, racketeers, kidnappers and other termites that would undermine with their greed one of the finest, noblest and truest movements and celebrations?"

In the 1930s, when the U.S. postmaster announced a Mother's Day commemorative stamp bearing the portrait of Whistler's mother, Jarvis went ballistic. *Whistler's mother!* They had the wrong mother on their stamp! Jarvis demanded an audience with President Franklin Roosevelt, and succeeded in having "Mother's Day" removed from the issue. The stamp was still embellished with a vase of white carnations, however, which appalled her: More profit for the profiteers.

About the same time, she stormed into a meeting of the American War Mothers and tried to break up their sale of white carnations for Mother's Day. The police had to drag the sputtering woman out kicking and screaming. Soon she began wandering the streets showing strangers old photos of her taken at the time of her mother's death. Eventually Jarvis shut herself away in her dilapidated house and hung a sign in her window that read

WARNING, STAY AWAY. She would sit for hours next to the radio, ear cocked, certain her dearly departed mother was trying to communicate with her through the radio waves.

In the end, she was sent penniless and babbling to a sanitarium. And though she was never told, perhaps as a safety measure, she was supported by contributions from the hated Florists Exchange.

24

William J. Burns:
"America's Sherlock Holmes"

Sleeping Angelenos were startled awake in the early morning hours of October 1, 1910, by a massive explosion many mistook for an earthquake. A cache of dynamite planted at the downtown headquarters of the *Los Angeles Times* had been detonated, flinging printing equipment and shooting flames high into the night sky. Inside the brick and granite structure known as "the Fortress," workers preparing the next day's newspaper were consumed in an inferno fueled by shattered gas lines or crushed under collapsing floors and walls. Firefighters made heroic yet mostly futile efforts to contain the angry blaze, while bystanders kept at bay by the intense heat watched helplessly as those trapped inside made desperate leaps from upper-story windows. All told, twenty-one *Times* employees lost their lives in the blast, with many more injured. It was one of the most horrific crimes of the young century, and it would take one of America's foremost detectives to find out who was responsible.

With his fiery red hair, flamboyant personality, and penchant for self-promotion, William J. Burns had already made quite a name for himself thwarting counterfeiters as the star detective of the United States Secret Service and tracking down public land thieves in the West under a mandate from President Theodore Roosevelt. His investigations into the corporate and political mal-feasance that had long infected the city of San Francisco made him a champion among progressives of the era. But it was his work solving the *Los Angeles Times* bombing that would thrust him to an entirely new level of renown and make him, at least for a time, an American folk hero. *The New York Times* declared him to be "the greatest detective certainly, and perhaps the only really great detective, the only detective of genius this country has produced." His fame would lead him into the thick of a celebrated murder case in Georgia, which nearly got him lynched, and eventually to become the head of what became the Federal Bureau of In-vestigation, where he was ultimately eclipsed in the national consciousness by his former deputy, J. Edgar Hoover.

The destruction of the *Times* building occurred during a pe-riod of intense class strife in America, when relations between industry and labor were dangerously volatile. This was particu-larly true in Los Angeles, where Harrison Gray Otis, the rabidly antiunion publisher of the *Times,* waged a relentless campaign against organized labor. Otis had no doubt who was behind the attack on his Fortress. UNIONIST BOMBS WRECK THE *TIMES,* blared the headline of the next day's abbreviated edition of the paper, which was printed at an auxiliary plant. "Oh, you anarchic scum," the publisher seethed in an editorial. "You leeches upon honest labor, you midnight assassins." Labor leaders, fearing the explosion would give Otis and his ilk the ammunition they needed to step up their assault on unionism, quickly entrenched themselves and vigorously denied any connection to the attack. Eugene Debs, the five-time Socialist candidate for president, even went so far as to accuse Otis of secretly blowing up his own building in order to blame it on organized labor and thus destroy it in California once and for all.

Los Angeles mayor George Alexander knew the simmering tension between Otis and the unions could easily erupt into war if the bombing wasn't solved quickly and decisively. He immediately hired Burns, who had recently left government service and formed his own agency. The detective had little to go on at first—except for an unexploded bomb that was intended to have been part of the mayhem wrought by the *Times* blast. The day the Fortress exploded, fifteen sticks of dynamite wired to an alarm clock were discovered at the home of Felix J. Zeehandelaar, secretary of the Merchant and Manufacturers Association, an antilabor organization founded by Otis and others to fend off the advances of unionism. Burns noticed that the design and components of the Zeehandelaar bomb were very similar to those of another unexploded bomb found in Peoria, Illinois, where he had been investigating a series of industrial explosions.

Burns was convinced there was a connection between the industrial sabotage in Peoria and the attack on the *Times,* but establishing it proved difficult. The unexploded Peoria bomb had been traced to a character calling himself "J. W. McGraw," who remained at large, while the Zeehandelaar bomb led to two anarchists named David Caplan and Matthew Schmidt, and their leader, an unidentified man operating under the alias "J. B. Bryce." All three of these men were also at large, and none matched the description of "J. W. McGraw."

The elusive connection between Peoria and Los Angeles had Burns stumped, plus he faced a new source of pressure as well. Otis and other powerful antilabor types, furious that Mayor Alexander refused to take it on faith that organized labor was responsible for the *Times* bombing, demanded that a grand jury convene and that a special prosecutor named Earl Rogers head the investigation. Both Otis and Rogers were inveterate foes of Burns, and opposed his involvement with the case because they believed his earlier San Francisco graft investigations proved he was an anticorporate tool of radical progressives. As the detective later related, "Otis sent vigorous protest to the mayor denouncing me and deriding the mayor for employing me, expressing his opinion of me and anticipating failure."

Otis and Rogers raised questions about the stalled progress of the investigation, suggesting that perhaps Burns wasn't earning the money he received from the city to solve the case. They exerted so much pressure that Mayor Alexander was eventually forced to withhold his fee. "The end of it," Burns reported, "was that I had to go ahead and finance the investigation myself. It cost me $14,000." That was a lot of money, but Burns sensed an imminent breakthrough and wasn't about to withdraw from such a potentially career-defining case. "I knew that our operatives were watching the right rat holes," he said, "and I intended to keep them there as long as I could raise the money to pay their wages."

Sure enough, the mysterious Peoria bomber known as "J. W. McGraw" was soon identified as Ortie McManigal, a labor extremist from Chicago. But his ties to the Los Angeles bombers Caplan and Schmidt, and their leader, "J. B. Bryce," were still obscured. All Burns could do was watch McManigal and wait to see what he would do next. As it turned out, he went on a hunting trip to Wisconsin with a companion who called himself Frank Sullivan but who matched the description of "J. B. Bryce." Burns immediately dispatched two of his agents to Wisconsin for a hunting trip of their own. After setting up camp near their quarry, the undercover detectives established an outdoorsman's rapport with the suspects. A souvenir snapshot of their time together was then shown to witnesses in Los Angeles and elsewhere who had seen "J. B. Bryce." They confirmed that he and Frank Sullivan were one and the same. Now it was time to find out who he *really* was.

The mystery man was trailed to Cincinnati, where he went to the home of a Mrs. McNamara, who turned out to be his mother. "J. B. Bryce" was at last identified as James B. McNamara, an alcoholic ne'er-do-well with a very important brother: John J. McNamara, secretary-treasurer of the International Association of Bridge and Structural Ironworkers. The union was one of the nation's most powerful and was suspected of being behind the explosions in Peoria and many others across the country. Could Otis have been right all along? Was it in fact a union bomb that had destroyed the *Times* Fortress? "Such an act is anarchy, pure and simple," John McNamara had asserted after the *Times* explosion. "No sane individual or organization would resort to anything of the kind under any circumstances." Did a terrorist lurk behind this seemingly sincere statement? Burns believed so, but he still needed proof.

Ortie McManigal and James McNamara were clearly guilty, but Burns believed that arresting them right away might destroy any chance of nailing John McNamara. "No one was likely to catch the Secretary-Treasurer of the International Association of Bridge and Structural Iron Workers—respected in the high circles of organized labor and a close friend of American Federation of Labor President Samuel Gompers—carrying dynamite around in a handbag," wrote Burns biographer Gene Caesar. "A conclusive link had to be established between John McNamara, the known bombers, and the bombings themselves, and Burns realized that it might take a long time to do it."

The detective again decided to watch and wait, but McManigal proved dangerous on the loose. In December 1910 he slipped out of Chicago and returned to Los Angeles to blow up the Llewellyn Iron Works, where a bitter labor strike was in progress. (He was also reportedly set to bomb the Los Angeles County Hall of Records, the *Times* auxiliary printing plant, and some other buildings, but abandoned the project when a detonating cap accidentally exploded and slightly injured him.) The following April, McManigal met up with James McNamara in Toledo, Ohio, from where the two took a train to Detroit with bags full of explosives. It was time to haul them in before anyone else got hurt. Burns operatives who had been trailing the pair swooped in on them at a Detroit hotel.

James McNamara seemed resigned, but when Ortie McManigal realized he was being arrested for the *Times* bombing (not on an unrelated charge, as he had been told), he was horrified. People had died in that explosion, and it was a hanging offense. "I didn't have anything to do with [it]," he protested. "Jim [McNamara] did that one with the help of a couple of anarchists named Schmitz and Caplan. I wasn't even there." When told it didn't matter, that he was still an accessory after the fact, McManigal panicked. "If I told you everything I know, would things go easy on me?" he asked. There were no guarantees, the Burns detectives replied, but his cooperation might weigh favorably. With that, McManigal started to sing. He admitted to planting the bombs in Peoria, as well as the one at the Llewellyn Iron Works in Los Angeles, and a long list of others—all under the direction of John McNamara. He also told the agents exactly what they would find at the Iron Workers union headquarters in Indianapolis, including a ledger with payments to him and James McNamara listed separately from legitimate union expenses, among other damning evidence. Based on the information provided by McManigal, John McNamara was arrested and extradited to Los Angeles.

The arrest of one of the nation's top labor officials was trumpeted in headlines across the country. Burns basked in the glory. He granted interviews to just about anyone who asked, and recounted his agency's initiative and daring in dramatic detail. The investigation, he told *The New York Times* with typical flair, "had led us among the tottering of wrecked buildings, where beneath impending dangers, we searched for clues." The media responded to the colorful detective with adoring accounts of his exploits, like this one in *McClure's* magazine:

> *He had been for three days in Indianapolis, cleaning up the evidence against the man who he had arrested for dynamiting the Los Angeles* Times *building in California; and during those three days he had been living like a celebrity on tour, in the eyes of all the reporters. . . . He had moved through this observation and surveillance with an easy, jovial manner, laughing and talking in the hotel lobby or on the street, without a trace of the manner of the traditional sleuth, without so much as a glance behind him or a confidential word out of the corner of his mouth. And during the whole time he had been secretly meeting and directing his operatives, consulting with police, and gathering by telephone and telegraph the evidence and corroboration of witnesses against the men whose movements for months past he had been carrying—mapped out to the last detail—in the silence that lay behind his breezy public manner and his candid, uncunning smile.*

Yet as the press fawned over Burns, organized labor rallied around the McNamaras, who maintained their innocence, and demonized the detective. Samuel Gompers, president of the American Federation of Labor, said the arrests were a vicious attempt to discredit unionism, and announced that the AFL was launching a nationwide campaign to raise a $300,000 defense fund for the brothers. "Labor has no intention of turning its back on John and Jim McNamara," he declared. Clarence Darrow, among the most famous lawyers of the day (even before the "Scopes Monkey Trial"), was retained to defend the McNamaras— victims, he said, of a "capitalist conspiracy" that had been financed by "the steel trust with its gold" and "masterminded by William J.

Burns." Darrow's decision to take the case, against his better judgment, "was the most momentous . . . of his life," writes his biographer Kevin Tierney, "for it was to be the bitterest culmination of the courtroom conflicts of capital and labor to take place prior to World War I—and would almost topple the AFL and Darrow personally at one fell swoop."

As the McNamaras were being hailed as "Heroes of Labor" at rallies across the country, Burns defended himself against charges that he was part of a capitalist conspiracy to destroy unionism. "When I'm employed to find out who committed a crime, I go out and find him," he said. "I don't care a row of red apples who he is or where he is. Those people who are calling me an 'enemy of labor' for running down these dynamiters are as muddleheaded as the jawsmiths in San Francisco who called me an 'enemy of capital' for going after the big fellows in the graft investigation out there. When I have my case against a criminal, I put my clamps on him just as quick whether he has diamond rings on his fingers or calluses as big as hoops."

Still, the agitation against Burns mounted as labor and defense attorneys continued to vilify him and aggressively promote the McNamaras' innocence. They financed a film portraying the brothers as martyrs and Burns as a thug hired by ferocious capitalists to destroy them. It was a successful piece of propaganda and only added to the luster of the brothers, who were being championed on buttons and banners in cities across the country. Burns appeared to be losing the public relations war. At one point he was even charged with kidnapping in Indianapolis due to alleged irregularities in John McNamara's arrest and extradition to Los Angeles.

Then, on December 1, 1911, came a stunning development: The McNamara brothers suddenly pleaded guilty. Darrow, who had planned to argue that a faulty gas line was responsible for the *Times* explosion (and even had a scale model of the Fortress made to demonstrate it), realized before the trial was set to begin that it was a hopeless case—even for him. The evidence Burns had accumulated was simply unassailable, especially after a search of John McNamara's office at the Ironworkers union—conducted after President William Howard Taft personally intervened—revealed that every element of Ortie McManigal's confession was true. "My God," the exasperated lawyer exclaimed to James McNamara, "you left a trail behind you a mile wide!" Darrow knew that if the documentation was ever presented in open court, his clients would surely hang and the union cause might be irreparably damaged. "There was no avoiding [the] step taken today," he wired Samuel Gompers on the day of the guilty plea. "When I see you I know you will be satisfied that all of us have done everything we had to do to accomplish the best."

But the plea shocked the labor movement, which had placed tremendous faith both in the McNamaras' innocence and in Darrow's ability to defend them. Now it was left crippled and humiliated. Many blamed the famed lawyer, who later wrote, "If perchance I allow myself to slip back the bolt, with which all mortals seek to lock away some of the sad and unpleasant memories of the past, at once my mind goes straight to the courtroom in Los Angeles on the evening of the plea of 'Guilty.' "

Things got worse for Darrow when he was indicted for attempting to bribe a juror in the McNamara case. Burns was one of the witnesses for the prosecution and faced a brutal cross-examination by his old nemesis Earl Rogers, who now served as Darrow's defense attorney. "It is doubtful if any witness of the prominence of Burns ever underwent the manhandling that Rogers subjected him to," wrote one biographer. "Sparks flew almost continuously and both men were frequently on the verge of physical encounters." During one particularly nasty exchange, Burns said of Rogers, "This man . . . made a statement in the presence of the jury [at the San Francisco graft trials] that I was a suborner of perjury." In response, Rogers sprang to his feet, stalked up to Burns with his finger pointed, and dramatically shouted, "I make it again, sir, and do not take it back!"

Darrow was ultimately acquitted, but Burns's reputation was hardly sullied by the episode, as he had feared it would be. He remained a hero—"America's Sherlock Holmes," as the fictional detective's creator, Sir Arthur Conan Doyle, called him. Not only had he snared the McNamaras, who, though spared the noose, were sentenced to long prison terms, he eventually caught the anarchists Caplan and Schmidt. The supersleuth was a now a bona fide superstar. "My name is William J. Burns," he wrote in his bestselling book *The Masked War*, "and my address is New York, London, Paris, Montreal, Chicago, San Francisco, Los Angeles, Seattle, New Orleans, Boston, Philadelphia, Cleveland, and wherever else a law-abiding citizen may find need of men who know how to go quietly about throwing out of ambush a hidden assassin or drawing from cover career criminals who prey upon those who walk straight." As it turned out, the great detective was needed in Georgia, where hate and ignorance would nearly consume him.

★

On April 27, 1913, the battered and sodomized body of thirteen-year-old Mary Phagan was discovered in the basement of Atlanta's National Pencil Factory where she worked as a machine operator for ten cents an hour. Georgians shocked by the ghastly deed were soon whipped into an anti-Semitic frenzy when factory superintendent Leo Frank, a Cornell-educated Jew, was charged with the murder of his young employee. Crowds gathered at his trial cheered for the prosecution that painted him as a predatory sexual deviant and chanted to the jury, "Hang the Jew or we'll hang you." Frank was convicted and sentenced to death, largely on the testimony of a black man named Jim Conley who claimed he had helped the superintendent dispose of the body in the factory basement and then helped him cover up the crime. By the time William J. Burns entered the case, nearly a year after the murder, Frank's appeal had been rejected by the Georgia Supreme Court and his defense attorneys were preparing an extraordinary motion for a new trial.

Burns had been retained by Chicago advertising magnate Albert D. Lasker, one of a number of powerful individuals, including *New York Times* publisher Adolph S. Ochs, who believed Frank had been unfairly tried and convicted in a racially charged circus of lies and intimidation. The celebrity sleuth took Atlanta by storm.

"Just the sight of Burns settling down to breakfast each morning in the fern-filled pink-and-white dining room of the grand Georgian Terrace Hotel suggested that a higher power was now at work," writes author Steve Oney in his book about the celebrated case, *And the Dead Shall Rise*. "Surrounded by half a dozen reporters, attended by a traveling secretary and assorted subalterns, and invariably clad in a crisp hounds tooth suit that set off his famous red hair and mustache, the detective exuded energy and confidence. This was America's greatest private investigator, and between bites of his soft-boiled eggs and toast, he would regale the table with war stories, pausing to dictate telegrams to clients and operatives in far-flung climes. Then, with the entire retinue in tow, he would stroll down Peachtree Street to his agency's local office, declaiming not just on aspects of the Phagan murder but on his certainty that he would solve it."

The detective's jaunty confidence remained abundantly evident throughout the early stages of his investigation—almost as a setup for the tragic course of events that was to follow. Burns broadly hinted that he had all but solved the murder and vindicated Leo Frank, even as he tried to give the impression that he was impartial enough to declare his client's guilt should the evidence so warrant. The crime had indeed been committed by a pervert, just as the prosecution had said, Burns told reporters. But, he added, Frank lacked all the qualities of a sexual deviant. Soon enough, he produced a series of obscene letters written by Jim Conley, indicating that the state's star witness *did* have the perverse characteristics needed to be Mary Phagan's murderer. Added to this, a group of physicians Burns had arranged to examine Frank "unanimously agreed that [he] was normal physically and mentally," reported *The New York Times*. To bolster that finding, Burns offered a $1,000 reward for definite "reports concerning acts of perversion on the part of Leo M. Frank."

Burns expected no responses to his offer and was therefore surprised when Newport Lanford, detective chief of the Atlanta Police Department, promised to share evidence of Frank's deviant nature. Yet when Burns arrived at police headquarters, Lanford refused to open his files. He cited the upcoming hearing on the motion for a new trial as his reason. Furthermore, he publicly maintained that the police had never accused Frank of perversion in the first place. Armed with that blatant lie, Burns triumphantly wired Adolph Ochs at the *Times*:

> *Police department today withdrew charge of perversion against Leo M. Frank. . . . Bearing in mind the numerous filthy charges of perversion which saturated the community prior to the Frank trial and aroused their passions, the charges of perversion injected into the case by the State upon the trial . . . and in the Supreme Court of Georgia, the statement made today by Chief Lanford is a severe indictment of the police department of this city and of the outrageous methods used in the prosecution of Frank.*

Burns seemed mighty pleased with the progress he was making, particularly as a number of prosecution witnesses retracted their testimony and new ones were found to implicate Jim Conley. But the detective failed to recognize the depth of resentment his presence in Georgia generated. To many he represented arrogant northern interests seeking to subvert local justice and free a depraved Jew. One of his most vociferous critics was the populist firebrand Thomas E. Watson, a former U.S. congressman and running mate of William Jennings Bryan in the presidential campaign of 1896. Watson used his publication, the *Jeffersonian,* to relentlessly attack Burns and "the conspiracy of Big Money against the law, against the courts, and against the poor little victim of hellish passion," Mary Phagan.

"This man Burns richly deserves a coat of tar and feathers, plus a ride on a fence-rail," roared Watson in the April 23, 1914, edition of the *Jeffersonian*. "He has been engineering a campaign of systematic lies tending to blacken this state and tending to provoke an outbreak of popular indignation. With all the bravado of a shallow bluffer, and with all the insolence of irresponsibility, he has gone to the extreme limit of toleration. There may not be a way by which the law can reach him, but there *is* a way to reach him."

This none-too-subtle call to violence was answered just a week later when Burns and one of his agents, Dan Lehon, found themselves under siege in Mary Phagan's hometown of Marietta, Georgia. They were on their way to interview a potential witness in Cedartown, the road to which ran through Marietta, when their car blew a tire. As they looked for a garage in town, a devotee of Watson's named Robert E. Lee Howell recognized Burns by his distinctive red hair and stormed up to him. "I have promised to beat you if ever came to Marietta," Howell announced, "and here goes." With that, he slapped Burns on both cheeks and wildly cursed him.

A large crowd started to gather at the scene, many of them readers of the *Jeffersonian,* and before long a cry of "Lynch him!" was heard. Burns and Lehon quickly recognized the very real peril they faced as the mob of several hundred grew more menacing. Both made a run for it: Burns to an adjacent neighborhood and Lehon to the local sheriff's office. "The great detective ran through several dark alleys as fast as his legs would carry him," reported one resident, "and those that saw him in action do say that he certainly showed a wonderful burst of speed." Burns eventually found refuge in a hotel on the outskirts of town, but the mob soon discovered where he was and reassembled outside. It was only when a circuit judge on the scene stepped in to calm the crowd that Burns, amidst a barrage of eggs, was whisked away in the car of a local furniture dealer. Lehon escaped separately.

Although disaster had been narrowly averted in Marietta, Burns still faced a number of troubling developments that boded ill for both him and Leo Frank. One of the worst came when a local pastor, Rev. C. B. Ragsdale, retracted his sworn statement that he had overheard Jim Conley confess to the murder of Mary Phagan. Ragsdale claimed that Burns operatives had bribed him. "They were just handing money out," he said. Burns dismissed the pastor's allegation as "a cowardly lie by a cowardly liar," but the damage was done. Tom Watson had a field day, of course, as did Leo Frank's prosecutors, who suggested that Rev. Ragsdale was merely one of many false witnesses assembled by the Burns agency.

The situation grew even bleaker when Burns was called to testify at the hearing for Frank's motion for a new trial. As prosecutors picked apart his investigative methods—challenging, for example, his declaration that Jim Conley was a deviant when he had never met the man, and mocking his failure to interview any witnesses favorable to the prosecution—the detective was frequently evasive or defensive. He distanced himself from some of the best defense evidence when the means of obtaining it was called into question, and was forced to acknowledge some other very suspect practices, such as his decision to send one sworn witness out of town beyond the reach of prosecutors. All in all, it was an unusually dismal performance by the celebrity sleuth.

The defense did their best to mitigate some of the damage, but they knew their case had been gravely compromised. "I regret to advise you that the situation here is desperate," one of Frank's attorneys wrote to Albert Lasker. "It is the belief of nearly all our friends that Burns's connection with the case has done us irretrievable damage." That sentiment was confirmed when the motion for a new trial was denied. "I have been disgusted at the farcical methods to which Burns has resorted," wrote Louis Marshall of the American Jewish Committee to Louis Wiley of *The New York Times*. "Every one of his acts has been a burlesque upon modern detective ideas. It is deplorable that a case so meritorious as that of Frank should have been brought to this point of destruction by such ridiculous methods."

What Marshall and others failed to realize was that Leo Frank's cause was doomed by a system determined to hang him, not by anything William J. Burns did. Indeed, the detective himself was hammered by that very same system. He was indicted for subornation of perjury in the Ragsdale matter, then had his license revoked by the Atlanta City Council, which forced him to close his local office. America's Sherlock Holmes had been effectively shut out—but not silenced. He continued to proclaim Frank's innocence in the press, while at the same time condemning overeager police and prosecutors, a rabidly anti-Semitic public, and the man he declared to be Mary Phagan's true murderer, Jim Conley.

Though the U.S. Supreme Court ultimately rejected the notion that Frank had not received a fair trial (with Oliver Wendell Holmes dissenting), public sentiment in much of America was with him, thanks largely to sympathetic press accounts. Leo Frank was no murderer, writer C. P. Connolly asserted in a *Collier's*

Weekly article that ran in December 1914, but a "shy, nervous, intellectual" who "looks through his prison bars with the eyes of a stoic." Three things have condemned him, Connolly wrote: "politics, prejudice, and perjury." That same month *The New York Times* devoted nearly a full page to Detective Burns's take on the case and the miscarriage of justice that he believed had occurred.

By June of the following year, there was enough doubt in the mind of Georgia's governor, John M. Slanton, that he commuted Frank's death sentence to life in prison. He was hanged in effigy for his courageous decision, a preview of what was to happen to Leo Frank less than two months later. Shortly before midnight on August 16, 1915, a group of vigilantes calling themselves the "Knights of Mary Phagan" and comprised of some of Georgia's leading citizens arrived at the Milledgeville prison farm where Frank was serving his sentence. With no resistance from either the warden or guards, they snatched the famous prisoner and drove him to a site two miles outside of Marietta known as Frey's Gin. There they bound and blindfolded him, placed a noose around his neck, and hanged him from a tree. Justice had been served, Georgia-style, after which Marietta's police chief sent Burns a jeering telegram: "Leo Frank lynched here. Come quick and help investigate."

★

William J. Burns continued to solve crimes and to make headlines until 1921, when he was tapped by his friend Harry Daugherty, the new attorney general under President Harding, to head what was then called the Bureau of Investigation. It was not an illustrious tenure. Like many detectives of his day, Burns often used whatever questionable methods necessary to achieve results. To his detriment, he employed them at the bureau as well.

"He had no qualms about search and seizure or about employing criminals and men of dubious reputation," wrote historian

Francis Russell. "Any inquisitive congressman or senator, any critic of Daugherty or the Department of Justice, would soon find his own affairs investigated by Bureau agents who did not hesitate to break into offices, riffle files, tap wires, and copy private correspondence."

Ultimately, though, Burns was brought down not so much by his own behavior as by the scandals of the Harding administration—one of the most corrupt in American history—and by an unsavory character named Gaston Means (see next chapter). He resigned from the bureau under pressure in 1924, and died less than a decade later. Since then his name has been all but obliterated from the history of the FBI, while his successor, J. Edgar Hoover, came to define that institution for the next half century. All in all, a rather sorry legacy for America's Sherlock Holmes.

25

Gaston B. Means: American Scoundrel

If William J. Burns was America's Sherlock Holmes, then Gaston B. Means was the nation's very own Moriarty. An unrepentant rogue with devilish charm and a gift for mendacity, Means thrived in that decade of lawlessness known as the Roaring Twenties. In fact, he helped shape it. His finely spun lies metastasized into the highest levels of government, wreaking havoc and ruining reputations—including that of his pal William Burns. He bilked bootleggers and other criminals by selling influence he didn't have, cruelly capitalized on the kidnapping of Charles Lindbergh's young son, and convinced many Americans that their president, Warren Harding, had been poisoned by his wife. He was so thoroughly rotten that he once bragged that he had been accused of every crime known in America—including murder—and convicted of none. Even when the law did finally catch up with him, Means was unbowed and continued to make sport of human lives until the day he died.

Francis Russell wrote of him: "In appearance a wastrel cherub with round face, dimpled smile, sharp chin, and beaming eyes that flickered from time to time with madness, [he] was a swindler for the joy of swindling, a liar proud of the credibility of his lies, a confidence man able to make his cheats and deceptions works of art."

Gaston Bullock Means was born on July 11, 1879, at his family's plantation outside Concord, North Carolina. By some accounts he was an affable, well-liked young man, if a bit of a rascal. It was only when he sustained a head injury after falling from the upper berth of a Pullman rail car that, intimates said, a darker, more sinister side of his personality began to emerge. Of course there were those who maintained that it was Means himself who had made the berth collapse by sawing through one of the chains that secured it. He certainly had the foresight to take out several accident insurance policies before boarding the train, and walked away with a tidy settlement.

After quitting his job as a salesman for the Cannon Cotton Mills (or being fired for lying, as the company maintained), Means used his family connections to approach the William J. Burns Detective Agency in 1915 for a job as an investigator. Burns was apparently impressed with Means's ideas about how to bring in new business and hired him for $25 a week, plus commissions. It was the beginning of a fateful friendship. About the same time, Means began working as an agent for the German government. There was nothing illegal about this because the United States had not yet entered World War I and was still officially neutral. Still, it was almost impossible for Gaston Means to operate inside the bounds of truth. To bolster German propaganda efforts against its enemy Britain, he contrived various situations that made it appear that Britain was breaking U.S. neutrality laws by, among other things, receiving American supplies. A minor tempest in the press resulted, but dissipated just as quickly when it was found that the allegations had no merit. By that time, Means had moved on to his next scam.

He managed to charm his way into the life of a wealthy, somewhat simple-minded widow named Maude King. Soon enough, he was managing her affairs and living off her money. Mrs. King had a tidy income from the estate of her late husband, but, as Means discovered, it was only a small portion of the estate. The bulk had been set aside in trust for the establishment of the James C. King Home for Old Men. Means thought himself far worthier of the money and settled on a way to get it. He fabricated a so-called second will that left the entire estate to his personal money vault, Mrs. King. The officers of the trust dismissed the forged will, however, after which Means tried to get former U.S. Supreme Court justice Charles Evans Hughes to pursue the case. When that failed, he started to get desperate. He had already squandered most of Mrs. King's money and he knew that if she ever found out, she might dismiss him as her manager, thus ruining his chance to profit from the bogus will. Plus, she had a met a young naval officer and wanted to marry him. That, too, would interfere with his plans. So, in an effort to isolate and distract her, he told Mrs. King that her life was in danger and sent her away to "safety" in North Carolina. When she grew restless there, Gaston Means settled on a more permanent solution.

On the evening of August 29, 1917, the well-trusted business manager took his client rabbit hunting. Only rabbits weren't the quarry: Mrs. King was. She was shot dead near a spring outside of Means's hometown of Concord. "As we came near the spring, she handed me [her] gun," he later recounted. "I said I wanted a drink of water from the spring. I placed her gun in the crotch of a tree and told her not to touch it. . . . Just as I was stooping down for a drink of water, out of the corner of my eye I noted her reaching for the gun, and I called to her not to touch it, as it was loaded. Then I took a drink and the next thing I knew I heard a shot."

Improbable as the story was, particularly since Mrs. King was shot in the back of the head, a coroner's jury ruled the death accidental. There were still strong suspicions of foul play, however, and an investigation was launched. Mrs. King's corpse was exhumed in Chicago, where the local coroner demonstrated how nearly impossible it would be for the woman to have shot herself. Other investigations in New York and North Carolina revealed, among other things, Mrs. King's missing fortune. As more and more suspicions were directed toward Means, he lashed out. "There is going to be a day of reckoning for those who are responsible for such insinuations," he declared. "As a southern gentleman I brand them as dastardly and I mean to defend to the limit the name of the woman who is dead and unable to protect herself."

Despite his dramatic protests, Means was indicted for murder. Clearly he was the killer, yet the prosecution faced a daunting obstacle—public opinion. Much like the Leo Frank case several years earlier, residents of Cabarrus County, North Carolina, resented the interference of New York authorities who arrived to help the state press its case. Gaston Means may have been a scoundrel, but he was *their* scoundrel. And he acquitted himself quite well in court. "Means was the smartest witness I have ever examined," Solicitor General Hayden Clement later said. A seasoned performer, he kept his cool and lied without blinking, all the while flashing his dimpled smile at the jury of his peers and his good pal the judge. When the verdict was returned, the prosecution was horrified to find that Gaston Means had gotten away with murder.

An ordinary criminal might have lain low for awhile after being acquitted of such a ghastly deed, but not Gaston Means. He got right back to the business of pursuing the matter of the second will, this time on behalf of Mrs. King's sister and beneficiary, Mrs. Melvin—the only member of her family who believed him to be innocent, and a woman now potentially worth millions. To increase his chances of prevailing in the Chicago probate court, Means launched a cynical public relations campaign designed to restore his battered reputation. He did it by fabricating a number of lies based on his stint as a German agent. In one instance, he convinced the district attorney who had prosecuted him in the King case to swear out a warrant for one "Otto Schumann," an imaginary German assassin who, he claimed, had inadvertently killed Mrs. King while firing at him after a dispute over money. The story was picked up in the Chicago and New York newspapers, just as Means intended. He also concocted an elaborate ruse in which he claimed to have damning papers from his German contact that could very well turn the tide of the war against America's enemy. (The United States had entered the war against Germany in April 1917.) The tale was so convincing that U.S. military intelligence agents got involved and tracked the lead to its inevitable dead end.

Though the nonexistent papers failed to give his reputation the boost he had anticipated, Means remained determined. He was invited to testify before Congress about German activity in the United States, a subject about which he claimed to be well versed. "Gaston was pleased to testify because he needed publicity," wrote his biographer Edwin P. Hoyt, "and he needed a podium from which he could shout to the world of the good citizenship of Gaston Bullock Means." Of course, much of what he had to say was pure bunk—a preview of the more significant, and equally untrue, congressional testimony he would later give.

Coinciding with his image enhancing appearance on Capitol Hill, Means filed a million-dollar lawsuit against those who had caused him to be brought to trial for the murder of Mrs. King. Among those named were officers of the King estate trust who had accused him of fraud. It was an obvious ploy to tarnish them and perhaps force a settlement of the second will. Yet this, like all his other efforts on the matter, came to naught. The probate judge ultimately upheld the validity of the first will and chastised Means and Mrs. Melvin for their efforts to profit from the spurious second will. Dogged as ever, Means appealed and was rebuffed again. "No fair consideration of this case can ignore the fact that Gaston B. Means is shown to be the controlling and determining spirit in the attempt to establish this will," the judge remarked. "Indeed, the conclusion is irresistible that Mrs. King and Mrs. Melvin were singularly under his influence and were largely dominated by his strong personality and inflexible will."

The estate of James C. King had at last proven to be a dry well, but Means wasted no time brooding. Before long, he was ready to exploit something entirely new—the government position he obtained courtesy of his friend and sometime employer, William J. Burns.

★

After Warren G. Harding was elected president in 1920 on the postwar promise of a "return to normalcy," he appointed as attorney general the political crony he credited for his sweeping victory, Ohio kingmaker Harry M. Daugherty, who in turn put William J. Burns in charge of the Bureau of Investigation. Burns then hired Means. At a time when the bureau seldom let civil liberties stand in the way of its agenda, the new director knew exactly what kind of work he could expect from his old friend. "If there were informers to be bribed," wrote Edwin Hoyt, "or offices to be searched, or if in other ways the law of the land was to be breached by the secret investigating arm of the Department of Justice, then Gaston Means was the best possible man to put on the job." Yet when it came to Burns's legacy, he was the worst. Because there is little documentation about the exact nature of the relationship between the two men, it remains mysterious. What is certain, though, is that Means profited well from the abuse of his position, and Burns, for some reason, protected him.

Was the heroic detective of a decade earlier really corrupt? Or was he, like so many others, a victim of Means's masterful deceit? Perhaps he was a bit of both.

No sooner had Means settled into his new job at the bureau than he began to exploit it. He started small, contracting to sell Justice Department investigative reports to the criminals named in them, or to fix federal indictments against them—all guarantees he made with no intention of delivering. He also used his new position to lash out at old enemies, including John T. Dooling, a New York assistant district attorney who had assisted the prosecution in his murder trial. Dooling related details of a troubling call he received from Means in a letter to Attorney General Daugherty: "Today he called me up on the telephone and said he was now at the Department of Justice and used foul and indecent language toward me and told me that he . . . would get me." Daugherty forwarded the letter to Burns, who vigorously defended Means and claimed that he had been unfairly prosecuted for the murder of Mrs. King and wrongly accused of forging her late husband's will. He was, said Burns, an asset to the bureau and ought to be left alone. It would take another year of his shenanigans before Daugherty finally suspended him.

The jig was up at the Justice Department, at least temporarily, but armed with a glowing recommendation from Burns, who called him "a resourceful, courageous, intelligent man," Means secured a temporary position at the Treasury Department. And he even got to keep his office at the bureau, much to the consternation of Burns's deputy, J. Edgar Hoover. Now Means had plenty of time and opportunity to concentrate on his influence peddling schemes. Through numerous contacts in New York and elsewhere, he established himself among rumrunners as the man to see. He convinced them of his powerful friends in Washington, and relieved them of thousands of dollars for services never rendered.

By October 1922, Means was "hand in glove with the boot-leggers," according to his wife. That month alone, she said, one gave him $5,000, another gave him $11,500, and a third forked over $13,000. And those were just the deals she knew about. No doubt even more illicit cash was pouring in. Ironically, it was during this period that Means actually did his duty as a government agent and helped bring down a prominent bootlegging ring known to service the Astors, Vanderbilts, and other members of the elite. But it wasn't a surge of conscience that motivated him; it was simply because he had tried to blackmail the bootleggers and they had refused to pay.

Means continued to perfect his role as the fix-it man for bootleggers and others who needed his help. He generated business by advertising his close association with such prominent government officials as Daugherty, whom he had actually only met once, and a man he never met at all, Secretary of the Treasury Andrew Mellon. Prohibition enforcement was notoriously corrupt, so Means had no problem convincing criminals that the officials could be bought. And when he failed to deliver, they obviously had no legal recourse against him. It was the perfect scam.

In one notable case, Means swindled more than $50,000 from Edward M. Salomon, president of the Val-Dona Drug Company of Chicago. The company's valuable permits to sell alcohol-based products had been revoked by the government, and Salomon was eager to get them back. Means promised to make it happen for $8,000 cash, which Salomon gladly paid in advance. To string him along, Means showed him forged papers that indicated that the approval process was moving along smoothly. He also offered him the job of Prohibition Director for Illinois, for the rock bottom price of $50,000. Salomon was thrilled. The post would allow him to manufacture and distribute alcohol products any way he wanted. Plus, Means had assured him that President Harding (another "close friend") would support his appointment. Giddy with excitement, Salomon returned to Chicago, sold out his interest in the Val-Dona company, and hired several assistants in preparation for the plumb post that never materialized.

And so it went, Means spinning his lies and living lavishly off the profits—until Treasury Secretary Andrew Mellon was informed of his nefarious activities and reported them to Harry Daugherty. The attorney general promised an investigation and encouraged Mellon to pursue one as well. After all, both departments had been tainted by Means's dirty work, more and more of which soon came to light. With the reputation and public trust of the Treasury and Justice departments at stake—and with a character as wily as Means at the center of it all—Daugherty knew a strong government prosecutor was necessary, even if it meant that some of his own questionable activities might be exposed. He settled on Hiram C. Todd, a U.S. attorney for the Northern District of New York, who managed to secure indictments against Means on over one hundred charges.

Never one to fold in the face of adversity, or the truth, Means began fabricating diaries from the past several years that would conveniently place him far away from any criminal activity. He even hired two full-time stenographers to assist with the task. At the same time, he and his lawyer connived to delay his day of reckoning, or avoid it altogether. They found a way when Senator Burton K. Wheeler of Montana launched an investigation of Harry Daugherty and invited Means to testify.

President Harding had died suddenly in August 1923, only two years into his term, and was succeeded by Calvin Coolidge, the so-called Puritan in Babylon. Soon enough, reports of astonishing malfeasance by some of Harding's cabinet members and cronies emerged as the Teapot Dome scandal and other instances of high-level corruption came to light.[1] Harry Daugherty had not been directly implicated in any of them, but Senator Wheeler was convinced he had profited from a number of criminal activities by failing to prosecute them. He was determined to bring the attorney general down. In Means, the senator believed he had the perfect witness—one who promised detailed records and other evidence of corruption at the Justice Department. And in Wheeler, Means saw his possible salvation. His perjured testimony could either destroy Daugherty, and thus Hiram Todd's prosecution of him, or it could at least delay the inevitable while he was under subpoena in the Senate.

"I am satisfied that [Means] is an unusually cunning crook," Todd wrote to the attorney general, "and now that he is cornered I believe he is scheming to use the examination before one of the Senate Investigating Committees as a ground for claiming immunity." On the eve of the Wheeler hearings, Means approached Daugherty to suggest that his testimony could be called off if the attorney general would simply stop Todd's prosecution. When Daugherty rebuffed him, Means stormed the Capitol with a fat file full of bogus documents and a glib tongue well practiced in the language of deceit. "Dimpled and beaming, he almost seemed to blow kisses to the spectators as he made his way to the witness chair," wrote Francis Russell. "Grandly he waived immunity, saying that he asked for no quarter and would give none."

---

1. Harding was never implicated in any malfeasance, but the weak and ineffectual president surrounded himself with a bunch of dirty dealers who corrupted his administration. One of the worst was his friend Albert Fall, Secretary of the Interior and architect of the great Teapot Dome swindle. Fall succeeded in transferring control of several oil reserves, including Wyoming's Teapot Dome (so named for its vague resemblance to a giant, sandstone teapot), from the navy to the Department of the Interior. He then leased out the reserves to various oil interests in exchange for $400,000 in undocumented "loans." Teapot Dome emerged as a sensational scandal that resulted in a prison term for Fall—the first cabinet member in American history to be incarcerated—and contributed to Harding's ranking as one of the worst presidents ever.

"The witness was a complete master of himself," *The New York Times* reported. "He knew all the members of the committee by name and answered questions, and sometimes asked them as if he and his inquisitors were old friends. He showed no evidence of nervousness or evasion." The performance was indeed magnificent, filled with what Treasury Secretary Mellon called "vicious piffle," but delivered with jaunty confidence and a cherubic smile. "While testifying in his easy, convincing voice," wrote Russell, "he kept smoking one cigarette after the other, mugging for the crowd, shooting the smoke through his nostrils or jetting it high in the air with a thrust of his mobile lower lip." Means regaled his audience with tales of corruption so deep and widespread that the entire government seemed to be infected. Delivered against the backdrop of the all-too-real scandals that were emerging at the time, his imaginary ones appeared frighteningly credible. Daugherty resigned under fire,[2] and Burns soon followed.

Senator Wheeler was so delighted with his star witness that neither he nor any of his fellow committee members bothered to question any of his stunning revelations. After all, Means seemed to have the corroborating evidence right there in his files, which he made a show of checking periodically throughout his testimony. Yet when it came time to enter the files into the record, they were nowhere to be found. Means told the committee that the files had already been picked up at his home by two men who said they were assistant sergeants at arms of the Senate. They had showed their badges, he claimed, and told him that Senator Smith Brookhart, chairman of the Wheeler Commission, had ordered them to collect the files. Means then produced a letter he said was the order from Brookhart. Brookhart instantly recognized it was a forgery. Now the committee's focus turned to an investigation

---

2. The former attorney general was later charged with a number of crimes while in office, but was never tried because the statute of limitations had expired.

of who had forged the letter and stolen the files—never once considering that Means might have been behind it all.

Means arranged for two false witnesses, one of whom was listed as a special agent for the Bureau of Investigation, to tell the committee that it was none other than Hiram Todd who had ordered the theft. The indignant prosecutor, still waiting to try Means, was hauled before Wheeler and the other members. Their interrogation had little to do with the stolen files. Rather, they wanted to protect their witness by impugning Todd. He was a tool of Daugherty's, they charged, out to destroy the man who had exposed the insidious corruption at the Justice Department. The members tried to probe into the evidence that had been gathered against Means, which Todd vigorously resisted. It was only after hours of tense exchanges with the committee on these matters that the prosecutor was allowed to address the issue of the stolen files. His testimony was so unassailable that members were left bewildered; perhaps Gaston Means wasn't so reliable after all.[3] On May 23, 1924, the Wheeler hearings concluded. A month later, Todd's prosecution began.

At last the spider was trapped in his own web, and his only recourse was to spin even more lurid tales of scandal in the Harding administration. The object was to inundate the jury with so many stories of wrongdoing at the highest levels that Means would appear to be only a minor cog in a massive corrupt machine. His defense attorney even went as far as to subpoena Treasury Secretary Mellon in the hopes of implicating him in a number of bootlegging conspiracies and thus demonstrate just how pervasive criminal activity was in the great halls of power. It didn't work. Gaston Means, ten days shy of his forty-fifth birthday, was convicted for the first time in his life and sentenced to prison.

---

3. Wheeler later ruefully admitted that "the rascally Means was more trouble to us than he was worth."

During his incarceration at the Atlanta Penitentiary he met May Dixon Thacker, wife of a prominent Southern evangelist as well as a contributor to such publications as *True Confessions*, who was doing research at the prison. As Means shared with her imaginative tales of his exploits, she assured him that they would make an interesting book and invited him to call on her in New York when he was ready to tell his story. On July 19, 1928, he was released from prison. Asked by a reporter what he planned to do in the future, he replied with a grin, "Anyone I can." Mrs. Thacker was his first target.

Means dictated his outrageous stories to Thacker, who excitedly compiled them into a book entitled *The Strange Death of President Harding*. In the book Means claimed to have been hired by First Lady Florence Harding to investigate her husband's extramarital dalliances. As a result, he had earned the wrath of the president, and all the legal troubles he had faced over the years were the direct result of an orchestrated campaign by Harding and his cohorts to destroy him. But the book's most shocking claim was that Mrs. Harding had killed her husband with poison in retaliation for his infidelities. It was a monumental hoax that became a bestseller. And though poor, gullible Mrs. Thacker eventually repudiated the book, the lies it contained still resonate.

About the time Means was dictating his nonsense to Mrs. Thacker, he met Ralph M. Easley, executive director of the National Civic Federation. Easley was obsessed with what he called "the menace of Socialism as evidenced by its growth in the colleges, churches, newspapers." Means had little trouble convincing him that he was the man to help root out the subversives. He produced several trunks filled with forged papers that purportedly documented Bolshevik activity in the United States, for which Easley paid him $25,000. The poor man was disgraced when the con was exposed; he was convinced it was part of a

Soviet plot to discredit him. As it turned out, he needed to look no further than Gaston Bullock Means.

★

After so many years perfecting his devilry, Means topped off his career with what was undoubtedly his cruelest con yet. When the young son of aviation hero Charles Lindbergh was snatched from his crib on the evening of March 1, 1932, Means sniffed opportunity. He was approached by Evalyn Walsh McLean, the wealthy grande dame of Washington society and owner of the Hope Diamond, who believed his connections with the criminal underworld might help her contact the kidnappers and get the child back to his heartbroken parents. "I had no illusions about Means," Mrs. McLean wrote in her autobiography, "except that I supposed the chance to act as go-between in the ransoming of the Lindbergh baby would seem a bigger prize to him than any other chance he might discern in his dealings with me." She was wrong.

Means invented an elaborate cloak-and-dagger story that cast Mrs. McLean into the center of the action. It appealed to her desire for excitement and intrigue, as well as to her genuine wish to rescue the little boy. The scheme also excited a brief flicker of hope in the Lindberghs, which made it particularly cruel. Mrs. McLean was instructed to go to Fairview, her estate outside Washington, D.C. There, Means said, the kidnappers would observe her carefully, and, once satisfied that it was safe, hand over the child. The ransom would be $100,000 in cash, plus $4,000 for his own expenses. The well-intentioned woman hocked the Hope Diamond and gave the money to Means. The kidnappers, however, never showed at Fairview. "Each night I waited there," she wrote, "and through the darkness tried to see along the paths. . . . Each dawn was just another disappointment; but with sunrise hope would grow again."

The kidnappers had been spooked, Means claimed. They expected Mrs. McLean to come to Fairview alone, not with members of her staff. But, he said, there was still an opportunity to get the boy back. A new rendezvous was selected in Aiken, South Carolina, where Mrs. McLean had rented a home while her son attended school nearby. An accomplice of Means's named Norman Whitaker appeared at the house and pretended to represent the kidnappers. He identified himself only as "the Fox," and made a show of checking the premises for wires or secret agents. Yet for all that, the baby still was not delivered. And so it went at the next arranged meeting place in El Paso, Texas, where the supposed kidnappers demanded an additional $35,000. Finally, Mrs. McLean grew suspicious and demanded her money back. Means, feigning dismay, told her he had already delivered it to the kidnappers. She had him arrested. By that time, Charles Lindbergh had identified the remains of his dead son.

J. Edgar Hoover, who had succeeded William J. Burns as bureau director and held a personal vendetta against Means for having sullied the reputation of the institution, was delighted to learn of his involvement in the Lindbergh scam. It was time for a little retribution. Means was charged with larceny after trust and put on trial. His only defense was that he had accepted Mrs. McLean's money in good faith and delivered it to the men he believed were the kidnappers. The prosecution aptly called him "the prince of liars." He was convicted and sentenced to fifteen years at Leavenworth. "The verdict of the jury in this case reveals that the defendant capitalized not only on the sweetest and tenderest emotions of the human heart," the judge said at sentencing, "but also the basest."

Means stood trial again the following year for having tried to extort the additional $35,000 from Mrs. McLean in Texas. Though his face appeared drawn and sunken, with a severe prison pallor, he still managed to sparkle. "He was the perfect picture of a man enjoying the crowd at his own hanging," *Newsweek* reported, and his testimony was suffused with the bold lies that had made him infamous. He claimed, for example, that one of the kidnappers was the head of the Communist Party in America, and that the Lindbergh baby was still alive and well in Mexico. The prosecution called his testimony "a figment of a weird imagination that makes Baron Munchausen look like a piker." But Means was rather proud of it.

"How did you like that story?" he asked J. Edgar Hoover at the trial.

"In all my life I have never heard a wilder yarn," the director replied.

"Well, it was a good story, just the same, wasn't it?" he concluded with a grin.

It may have been, but no one believed a word of it. Means was convicted and sentenced to two more years in prison. He was now desperate for an escape, or at least some attention. To that end, he continued to torment the Lindberghs when he "confessed" that it was he who had taken and killed their child—not Bruno Richard Hauptmann, who had been convicted of the crime and sentenced to death. He also taunted authorities with false leads as to the location of Mrs. McLean's money, which was never found. The secret died with him when, on December 12, 1938, the black heart of Gaston Bullock Means finally gave out.

26

Louise Arner Boyd: The Socialite Who Conquered the Arctic Wilderness

She was the unlikeliest of Arctic explorers: a San Francisco socialite who plumbed the icy mysteries of Greenland with her nose always freshly powdered and a personal maid to attend her every need. But Louise Arner Boyd was far from a pampered blue blood who liked to play adventuress. The numerous expeditions she led to the frozen North yielded a valuable photographic record of a region almost as alien as the lunar landscape, and earned her recognition from some of the most prestigious scientific societies. There's even a spot on the map that attests to her impressive accomplishments—a previously uncharted area of Greenland that she discovered and which now bears her name: Weisboydlund (Miss Boyd Land).

Born into fabulous wealth in 1887, Louise enjoyed all the privileges of an American aristocrat. But tragedy intruded when her two brothers passed away from rheumatic fever and both of her parents died within a year of each other. Left alone in the world at age thirty-two with a fortune to realize whatever she dreamed of doing, she stumbled upon her life's passion in 1924 while on a cruise from Norway to the frozen archipelago of Spitsbergen in the Arctic Sea.

"Far north, hidden behind grim barriers of pack ice are lands that hold one spellbound," Louise later wrote of the new world that had been revealed to her. "Gigantic imaginary gates, with hinges set in the horizon, seem to guard these lands. Slowly the gates swing open, and one enters another world where men are insignificant amid the awesome immensity of lovely mountains, fiords, and glaciers."

It was a world she would return to again and again, not as a mere tourist but as a scientific patron and well-respected explorer in her own right. "There is no question that she was a pioneer for women in expedition science," Melvin Marcus, a professor of geography at Arizona State University, told *The Washington Post* in 1996. "If you consider the times, it was a big deal to have a woman in charge." Lacking any scientific credentials or even a college education would normally have made the attainment of such a position impossible, but Miss Boyd was paying the bills and that made her the boss. Respect was another matter; she earned that.

"Not only did she hold the purse strings," writes her biographer Elizabeth Fagg Olds, "but her systematic attention to detail, and her passion for converting her expeditions into serious instruments for contributing to knowledge of the polar regions, elevated her from the initial role of wealthy socialite indulging in an expensive hobby. She became a true leader, a presiding patron of scientifically trained personnel, a sponsor of science."

After her enchanting introduction to the Arctic in 1924, Louise returned in 1926—stopping off in London along the way to be presented at the Court of St. James's. She was still a full-time grande dame, not yet the intrepid explorer she was to become.

Science, in fact, played no part in this trip. Louise and her society pals were there to shoot polar bears, reportedly bagging twenty-nine of the great Arctic creatures in one day. Frivolous as the expedition was, she did begin the photographic documentation of the region that would one day become her legacy.

A third trip in 1928 began as another lark, but turned into a rescue mission instead. Roald Amundsen, the famed Norwegian explorer who in 1911 became the first to reach the South Pole, was declared missing while searching for the crew of a crashed dirigible. His disappearance stunned the world at a time when polar explorers were revered the way astronauts would be by later generations. Upon hearing the news, Louise immediately volunteered the ship and crew she had chartered for her pleasure trip, and joined the search. For months they cruised the coastlines of Greenland, Spitsbergen, and the collection of tiny frozen islands known as Franz Josef Land, eventually covering ten thousand miles.

Vivid mirages produced by the unstable Arctic atmosphere often led the searchers astray. "Four of us stood watch round the clock," Louise reported. "We would just stand there and look. Ice does such eerie things. There are illusions like mirages, and there were times we clearly could see tents. Then we'd lower boats and go off to investigate. But it always turned out the same—strange formations of the ice, nothing more."

Though Amundsen was never found, Louise was awarded for her efforts by the king of Norway with the Knight Cross of St. Olaf, First Class, the first non-Norwegian woman to be so honored. The search also allowed her the opportunity to meet some of Scandinavia's top Arctic explorers, who inspired her with stories of Greenland's legendary east coast—a "dramatic alpine complex of waterways, mountains, and glaciers," as she described it, "where the approach to land is rendered difficult by an exceptionally wide belt of ice." Polar bears were no longer her quarry. She was now determined to break through this hazardous, ice-crusted barrier, having understood that "the reward of crossing this belt is access to a land of extraordinary grandeur and beauty."

The expedition that resulted in 1931 was more rewarding than she might ever have imagined. "The luck of the beginner, as well as a season of favorable weather, smiled upon Louise on this trip," writes Olds, "so that despite the lack of scientists in her party (she would assemble these for her next and all subsequent trips), she achieved astonishing results." Perhaps the most impressive of these was the discovery of the uncharted area in Greenland's eastern fiord region that now bears her name, as well as other previously unknown geographic features that she literally put on the map. All this from a dainty, upper-crust hostess who insisted upon wearing a fine wool suit while gardening and who wouldn't dream of leaving her mansion without a hat.

Louise had indeed accomplished much on this journey, but she came to realize that it would take expertise in a number of scientific fields to begin plumbing Greenland's many mysteries. This desire to better understand the land she loved prompted her to gather some of the world's top surveyors, physiographers, and geologists for her subsequent expeditions. Although she also brought along botanists, Louise herself collected hundreds of plant specimens and learned how to professionally preserve them. In Greenland, she wrote, "nature has created . . . rock gardens that have a beauty almost beyond description—masses of brilliantly colored blooms in exquisite arrangement."

Though she traded her fine gowns and high heels for parkas and hobnailed boots when the Arctic beckoned, Louise always carried a little of her gilded life in San Francisco with her. That included her personal maid and a touch of her fashion sense. "I don't feel dressed unless I'm wearing flowers," she said. "Even in Greenland, I'd find something and wear it with a safety pin." A few of the scientists on the expeditions tended to denigrate her because of her wealth. "Louise was not only a woman in a man's realm, a nonscientist among scientists, but a capitalist who inadvertently riled the chip-on-the-shoulder have-nots," writes Olds. "She chose to ignore these tensions and sailed along in serene indifference; but she did not later issue second invitations."

And woe to anyone foolish enough to underestimate her. One time she sent two scientists inland to examine a specific site, but for whatever reason the pair decided the task wasn't worth their effort and turned back without reaching their goal. Upon their return, they reported that the mission had been completed—unaware that Louise had elected to make the same trek. When they saw her making her way back to the ship, they knew they were caught. "This is where we had better duck," one of them reportedly said. Neither was asked back.

Taskmaster though she was, Louise shared in many of the difficulties her team faced. She often trudged through extremely difficult terrain, laden with her photographic equipment, without benefit of sleds or marked trails. These excursions, though strenuous, allowed her to witness more intimately the magnificence of a world unknown to most; a world where, she wrote, "inanimate nature seemed almost alive."

> Icebergs provide the chief source of noise in what [Arctic explorer Vilhjalmur] Stefansson calls the "misnamed Silent North!" You hear the trickle of small rivulets on the larger bergs, and the drip-drip of water splashing from their sides. The smaller ice formed from the calving of bergs makes a cracking sound in warm weather. Occasionally there is a swish against the shore of waves produced by the overturning

and breaking up of some ponderous mass. Loudest of all, like
the sound of cannonading, is the boom of a berg as it splits
off from the parent glacier or the crash of bursting ice as a
mighty berg collapses. These extraordinary sounds echo and
reecho through the fiords.

In the midst of all the natural splendor, danger always
lurked—particularly the grim possibility of being trapped in the
ice if the brief summer window that made exploration possible
suddenly slammed shut. Louise and her crew very nearly faced
this ordeal in 1933 when their ship, the *Veslekari,* ran aground at
the end of the summer season. Stuck in a fiord with no hope of
rescue, dramatic action had to be taken to buoy the ship. "By
the removal of 30 tons of sea-water ballast, 2 motor boats, 1
rowboat, 3½ tons of fuel oil, and 17 barrels of petrol she was
lightened," Louise reported, "and we hoped that the incoming
tide would free her." It didn't. Next, fifteen tons of coal were
tossed overboard, yet the *Veslekari* still remained mired. It was
then that the ship's captain devised a brilliant plan utilizing a
nearby iceberg. A cable was thrown around it and connected
to the ship's winch. "The motor dory shoved the berg as the
winch pulled on the cable," she continued, "and the iceberg
was grounded in a desired position aft of us. Fortunately for us,
the next tide was the spring tide, and at high water (11:30 A.M.)
on September 4, with the engines full speed astern and the
winch pulling on the cable connected with the iceberg, the ship
was floated undamaged. Here was a case when an iceberg was a
friend."

They had narrowly avoided entrapment in the soon-to-be
frozen fiord, but still had to escape the Greenland coast as winter
rapidly approached. Fierce gales twice forced them back. "Nature
was closing her doors on us!" Louise wrote. "We had arrived in
early July when the last winter's ice was still blocking the entrance

to the fiords and on shore spring flowers were in full bloom! Now the snow of coming winter had appeared. Extending from summit to sea level, as far as one could see, Greenland was white. Overhead were foehn clouds and northern lights, not in their real glory, but sufficiently to show that we had passed from one season into another—from a season of perpetual sunshine into one of darkness. Nature's warning to us was: 'Go Home!' " They heeded it just in time.

Harrowing as the experience had been, Louise returned to Greenland in 1937, after representing the U.S. government as a delegate to the International Geographical Congress in Warsaw and coauthoring *The Fiord Region of East Greenland,* the first of her three books.[1] She had purchased a high-tech depth finder prior to the expedition, and used it to discover an entirely unknown ocean bank. It was appropriately named the Louise A. Boyd Bank, and joined Louise Boyd Land and the Louise Glacier as a geographical monument to a "dauntless leader of scientific expeditions into the Arctic," as the American Geographical Society described her when awarding her its prestigious Cullum Medal in 1938.

The medal, which put Louise in the august company of the great polar explorers Robert E. Peary and Robert F. Scott, both previous recipients, was awarded right after she achieved another remarkable milestone. A push to the northernmost limit a ship could travel along Greenland's east coast placed Boyd and her crew only eight hundred miles away from the North Pole, a place she had dreamed about since childhood. The feat was reported in *The New York Times* on September 9, 1938, with a declaration from Dr. John K. Wright of the American Geograph-

---

1. Her second book, *Polish Countrysides,* documented that nation's rural heritage just before it was forever transformed by World War II.

ical Society: "Miss Boyd may claim the credit of having gone further in a ship along the East Greenland shore than any other American and of having attained what is probably the second highest latitude ever reached by a vessel in these waters." It would be her last expedition to the region.

The splendid isolation of Greenland, a Dutch possession, was shattered when Nazi forces arrived after conquering Denmark in 1940. With the great northern land mass suddenly of strategic importance to the United States, Louise was called upon by her government to withhold publication of her third book, which contained photographs and data from her 1937 and 1938 expeditions, because of its potential value to the enemy. "Immediately I put into 'security' not only the material contained in this book," she wrote in the introduction to *The Coast of Northeast Greenland*, which was finally published in 1948, "but also my extensive library of photographs taken on these and my previous Arctic expeditions and the hundreds of maps and miscellaneous publications, dealing with the northern countries of Europe as well as with the Arctic, that I had collected over the years. All this material was turned over to departments of our government upon request and restricted to their use for the duration of the war." Given the extreme level of American ignorance about the region, the contribution was significant and, wrote Rear Admiral Edward H. Smith of the U.S. Coast Guard, it provided "great assistance in the navigation of these little known ice-infested waters."

As part of the war effort, Louise led a secret expedition she funded into Canadian Arctic waters to obtain data affecting long-distance radio transmission in the Arctic ionosphere. "Many thrilling experiences were reported by Miss Boyd," a Department of Commerce report read. "At one time the *Morrisey,* a small but stout vessel, was battered by a 100-mile gale, with waves 60 feet high. Everything movable on board was thrown about, including members of the party. Nobody knew whether the vessel would survive, but there was no sign of panic among either members of the crew or technical personnel."

Having served her country valiantly in World War II, Louise had one more ambition to satisfy. In 1955, at age sixty-seven, she chartered the first private flight over the North Pole. She later wrote of this, her last great adventure, in *Parade* magazine:

> *North, north, north we flew. Soon we left all land behind us. From the cabin window I saw great stretches of ocean flecked with patches of white floating ice. Now the ice became denser, its jagged edges surrounding open pools of sea. And as I saw the ocean change to massive fields of solid white, my heart leaped up. I knew we were approaching my goal.*
>
> *Then—in a moment of happiness which I shall never forget—our instruments told me we were there. For directly below us, 9,000 feet down, lay the North Pole. No cloud in the brilliant blue sky hid our view of this gorgeous field of shining ice. Suddenly I felt we had an invisible passenger—the Almighty.*
>
> *In a moment of silent and reverent awe the crew and I gave thanks for the priceless sight. We crossed the Pole, then circled it, flying "around" the world in a matter of minutes. Then we departed. My Arctic dream had come true.*

After nearly a lifetime of grand adventure and scientific achievement, Louise Boyd spent her remaining years in relative poverty.[2] Forced to sell the estate where she had once entertained the world's

---

2. "The evaporation of her wealth, particularly in view of her earlier sagacity and attention to careful investment, remains a mystery," writes biographer Elizabeth Fagg Olds.

elite, she lived in a San Francisco nursing home supported by a group of loyal friends. When she died in 1972 at age eighty-four, there wasn't enough money to honor her final wish that her ashes be scattered over Greenland. Instead they were dropped over Alaska, where at least there was ice.

27

Beulah Louise Henry:
"Lady Edison"

None of her inventions revolutionized the world, but the sheer number of them earned Beulah Louise Henry the appellation "Lady Edison." A mechanical genius who knew next to nothing about physics or engineering, she created a remarkable array of products and devices, forty-nine of which were patented. Many are obsolete now. In an era of laser-jet printers, for example, there is little use for her Protograph, a typewriter attachment that could produce four original copies without the use of carbon paper. Still, that does nothing to diminish her achievements.

"She astonished scientists and patent officials alike," writes historian Autumn Stanley, "not only with the number and variety of her inventions, but with their technical nature, particularly since she was completely innocent of technical training."

Henry, who, one reporter wrote, "looks more like Mae West than the movie conception of an inventor," received her first patent in 1912 for a vacuum-sealed ice-cream freezer. Many more followed, from mechanically animated dolls to a bobbinless sewing machine, and by 1924 *Scientific American* was glowing with details of her inventive prowess. "I know nothing about mechanical terms," she said at the time, "and am afraid I do make it rather difficult for draughtsmen to whom I explain my ideas, but in the factories where I am known they are exceedingly patient with me because they seem to have a lot of faith in my inventiveness. I have my inventions patented in four different countries, and I am President of two newly incorporated companies."

A monument to Henry's success was her headquarters at New York's Hotel Victoria, where she also made her home. Crammed into her room were models of all her patented inventions, leaving very little space to move around. On the walls were the watercolors she had painted. "I think literature and art are far above things mechanical," she once said. "I have painted many watercolors, but the world calls me an inventor." Given her prolific output, it was a label she would have to live with. For not only did she work on her own projects, she was also employed as an inventor by the Nicholas Machine Works in New York. In addition, she served as a consultant to a number of companies that manufactured her creations. Clearly, her admitted lack of scientific credentials were no handicap, though her art did go unheralded.

Henry attributed her inventiveness to some "inner vision" that she said she had possessed since early childhood. An idea would emerge in her mind fully formed and three-dimensional. But it took a large laboratory and a staff of mechanics who understood her layman's language to translate her visions. She also paid pattern makers thousands of dollars to create models of what she had conjured. "Sometimes when I am trying to explain an idea to model-makers and engineers, they tell me it is against all the laws of physics," she said, "but as that means nothing to me I just have to carve my ideas from bits of soap, complete them with rubber tubing, tape, etc., and keep talking until I get it over."

One illustrative example of Beulah Henry's inventive process was her early idea for an umbrella with detachable snap-on covers of various colors to fit a single frame—a perfect way to match one's parasol with the day's outfit. It was a rather simple concept, but with one big problem: the snappers. A number of manufacturers turned down the idea because they said it would be impossible to pierce the frame of the umbrella with the kind of snappers she proposed. Discouraged, Henry reported that she went home one day, and "with a stone for a work bench and a hammer and nail for implements, I made a hole in the tip of that steel rib. Then I got a cake of soap and a nail file and modeled the style of snapper that would be strong enough to do duty on a windy day." It was enough to convince one manufacturer to produce the umbrella, which went on to become a popular seller. Beulah Henry received a patent for the snapper, as well as a fat check for her idea.

"If necessity is the mother of invention," she said years later, "then resourcefulness is the father."

28

Guy Gabaldon:
"The Pied Piper of Saipan"

On July 8, 1944, one of the more astonishing, uncaptured scenes of World War II took place in the Pacific. The bloody battle of Saipan was near its end, but the Japanese forces defending the island had given no indication that they were ready to capitulate. Just the day before, in fact, they had carried out one of the largest banzai attacks of the war—a suicidal last stand in which an enemy horde, many of them wounded and armed only with bamboo spears, swarmed over the American lines. Surrender was an anathema to these people, an act of cowardly betrayal that led a number of soldiers and civilians to hurl themselves off Saipan's sea cliffs rather than give themselves over to the American "barbarians" they had been indoctrinated to fear and despise. It was this mindset, therefore, that made the scene on the island's northern end that July day truly remarkable: A lone marine private—all five feet four inches of him—corralling eight hundred battle-hardened Japanese he had personally coaxed out of their caves into willing captivity.

His name was Guy Gabaldon, an eighteen-year-old Chicano from the East Los Angeles ghetto who had joined the service the year before and was with the Second Marine Division when it stormed Saipan's beaches on June 15, 1944. From the moment he arrived on the island, the "Pied Piper of Saipan," as he came to be called, made it clear that he would be fighting the war the way *he* saw fit. With only a smattering of Japanese he'd picked up from a Japanese American family that had semiadopted him as a kid—and an extraordinary amount of gumption—Gabaldon began making lone forays into enemy territory, usually at night, to take prisoners.

"My plan, impossible as it seemed, was to get near a Japanese emplacement, bunker, or cave, and tell them that I had a bunch of Marines with me and we were ready to kill them if they did not surrender," Gabaldon wrote in his privately published memoir. "I promised that they would be treated with dignity, and that we would make sure they were taken back to Japan after the war."

It was audacious, but it worked. His first night out, right after his arrival on Saipan, Gabaldon returned with two prisoners. The next night he captured fifty. "When I began taking prisoners it became an addiction," he wrote. "I found that I couldn't stop—I was hooked." Though at first his commanding officers were infuriated by these freelance excursions, they quickly realized that the captured enemy troops were providing valuable information that saved lives. After that, Gabaldon wrote, "I won approval for my 'Lone Wolf' escapades. I was on my own."

Gabaldon used a similar routine each time he ventured out. He would approach an enemy cave or bunker, shoot any guards outside, then trick the troops inside into believing that they were surrounded. Bribes of candy and cigarettes, plus the assurances he gave in his broken Japanese that they would be well treated, achieved the desired results and hundreds were cajoled into surrendering over the course of the campaign.

"Making these daily ventures into enemy territory, getting shot at daily, and not getting wounded (yet),[1] had given me a sense of self-confidence, a feeling that I would not get killed as long as I worked alone," he recalled. "As I look back on these escapades I wonder how I survived. I believed that working alone in the jungle was the best manner in which to escape detection, and I was right. I took it upon myself to go into Japanese territory to kill and capture the enemy—my actions prove that God takes care of idiots."

Yet for all the success the young private achieved on his "lone wolf" expeditions, they were merely practice runs for his staggering achievement on July 8. After weeks of fighting, the Japanese—many of them survivors of the previous day's ban-zai charge—had been pushed to Saipan's northern tip, where they hunkered down in cliff-side caves. Gabaldon managed to take two prisoners atop the cliffs that morning. They would be his conduit to the enemy entrenched below—his spokesmen, of sorts—but first they would have to be persuaded that surrender made sense. "I talked with them at length trying to convince them that to continue fighting would amount to sure death for them," he wrote. "I told them that if they continued fighting, our flame throwers would roast them alive."

An even bigger challenge was to make them see that surren-der would be honorable; that they would be well treated, and then have them relay that message to the fanatical troops lurking in the caves below. One prisoner agreed to deliver the offer. The other, fearing he would be killed for even speaking of surrender, refused. "The one that descended the cliff either had lots of guts or he was going to double-cross me and come back with his troops firing away," Gabaldon wrote. "Who was the prisoner,

---

1. He was wounded later in the war.

me or the Japs? This was the first time that I was caught in this type of predicament."

The bold marine would soon have his answer when his messenger returned from the caves accompanied by twelve armed military personnel. He recalled the moment: "This is it! This time I can't tell them to drop their weapons. I can't tell them they are surrounded. . . . They don't say a word. They just stand there in front of me waiting for the next move. They're not pointing their weapons at me, but on the other hand, they don't have to. If I go to fire they would have the drop on me. They'd chop me down before I [could] fire a round. I must keep my cool or my head will roll."

Gathering all the courage that had sustained him throughout the Saipan campaign, Gabaldon sat the Japanese down, offered them cigarettes, and delivered a message he said was from General Holland "Howlin' Mad" Smith, U.S. commander of the operation, whom he called Shogun—a word to which the Japanese seemed to respond. "General Smith admires your valor and has ordered our troops to offer a safe haven to all the survivors of your intrepid [banzai] attack yesterday," he told them. "Such a glorious and courageous military action will go down in history. The General assures you that you will be taken to Hawaii where you will be kept together in comfortable quarters until the end of the war." The alternative, he reminded them while pointing to the American fleet offshore, was certain death.

To the lone marine's relief and surprise, he seemed to be making progress. The enemy gathered around him and smiled at his broken Japanese, while their leader, a second lieutenant (known as a Chuii), asked about medical treatment for his wounded comrades. Gabaldon assured him that it would be provided. "So be it!" the Chuii responded after a time. "I become your prisoner!" With that, he rose and took his men back over the cliffs, leaving four with Gabaldon. The hour that followed was exceedingly tense as Gabaldon waited for him to return. When he did, with over fifty men in tow, he demanded water and medicine—immediately. "Be patient," Gabaldon responded, "I give you my word that once you have all your people here I will make contact with my troops."

The Chuii appeared uncertain, yet agreed. And then began the mass exodus from the caves. "They started coming up," Gabaldon wrote. "The lines up the trails seem endless. My God, how many are there? I might as well throw my carbine and side-arm away. If they rush me, sayonara! But they seem to know that they are surrendering." As more and more Japanese emerged, their lone captor set about organizing them, separating military personnel from civilians and moving the wounded into one area. It was a nearly overwhelming task, made all the more difficult by the uncertainty of the enemy. "They want food and water and medical care," he wrote. "If it is not forthcoming it is a sure thing that they will kill me and go back to their caves."

Fortunately, a few marines on a nearby hill observed what must have seemed surreal to them: Private First Class Guy Gabaldon, unharmed, in the midst of an enormous swarm of enemy combatants. Gabaldon ordered one of the Japanese to use a white shirt to signal the marines, who immediately burst into action. "I was so damn busy trying to get a semblance of order, I can't remember how long it took help to arrive," he wrote, "but I remember hundreds of Marines arriving on the scene."

Late that night, after single-handedly capturing eight hundred enemy prisoners, the Pied Piper of Saipan did something rather ordinary: He wolfed down a K ration and went to sleep.

★

Extraordinary as Guy Gabaldon's actions were on Saipan, he was only awarded the Silver Star during the war—despite the recommendation of his commanding officer, Captain John Schwabe, that he be given the highest award for valor, the Medal of Honor.

It was only after he achieved a measure of fame on the television program *This Is Your Life,* and from the 1960 film *Hell to Eternity,* which chronicled his exploits, that the Marine Corps saw fit to upgrade his award a notch to the Navy Cross—one designation shy of the Medal of Honor. "It was only with a twinge of conscience that they upgraded my Silver Star to a Navy Cross," Gabaldon told the *Honolulu Star-Bulletin* in 2004, "and to me that indicated they knew they had made a mistake." Still, the highest award for valor remained elusive, despite the fact that he had taken ten times as many prisoners as Sergeant Alvin York, who won the Medal of Honor in World War I. Though there were some congressional efforts to properly honor the Pied Piper of Saipan, Gabaldon was still waiting when he died in 2006.

29

Elizabeth Bentley:
"Red Spy Queen"

The witness, wearing a conservative dark dress, walked into the crowded House Ways and Means Committee room on the morning of July 31, 1948, apparently undaunted by the wall of newsreel cameras and blinding klieg lights set up for the occasion. Taking her seat behind a desk with a phalanx of microphones placed upon it, she sat poised and erect, her hands clasped. On a raised platform in front of her sat members of the notorious House Un-American Activities Committee, still basking in the destruction of the "Hollywood Ten" the previous fall. Having ferreted out dangerous subversives in the film industry, they now wanted the names of traitors working within the government so they could, in the words of one committee member, "drive these rats from the federal . . . payroll." This witness was there to oblige them.

★

Some called her a kook, and worse, but Elizabeth Bentley was telling the truth when she declared that Soviet spies were operating at the highest levels of government. She knew, because she controlled them. Fifty years after her revelations helped launch America's second Red Scare and all the excesses of the

McCarthy era, the release of decrypted Soviet communications confirmed much of what she had to say (while debunking some of her more blatant lies). It was only then that it became clear how the Right had overplayed the Communist menace she exposed, and the left seriously underestimated it. In the meantime, while the Cold War raged, Elizabeth Bentley gradually faded into the footnotes—a curious place for a woman who managed first to betray her country, then outmaneuver the murderous NKGB, manipulate the FBI, and, in the words of one biographer, "initiate one of the most destructive episodes in U.S. political history."

The life of the "Red Spy Queen," as Bentley came to be called, had a rather unremarkable beginning. She described herself as a "lonely, withdrawn child" growing up in Connecticut, with overly strict parents who allowed her very little freedom to socialize. As a student at Vassar she was alienated from most of her classmates, one of whom later remembered her as "kind of a sad sack, plain, dull, very teacherlike. She didn't have a single boyfriend . . . a pathetic person really. Everyone that knew her just called her Bentley. She was a sad and lonely girl."

However, a dramatic change overcame Elizabeth when she went to Italy in the early 1930s as part of a Columbia University graduate program. The once withdrawn girl became wildly promiscuous and indulged a taste for booze that would plague her for the rest of her life. She also showed herself to be a liar who blithely disregarded the rules, as when she delivered a master's thesis written by someone else. "Throughout her life, she seemed to believe that other people's regulations and laws did not apply to her," writes biographer Kathryn S. Olmsted. "If egotism is a central ingredient for treason, as Rebecca West has said [in *The New Meaning of Treason*], then Elizabeth Bentley had it in abundance."

While in Italy, Bentley developed a tendency toward political extremism and joined a student group that agitated for Benito

Mussolini's Fascist regime. But she returned home in 1934 to dismal prospects, thanks to the Great Depression, and was introduced to a group of anti-Fascists who warmly welcomed her— particularly since she conveniently altered the details of her time abroad and presented herself as having been a militant opponent of Mussolini. Elizabeth immersed herself in the group's activities and basked in the fellowship she found among them. "Surprisingly enough," she later wrote, "from then on my life took on a new zest. I seemed to have cast off the old feelings of listlessness and despair." Before long, she learned that her new friends were not only anti-Fascists, but Communists as well. Comradeship now took on an entirely new meaning.

The Communist Party of the United States of America (CPUSA) was near its peak membership when Bentley joined in 1934, and perfectly legal. With the nation in the midst of the Depression and Adolf Hitler on the rise in Europe, the party's seemingly progressive agenda appealed to many who saw it not only as a bulwark against Fascism, but an enlightened alternative to a demonstratively corrupt and unworkable capitalist system. They looked to the Soviet Union and came to believe that Joseph Stalin had built a model state, free from class strife and geared toward the common good—yet they were unable or unwilling to see that it was a massive fraud costing millions of lives and denying every vestige of freedom. "I have been over to the future," journalist Lincoln Steffans famously said after a visit to Russia in 1919, "and it works."

Ideology always meant less to Bentley than a sense of belonging. She found Communist literature tedious and difficult to grasp. "If you ever tried to read Marx, you will understand what I mean," she later said. "I used to read one page ten times and give up." Still, she was a dutiful Communist and met all the party's stringent requirements. Her diligence was recognized by the Soviets, who saw great potential in her and several times approached her for underground spy work. Nothing came of it, however, until Elizabeth essentially activated herself and infiltrated Mussolini's propaganda bureau in New York, the Italian Library of Information. This secret work put her in contact with Jacob Golos, who was, according to historian Anthony Cave Brown, "among the cleverest, most mysterious, and most powerful" Communist spies in the United States. He was also the love of Elizabeth Bentley's life.

Golos, born Jacob Raisin,[1] had been a Bolshevik revolutionary in his native Russia before he escaped the czarist secret police and immigrated to America, where he became a founding member of the U.S. Communist Party. Though an American citizen, Golos remained fanatically loyal to the Soviet Union and performed many valuable services for the regime there, from forging passports to plotting the assassination of Stalin's rival, Leon Trotsky. "Our reliable man in the U.S.," as intercepted Soviet cables referred to him, also served as the feared enforcer of Stalinist doctrine among American party members. "As with Tomás de Torquemada and Isabella I of Spain [during the Spanish Inquisition]," wrote Anthony Cave Brown, "so with Golos and Stalin."

Bentley knew little of her contact's power or position, at least initially. All she saw were his "startlingly blue" eyes, as she described them, and his "powerfully built" frame. Soon enough she fell into bed with him and was more than willing to do his bidding. Golos taught his new source all the skills of espionage and reminded her of the sacrifices that were necessary for their great cause. "You are no longer an ordinary Communist, but a member of the underground," he told her. "You must cut yourself off completely from all your old Communist friends." This was to ensure that the Fascists at the Italian Library of Information would

---

1. Golos (Russian for "voice") was an alias that Raisin adopted after coming to the United States.

be convinced of her loyalty. As it turned out, Bentley's job at the library didn't last long. But her undercover work with Golos continued as she assisted him in various capacities. "Elizabeth fairly glowed with satisfaction and self-importance," writes Kathryn Olmsted. "A few years earlier, she had been an unemployed, unattached virtually friendless young woman. Now she had a powerful, caring lover who was training her to play a critical role in the coming worldwide revolution."

That critical role came sooner than expected when a Justice Department investigation exposed Golos as a Soviet agent and effectively neutralized him. It was under these circumstances that his lover and protégée took over many of his responsibilities and reached a new level of importance. Now she would control his highly placed sources, some within the U.S. government, and operate a newly created front organization, U.S. Service and Shipping, that provided cover for various espionage activities. With barely a blink, Elizabeth Bentley set off on the road to treason. "I had made my choice," she later wrote, "and I would stick to it."

Soviet espionage in the United States was at its most aggressive when Bentley took over for Golos during World War II. Although the USSR was a close ally in the effort to defeat Nazi Germany and Imperial Japan, and received billions of dollars in American aid, Stalin nevertheless recognized that the United States would emerge from the conflict as the strongest power in the world. He was determined to avert such an outcome. Messages to and from Moscow, decrypted shortly after the war in a secret operation known as Venona, indicate that he had plenty of assistance in this effort from members of the CPUSA and other so-called "fellow travelers"—a term coined by Stalin to describe people who were not members of the party but who sympathized with the revolution and were willing to work toward it. "While not every Soviet spy was a Communist, most were," write historians John Earl Haynes and Harvey Klehr. "And while not every American Communist was a spy, hundreds were."

Some of the most influential spies of all were controlled, directly and indirectly, by Bentley. Among them were members of what was known as the Silvermaster Group, one of the most productive espionage operations in the United States. Nathan Gregory Silvermaster, an economist with the Agriculture Department and a committed Stalinist, led the spy ring and had powerful sources within the government who willingly assisted him. Two of the most prominent by far were Lauchlin Currie, President Roosevelt's White House economic adviser, and Harry Dexter White, who in 1945 became the second-highest ranking official in the Treasury Department. There were also a number of "singleton" spies who operated outside any organized ring, but reported to Bentley. Some of these lone sources worked for the Office of Strategic Services, forerunner of the Central Intelligence Agency; one in particular, Duncan Lee, was actually the personal assistant to the agency's director, William Donovan.

The majority of such sources within the government were motivated by principle, not profit. A few, like Silvermaster, were fanatical Stalinists; most were terribly misguided idealists who foolishly believed they were helping to build a better world—not betraying their country. The Soviet Union was an ally, after all, and as far as some of these men and women were concerned, secrets should be shared among friends. As for Bentley, her motives tended to be a bit less lofty. "She had only the vaguest grasp of Communist doctrine, which of course made it easier for her to abandon it later," writes Kathryn Olmsted. "For her, spying offered the chance to take risks and break the rules, all the while earning a good income [mostly from U.S. Service and Shipping]. Most important, her supervisor [Golos] loved her and kept her bed warm at night."

Interestingly, Bentley's career as a spymaster nearly collapsed before it even really began. Her association with Golos attracted the attention of the FBI in 1941, but after only a few months the bureau determined that she was of little importance and the surveillance stopped. Now, having assumed more and more of her lover's responsibilities as his health failed, in addition to his exposure by the Justice Department, she became a powerful agent in her own right—code-named *umnitsa* by the Russians, which loosely translated into "clever girl" or "Miss Wise." That was a bit of a misnomer, though, for while the Soviets found Elizabeth intelligent, they also thought the way she and Golos operated and controlled their sources was dangerously lax. In fact, they eventually ordered Golos to turn over all his agents, including Elizabeth, to their direct control. He resisted, and after his death in 1943, she continued to defy Moscow.

Bentley was bitter, and drinking hard. She believed that the pressure the Russians put on Golos had killed him, and she was in no mood to bow to their demands that she turn over the Silvermaster Group and some of her other sources. Iskhak Abdulovich Akhmerov, the NKGB agent who replaced Golos, reported his new charge's intransigence to his bosses back home. "She, as a rule, carries out my instructions gladly and reports everything about our people to me," he wrote. "However, her behavior changes when I ask her to organize a meeting with [Silvermaster]. . . . Sometimes, by her remarks, I can feel that at heart, she doesn't like us." The Soviets eventually bypassed Bentley entirely and went to Earl Browder, head of the CPUSA, who agreed to give them the Silvermaster Group. Elizabeth was livid, and her disenchantment would soon lead her to the FBI.

In the meantime, though, she would play a subversive game with the Soviets who she believed had betrayed her. She pretended to repent of her defiant ways and became a model agent.

Akhmerov was stunned by the apparent transformation. "Now she tells me that her life is connected with us," he reported to Moscow, "that she doesn't have any other interests besides her work, and that she loves our country more than anything else." Bentley also lied to the Russians by reporting detrimental information about the sources she still controlled in an effort to discredit them. This, she later claimed, was to save them. "I would slant the information I had on them to such a degree that they would look like poor risks to the Russian Secret Police, who perhaps would drop them," she wrote. Revenge, however, was the more likely motive.

"As the end of World War II and its grand alliance approached," writes Kathryn Olmsted, "one of the top Soviet agents in the United States was an unstable, alienated, mendacious American who drank too much and was doing all she could to sabotage her own agent network. She was not, in short, the perfect spy."

Antoly Gorsky, chief of NKGB operations in America, became Bentley's final handler and the one she came to truly fear. There was something about this hardened Stalinist that made "shivers run up and down your spine," she later recalled. Gorsky feared Elizabeth, too. Her undisciplined approach to espionage was simply too risky to tolerate. "I'm afraid our friend Golos was not too cautious a man," Gorsky told her, "and there is the risk that you, because of your connection with him, may endanger the apparatus." Elizabeth was ordered to give up the rest of her contacts, quit her job at U.S. Service and Shipping, and move out of the apartment she had shared with Golos. The final breach in the poisoned relationship came when she started sleeping with a man who claimed after a few dates to be a federal agent. He wasn't, as it turned out, but Gorsky had no way of knowing that. Bentley, he reported, "is a serious and dangerous burden for us here." All too aware of what could happen to anyone the NKGB found burdensome, Elizabeth finally came in from the cold.

★

On August 23, 1945, the week after World War II ended, Elizabeth Bentley walked into the FBI offices in New Haven, Connecticut. It was only a tentative step, however. She said little of substance at that first meeting, and was so vague that the agent in charge had no idea that the most significant American agent of Soviet espionage was sitting right in front of him. And it was evident the following month that she wasn't quite ready to sever her ties to the past when she returned to her job at U.S. Service and Shipping, mostly for the money.

This was against express Soviet orders and led to a drunken confrontation with Antoly Gorsky, during which Elizabeth made some rather unwise threats that left her even more vulnerable to reprisal. "Judging by her behavior," Gorsky wrote to Moscow, "she hasn't betrayed us yet, but we can't rely on her. Unfortunately, she knows too much about us." There was only one remedy left, he concluded, "the most drastic one—to get rid of her."

Bentley knew she was "living on borrowed time," as she later related. But that's not what drove her back to the FBI. One of her sources, Louis Budenz, editor of the Communist newspaper the *Daily Worker,* suddenly left the party amidst a flurry of publicity, and Elizabeth feared he would expose her. As a preemptive maneuver she went back to the feds, but was still less than forthcoming. She said that "she was closely tied in with people of whom she had suspicions and whom she believed to be Russian espionage agents," according to bureau files, but gave few details. The FBI still had no idea about who they were dealing with. It was only when Lem Harris, a leading fund-raiser for the CPUSA, questioned the finances of U.S. Service and Shipping and demanded the return of the $15,000 the party had invested in the front organization that she became indignant and made her third trip to the FBI. This time she told all.

"There wasn't any question in my mind that we hit gold on this one," agent Don Jardine told Kathryn Olmsted in 2001. Thanks to earlier revelations by another Soviet agent, Whittaker Chambers, the bureau already had suspicions about a number of sources named by Bentley, including Harry Dexter White and Lauchlin Currie. But the information was fragmented, in part due to the fact that the bureau had failed to give much weight to what Chambers had to say. "We had files here, there, and everywhere," Jardine said, "and [Bentley] kind of sewed it all together." In addition to the sources she knew personally, Elizabeth also offered clues to ones she had heard about from Golos and others. One turned out to be Alger Hiss, a high-ranking State Department official also named by Whittaker Chambers; another was the atomic spy Julius Rosenberg.

By December 1945, seventy-two special agents were working on the biggest espionage case in the FBI's history. Bentley herself was part of the effort, although she didn't have much choice in the matter. The plan was for her to act as if she were still loyal to the Soviets and thus help the bureau gather critical evidence against the sources she had named. Only problem was, the Russians already knew that she had turned courtesy of Kim Philby, chief of Soviet counterintelligence for the British Secret Service and, as it turned out, a major Soviet spy.[2] As a result of Philby's disclosure, all Soviet espionage in the United States ceased. The Russians acted as if they were unaware, however, which left the FBI to conduct a massive investigation that was stymied at every turn.

---

2. The source of the leak was probably FBI director J. Edgar Hoover, who told Sir William Stephenson, the British station chief in the United States, that Bentley had defected. Stephenson is believed to have then told Philby, who passed the information on to the Russians.

The bureau faced an almost insurmountable problem. After a year of investigation, they had no evidence of illegal activity against anyone Bentley had named. Any potential prosecutions would "hang by the thread" of her testimony alone, noted an aide to FBI director J. Edgar Hoover; she had no documents or other proof to back up her allegations. "[T]he case is nothing more than the word of Gregory [the bureau's code name for Bentley] against that of the several conspirators," wrote one of Hoover's top lawyers. The FBI's frustration was perhaps best summarized in a memo by Louis Nichols, the bureau's public relations chief: "Obviously this whole group is wrong and as far as I am concerned they could be shot, but that is not legal proof."

Hoover's solution was to secretly feed Bentley's allegations to the notorious House Un-American Activities Committee, which would serve two desirable purposes: First, it would expose the traitors within the government; even better, it would embarrass President Harry Truman, whom the FBI director not only despised, but sincerely believed was criminally soft on Communism. Attorney General Tom Clark pursued a different course and presented the Bentley case to a grand jury. Though there was little chance of any indictments, Clark wanted to cover himself should questions arise as to what the Justice Department had done with the information Bentley provided. As one internal memo noted, "it would be possible to answer by saying that the Grand Jury had considered the evidence and had not deemed it sufficient to justify criminal action."

While the Justice Department fretted over the case, Elizabeth was eager to profit from it. Her first thought was to write a book, but the FBI quickly put a stop to that idea. Undeterred, she approached two reporters from the *New York World-Telegram,* a staunchly anti-Communist newspaper. "This was one of the most fateful choices of her life," writes Olmsted. "She had decided to spy; she had decided to defect; and now she decided to tell the world about it. None of these decisions worked out well for her, but in many ways the last one was the most disastrous."

Hoover was furious when he learned what Bentley had done. "This certainly is outrageous acting upon part of informant," he jotted in the margin of one memo. Though Elizabeth assured the FBI that she had "absolutely made no proposition toward developing her story on a commercial basis," within a few weeks she signed a contract with reporter Nelson Frank to ghostwrite her autobiography and serialize the story in the *World-Telegram*. Frank himself promised the bureau that nothing would be published while the grand jury was still in session. But when the *New York Sun* made an oblique reference to a mysterious female informant, he wasn't about to jeopardize his scoop.

RED RING BARED BY BLOND QUEEN, read the *World-Telegram*'s front page headline on July 21, 1948, and an equally sensational story followed. Bentley was unnamed in the article, but described as a "svelte and striking blond"—a generous representation of a middle-aged woman who, on a good day, could only be described as frumpy. The information she had given the FBI was exaggerated as well. Over the days that followed, the paper continued to run stories about the alluring spy queen, always protecting her identity until Frank felt it would be most advantageous to reveal it. He hoped to manage Elizabeth's debut by arranging her first public appearance before Senator Homer Ferguson's respected Committee on Expenditures in the Executive Departments, thus avoiding the Red-baiting House Un-American Activities Committee and some of its more unsavory members. Yet HUAC got her name anyway—probably from an FBI leak—and promptly subpoenaed her.

J. Parnell Thomas, the Republican chairman of the committee, was eager to show how the Democratic administrations of Franklin Roosevelt and Harry Truman were, as he put it, "hand in glove with the Communist Party." Bentley seemed only too eager to help him prove it by burnishing her story with lies and distortions. She falsely testified, for example, that sources within the government provided her with advance notice of the D-Day invasion. "Elizabeth's testimony did not need any embellishments," writes Kathryn Olmsted. "Her true story was scary enough. In her eagerness to please the congressmen and generate headlines, though, she was not satisfied with the truth."

Bentley's appearances before Congress at the end of July 1948 did indeed generate headlines. But if she expected to emerge as a heroine, she was no doubt disappointed. Certainly the Right celebrated her revelations, which, in an election year, provided excellent ammunition against President Truman and the New Deal Democrats. Yet the anti-Communist press also caricatured her as a temptress who seduced secrets out of treasonous Reds in the government. The Left, on the other hand, dismissed her altogether. Her charges, writes historian Earl Latham, were treated as the "imaginings of a neurotic spinster."

The Red Spy Queen's image was hardly enhanced after Harry Dexter White, the prominent Treasury official whom she accused of disloyalty, passionately defended himself before HUAC and then dropped dead of a heart attack three days later. Many believed Bentley's charges were baseless and drove a good man to his grave. Other men and women she named vigorously denied her charges as well. One in particular, an official with the War Production Board by the name of William Remington, would harass her for years with libel charges and batter her reputation with revelations his lawyers uncovered about her sordid past. Still, the fact remained that Remington, like the others, was indeed guilty of espionage.

Stories started to circulate, some of them from the highest levels of the Truman administration, that Elizabeth was a lunatic. Yet her charges were soon bolstered by Whittaker Chambers.

His testimony before Congress, which was prompted by Bentley's own, verified much of the undocumented information she had provided. (This in addition to his startling revelations about Alger Hiss, the State Department official Whittaker famously accused of espionage.)

Decoded Soviet communications from the Venona project also proved much of what Elizabeth said. But Venona remained a secret to all but a few, and would remain so until 1995. Even President Truman was unaware of it. Had the president known, he might not have been so quick to dismiss Elizabeth Bentley and what he termed "the Communist bugaboo."[3] Furthermore, as John Earl Haynes and Harvey Klehr point out in their study of Venona, if the project had been made public, the very real threat of Communist infiltration of the government probably would not have been reduced to the dangerous partisan rantings of the Far Right. Conversely, the limits of the conspiracy would have been clearly defined by Venona, and such demagogues as Senator Joseph McCarthy would have been denied the platform to smear loyal Americans including Secretary of State George Marshall and others who he claimed were part of "a conspiracy on a scale so immense as to dwarf any previous such venture in the history of man." With the secrets of Venona well concealed, one of the ugliest chapters in American history began.

Bentley became the avenging angel of the Right as she made more appearances before Congress and various grand juries investigating Communist infiltration of the government. Her testimony thrilled newfound pals such as Joe McCarthy, but she continued to embellish it with distortions and fabrications that further inflamed the Red hysteria she had helped ignite. For

---

3. Despite his skepticism about Communist infiltration in the government, Truman had already issued Executive Order No. 9835, which established the sweeping Federal Employees Loyalty and Security Program. The president had misgivings about the order, however, and years later admitted to friends that "it was terrible."

instance, just as she had earlier lied about the D-Day invasion, she also falsely claimed that a source inside the Pentagon had given advance notice of General Jimmy Doolittle's famous raid on Tokyo in 1942. "Yes," she declared, "we knew about that raid, I guess, a week or ten days ahead of time." Over time, her tales would become even more fantastic.

Although she was always cool and collected when she testified, Elizabeth was a drunken, paranoid mess out of the spotlight. The FBI worried that she was "bordering on some mental pitfall," as one agent put it. Unstable as she was, however, she remained a valuable asset to the bureau and had to be protected, particularly since she would be a key prosecution witness in several important trials—most notably that of Julius and Ethel Rosenberg.[4] Bentley knew the FBI needed her and, as a result, her demands for cash and other perks became increasingly outrageous. "You should inform her," an exasperated J. Edgar Hoover wrote in a memo, "that any further trouble may necessitate our terminating any further weekly payments to her." Yet no matter how irksome she became, the bureau continued to compensate its star witness.

Profit was always a major motivating factor for Elizabeth. She went on what she hoped would be lucrative lecture tours (they weren't), and converted to Catholicism to boost her anti-Communist credentials and thus her income potential. (Her new faith did little to improve her morals, however: She was dismissed from a teaching job at Mundelein, a Catholic college in Chicago, for her rather uninhibited lifestyle.) Bentley also hoped to make money from her autobiography, *Out of Bondage,* a book many found to be a bit disingenuous. "She decided to portray

---

4. Bentley's connection with the Rosenbergs was remote. Julius Rosenberg was one of Golos's sources and Elizabeth had only seen him once, from a distance. However, she did have telephone contact with him when he would call the apartment she shared with Golos.

herself as a sort of Communist June Cleaver," writes Kathryn Olmsted—a devoted companion led down the path to treason by the man she loved. "It is very hard to decide whether to treat *Out of Bondage* . . . as tragic, or as ludicrous, or as terrifying, or as pathetic," journalist Joseph Alsop wrote in one review. Whatever it was, the book was definitely not a bestseller.

Success from the Red Scare continued to elude Elizabeth, leaving her broke, demoralized, and as dependent as ever on the FBI. The bureau needed to protect her "credibility as a witness," as it was noted in her file, and repeatedly extricated her from the endless problems she created for herself. These included an abusive boyfriend, several car crashes, and debts to the Internal Revenue Service.[5] On one occasion, when she demanded that the FBI pick her up at her home in Connecticut and drive her to her doctor in New York, an agent took note of her unsettled state: "Throughout the trip from Madison to New York City she was rambling and incoherent in her speech . . . engaged in back-seat driving, weeping, sleeping, fingering a small crucifix, chain-smoking and was quarrelsome and demanding throughout the trip." Still, she was a great witness, and whatever problems she caused the FBI were mitigated by her compelling testimony.

For Elizabeth to remain compelling, though, she had to keep telling lies, which battered her credibility. So many questions were raised about her that J. Edgar Hoover was forced to publicly defend his informant before Senator William Jenner's Internal Security Subcommittee in 1954. "All information furnished by Miss Bentley, which was susceptible to check, has proven to be correct," he testified. The director's endorsement thrilled Elizabeth and, she said, "made her feel like a different person." Nevertheless, she became increasingly marginalized and sank

---

5. Roy Cohen, an assistant U.S. attorney who would soon become infamous as Senator McCarthy's henchman, was often called in by the FBI to solve Bentley's myriad problems.

deeper into an alcoholic stupor. A series of teaching jobs all ended the same way—with her dismissal—until she finally landed a position with a penal institution for girls. It was an ignominious end for the Red Spy Queen who had once commanded the attention of the nation and helped set its course during the early Cold War. On December 3, 1963, at age fifty-five, she died of abdominal cancer, already well on her way to obscurity.

30

Dick Fosbury:
Father of the Flop

The obscure Americans chronicled thus far all have the distinction of being dead. The fact that Dick Fosbury is alive and well (as of 2007) should probably have been an impediment to his inclusion here, since time is the ultimate arbiter of historical status. But Fosbury bent over backward to get in anyway—with an awkward maneuver known as the Fosbury Flop. It was a technique that transformed a third-rate athlete into an Olympic champion, and in the process revolutionized the sport of high jumping. Roy Blount Jr. described the still-unconventional flop in a 1969 edition of *Sports Illustrated:*

> In detail, Fosbury charges up from slightly to the left of center with a gait that may call to mind a two-legged camel, hooks to the right at the last moment, plants his outside (or right) foot action of a "screw," as he says, so that his back turns abruptly to the bar and, ideally, rises seven feet and change into the air. Then, cocking an eye over his shoulder at the bar, he extends himself like a slightly apprehensive man

lying back on a chaise lounge that's too short for him and
finally kicks his legs up—and falls flat on his back.

Before the flop became standard, high jumpers cleared the bar with the traditional straddle method—kicking the outside leg straight up, ascending after it, stretching out facedown along the bar, and swiveling over it. Fosbury, a self-described gangly and uncoordinated wannabe athlete, never could master the straddle. To compensate, he adopted an antiquated style as a young jumper known as "the scissors," where the athlete runs at the bar and goes over sitting up, with the legs positioned like an open pair of sheers. It was terribly inefficient, as the center of gravity was too high to achieve competitive results. But Fosbury began to modify the scissors jump by laying out more and landing on his back—the larval form of what would become the flop. The evolution of the unique form was gradual and intuitive.

"You'll read that I'm a gymnast," Fosbury told Roy Blount in 1969. "You'll read that I'm a physicist and that I sat down one day and figured out a better way to jump. You'll read that I ran up and tripped one day and fell backward over the bar." In reality, he said, "I didn't change my style. It changed inside me."

Fosbury and his slightly ridiculous flop reached their apotheoses at the 1968 Olympics in Mexico, when the twenty-one-year-old cleared the bar with a record jump (7 feet; 4¼ inches) and won the gold medal. Spectators roared their approval. Traditionalists were aghast. "Kids imitate champions," U.S. Olympic coach Payton Jordan said at the time. "If they try to imitate Fosbury, he will wipe out an entire generation of high jumpers because they will all have broken necks."

The kids did indeed mimic Fosbury, hurling themselves over sofas and landing on their backs. But instead of maiming themselves, they eventually helped make the Fosbury Flop the standard it is today. Still, the man behind it all—now an engineer in Ketchum, Idaho—has a rather subdued legacy, perhaps because the sport he transformed lacks the rabid following others have. That may change someday, and millions will gather to watch *Monday Night High Jumping*. But until that happens, Dick Fosbury's place here among some of America's more overlooked characters seems fairly secure. He's certainly in good company.

Select Bibliography

Books

Andrews, William L., ed. *Sisters of the Spirit: Three Black Women's Autobiographies of the Nineteenth Century.* Bloomington, Indiana: Indiana University Press, 1986.

Black, Clinton V. *Pirates of the West Indies.* New York: Cambridge University Press, 1989.

Blackman, Ann. *Wild Rose: Rose O'Neale Greenhow, Civil War Spy.* New York: Random House, 2005.

Brands, H. W. *Andrew Jackson: His Life and Times.* New York: Doubleday, 2005.

Brekus, Catherine A. *Strangers & Pilgrims: Female Preaching in America, 1740–1845.* Chapel Hill and London: The University of North Carolina Press, 1998.

Brodhead, Michael J. *Isaac C. Parker: Federal Justice on the Frontier.* Norman, Oklahoma: University of Oklahoma Press, 2003.

Brookhiser, Richard. *Alexander Hamilton: American.* New York: The Free Press, 1999.

Caesar, Gene. *Incredible Detective: The Biography of William J. Burns.* Englewood Cliffs, New Jersey: Prentice-Hall, 1968.

Canfield, Gae Whitney. *Sarah Winnemucca of the Northern Paiutes.* Norman, Oklahoma: University of Oklahoma Press, 1983.

Davis, Burke. *Old Hickory: A Life of Andrew Jackson.* New York: Dial Press, 1977.

Donald, David Herbert. *Lincoln.* New York: Simon & Schuster, 1995.

Duncan, Russell. *Freedom's Shore: Tunis Campbell and the Georgia Freedmen.* Athens and London: University of Georgia Press, 1986.

Durey, Michael. *With the Hammer of Truth: James Thomson Callender and America's Early National Heroes.* Charlottesville and London: University of Virginia Press, 1990.

Eastman, Tamara J., and Constance Bond. *The Pirate Trial of Anne Bonny and Mary Read.* Cambria, California: Fern Canyon Press, 2000.

Fischer, David Hackett. *Raul Revere's Ride.* New York and Oxford: Oxford University Press, 1994.

Flynn, John T. *Men of Wealth: The Story of Twelve Significant Fortunes from the Renaissance to the Present Day.* New York: Simon & Schuster, 1941.

Gabaldon, Guy. *Saipan: Suicide Island.* Privately printed, 1990.

Gaustad, Edwin, and Leigh Schmidt. *The Religious History of America: The Heart of the American Story from Colonial Times to Today.* San Francisco: HarperCollins, 2002.

Hatfield, Mark O., with the assistance of the Senate Historical Office. *Vice Presidents of the United States, 1789–1993.* Washington, D.C.: U.S. Government Printing Office, 1997.

Haynes, John Earl and Harvey Klehr. *Venona: Decoding Soviet Espionage in America.* New Haven and London: Yale University Press, 1999.

Herman, Arthur. *Joseph McCarthy: Reexamining the Life and Legacy of America's Most Hated Senator.* New York: Free Press, 1995.

Hopkins, Sarah Winnemucca. *Life Among the Piutes: Their Wrongs and Claims.* 1883. Reprint, Bishop, California: Sierra Media, 1969.

Hoyt, Edwin P. *Spectacular Rogue: Gaston B. Means.* Indianapolis and New York: Bobbs-Merrill, 1963.

Hunt, William R. *Front Page Detective: William J. Burns and the Detective Profession, 1880–1930.* Bowling Green, Ohio: Bowling Green State University Popular Press, 1990.

Kauffman, Michael W. *American Brutus: John Wilkes Booth and the Lincoln Conspiracies.* New York: Random House, 2004.

Klement, Frank L. *The Limits of Dissent: Clement L. Vallandigham and the Civil War.* Lexington, Kentucky: University of Kentucky Press, 1970.

LaPlante, Eve. *American Jezebel: The Uncommon Life of Anne Hutchinson, The Woman Who Defied the Puritans.* New York: Harper Collins, 2004.

Lewis, Arthur H. *The Day They Shook the Plum Tree.* New York: Harcourt, Brace, 1963.

Lewis, Charlene Boyer. "Elizabeth Patterson Bonaparte: Napoleon's American Sister-in-Law," in Racine, Karen, and Beatriz Gallotti Mamigonian, eds., *The Human Tradition in the Atlantic World, 1500–1850.* Lanham, Maryland: Rowman & Littlefield, forthcoming.

Macdonald, Anne L. *Feminine Ingenuity: How Women Inventors Changed America.* New York: Ballantine Books, 1992.

Marszalek, John F. *The Petticoat Affair: Manners, Mutiny, and Sex in Andrew Jackson's White House.* New York: Free Press, 1997.

McCullough, David. *John Adams.* New York: Simon & Schuster, 2001.

McPherson, James M. *Battle Cry of Freedom: The Era of the Civil War* (Oxford History of the United States). New York: Oxford University Press, 1988.

Moody, Richard. *The Astor Place Riot*. Bloomington, Indiana: Indiana University Press, 1958.

———. Edwin Forrest: *First Star of the American Stage*. New York: Knopf, 1960.

Nicolay, John G., and John Hay. *Abraham Lincoln: A History* (ten volumes). New York: Century Co., 1890.

Old, Elizabeth Fagg. *Women of the Four Winds: The Adventures of Four of America's First Women Explorers*. Boston: Houghton Mifflin, 1985.

Olmsted, Kathryn S. *Red Spy Queen: A Biography of Elizabeth Bentley*. Chapel Hill, North Carolina: University of North Carolina Press, 2002.

Oney, Steve. *And the Dead Shall Rise: The Murder of Mary Phagan and the Lynching of Leo Frank*. New York: Pantheon, 2003.

Pitch, Anthony S. *The Burning of Washington: The British Invasion of 1814*. Annapolis, Maryland: Naval Institute Press, 1998.

Purcell, L. Edward, ed. *The Vice Presidents: A Biographical Dictionary*. New York: Facts on File, 1998.

Remini, Robert V. *Andrew Jackson: The Course of American Freedom, 1822–1832*. Baltimore, Maryland: The Johns Hopkins University Press, 1998.

Rogers, Horatio. *Mary Dyer of Rhode Island: The Quaker Martyr That Was Hanged on Boston Common, June 1, 1660*. Providence, Rhode Island: Preston and Rounds, 1896.

Ross, Ishbel. *Rebel Rose: The Life of Rose O'Neal Greenhow, Confederate Spy*. New York: Harper, 1954.

Russell, Francis. *The Shadow of Blooming Grove: Warren G. Harding in His Times*. New York and Toronto: McGraw-Hill, 1968.

Safire, William. *Scandalmonger: A Novel*. New York: Simon & Schuster, 2000.

Sandburg, Carl. *Abraham Lincoln: The War Years* (four volumes). New York: Harcourt, Brace, 1939.

Schom, Alan. *Napoleon Bonaparte*. New York: HarperCollins, 1997.

Seaver, James E. *A Narrative of the Life of Mary Jemison, De-He-wa-mis, The White Woman of the Genesee*. Seventh Edition. New York: The Knickerbocker Press, 1910.

Slack, Charles. *Hetty: The Genius and Madness of America's First Female Tycoon*. New York: HarperCollins, 2004.

Spargo, Tamsin. *Wanted Man: The Forgotten Story of Oliver Curtis Perry, an American Outlaw*. New York: Bloomsbury, 2004.

Sparkes, Boyden, and Samuel Taylor Moore. *Hetty Green: The Witch of Wall Street*. Garden City, New Jersey: Doubleday, Doran & Co., 1935.

Stanley, Autumn. *Mothers and Daughters of Invention: Notes for a Revised History of Technology*. New Brunswick: Rutgers University Press, 1995.

Tierney, Kevin. *Darrow: A Biography*. New York: Thomas Y. Crowell, 1979.

Tuller, Roger H. *Let No Guilty Man Escape: A Judicial Biography of "Hanging Judge" Isaac C. Parker*. Norman, Oklahoma: University of Oklahoma Press, 2001.

Widmer, Ted. *Martin Van Buren*. New York: Times Books, Henry Holt, 2005.

Willison, George F. *The Pilgrim Reader: The Story of the Pilgrims as Told by Themselves and Their Contemporaries, Friendly and Unfriendly*. Garden City, New York: Doubleday, 1953.

Zanjani, Sally. *Sarah Winnemucca*. Lincoln and London: University of Nebraska Press, 2001.

Zug, James. *American Traveler: The Life and Adventures of John Ledyard, The Man Who Dreamed of Walking the World*. New York: Basic Books, 2005.

Periodicals

Blount, Roy Jr. "Being Backwards Gets Results." *Sports Illus-trated,* February 10, 1969.

Gillis, Anna Maria. "A Socialite Conquers an Arctic Wilderness." *The Washington Post,* April 10, 1996.

Kakesako, Gregg K. " 'Pied Piper' Returning to Saipan." *Hono-lulu Star-Bulletin,* June 6, 2004.

Acknowledgments

Even the most obscure Americans in the nation's history usually have at least one historian or biographer who has found their lives worthy of study. It is to these scholars that I am most grateful for providing so much of the material found in this book. I couldn't have written it without them.

I am also indebted to my friends, family, and colleagues who either suggested some of the footnote Americans found here, or supported me through the publishing process—especially my editors, Karen Anderson and Caroline White; my agent, Jenny Bent; Ginny Bride, Bill Broadway, Peter Carlson, Marguerite Conley, Kristin Inglesby, Ann Marie Lynch, Peggy McDonough, Heming Nelson, Brendan O'Neill, Lance Robinson, Raoul Socher, Christie Tolson, David Von Drehle, Gene Weingarten, and Tom Wilkinson.

Finally, I want to thank my good friend Mary Hadar of *The Washington Post,* a generous editor whose imprint may be found not only in this book, but on my entire career.